STORIES THAT NEED TO BE TOLD
2019

I0640235

STORIES
THAT NEED
TO BE TOLD
2019

EDITED BY
JENNIFER TOP

TULIPTREE
PUBLISHING, LLC

CONTENTS

MESSENGER OF GOD
MORGAN SMITH

THE FIVE MEXICAN SOLDIERS TURNED IN UNISON AS IF THEY had been waiting for him. Then Carter saw something that he had never seen before—their eyes glowing in the reflection of the fire that was warming them in the predawn darkness. In daylight, soldiers' eyes were always hidden by dark glasses or goggles.

It was 6:00 a.m., New Year's Day at the Santa Teresa border crossing west of Juárez and Carter's station wagon was so stuffed with clothing, paint supplies, candy, and cigarettes that he could barely see out the rear-view mirror. Whenever he crossed, he was afraid that he would be stopped and the soldiers would confiscate everything. Or, worse, that they would just take him away. Then one of them waved him on and, relieved, he continued south.

After more than four years of these monthly trips, he knew every section of the narrow, two-lane highway from here to the mental asylum—the area before the customs line where the little clan of Mixteca Indians would shiver in the frigid wind, trying to sell sombreros and crosses with Jesus on them; the rickety stand where he would often buy a Coke and gird himself for the journey ahead; the area where vendors array their tacky ceramic statues in the sand with the border fence looming in the background. But now the highway was dark, empty, and windswept.

He thought of Paula, the woman in Las Cruces who had given him paint supplies and a dozen freshly pressed shirts on wire hangers. Months earlier, she had read one of his articles about the border and emailed him with an offer of help. Driving down from Santa Fe, he would meet her in a Burger King parking lot where they would transfer food, plastic bags of used clothing, whatever she had from her car to his. Although they met like that every month, he had no idea where she lived, if she had a husband, or what her life was like.

"I'd like to go with you," she had said yesterday afternoon. They were looking at each other over the hood of her car, the wind blowing her dark hair across her face. When she pushed her hair back, it was like she was opening herself up to him and he had almost said yes. Later, he had started to dial her number, but, instead, he called his daughter in Colorado, who told him that he was in mourning and not thinking straight, that it was too dangerous to be going across the Mexican border again. He could hear the shrill sound of his granddaughter's flute in the background.

Now once again he thought of calling Paula but he was out of cell phone range. And what do you say to a woman you hardly know at six a.m. on New Year's morning? Laughing to himself, he continued south, suddenly elated by the sense of movement. This was what kept him alive, he thought. Movement. Pushing ahead. When Pantoja, the founder of the mental asylum had heard of Carter's wife's death, he had knelt before him in the patio with a semicircle of his "loquitos," or mental patients, and prayed for him. Carter laughed. How could life have come to this? Then Pantoja said that most people have to drink Red Bull to get going. "Pero, Carter, tú tienes adentro el Red Bull." "You've got Red Bull inside you." Carter hoped that he was right, hoped that something—maybe this predawn New Year's Day visit—would keep him going.

To the east toward Juárez, the skyline was turning pink and the early light illuminated the white, curved lines of a huge, elongated horse painted on the side of a barren mountain. Who had done that? What did it mean? Who had had the time to create a work of art in this land where every instant had to be devoted to survival? These questions churned through him. But wasn't that why he too was here? To bring attention to the beauty he had found along this brutalized frontier?

Then he passed the battered sign that had been erected by a woman whose daughter had been murdered, a sign that announced her thirst for revenge. Carter could imagine the woman appearing some night and standing over the killers with a knife in her hands. "Now it's your turn to die," she would say to them. He would like to meet her. Simply putting up the sign with all the suspicious cars and trucks cruising by or leaving her phone number so that anyone who had information about the killers could call her—that had taken courage. But it wasn't courage that women like her felt; it was rage.

Finally, he passed a now-abandoned Mexican Army checkpoint with two buses partially submerged in the sand, a big tent, sandbag bunkers for soldiers with machine guns, and several outhouses. He'd heard that the president of Mexico was pulling most of the soldiers out of Juárez, leaving just a few at the border crossings. The stocky, unsmiling soldiers from Indian villages in southern Mexico; the federal police in dark blue pickup trucks, their faces covered by balaclavas; the convoys of local police with their automatic weapons. They might look different, but he didn't trust any of them. Many are killers, just like the narcos.

To the right, the highway disappeared off into the desert, straight as an arrow toward the city of Chihuahua some three or four hours south. Just driving these few miles was scary enough; the thought of continuing deeper into Mexico made him gasp.

Juárez, the murder capital of the world, was to the left. And along the way, huddled in a little swale in the desert, was the asylum.

It was still semi dark and too early to go to the asylum so he drove into an area of shattered, abandoned buildings and "yonkes" or junkyards. One building had a rotary sign on top that said "Hamburgers." The sign was slowly turning in the wind as if to invite him in, but the windows were broken and the building empty. Stopping to take a leak, the only noise he could hear was the roaring of the wind and the grinding sound of metal rubbing together, the sheet metal that was loosely tacked to the fences surrounding the yonkes. Aimless, killing time before going to the asylum, looking for a photograph or perhaps just a feeling, he saw a sign for a church—Iglesia de Paz—and drove down a stony road into a barrio of shacks. Each shack had a wind-scoured yard that was surrounded by a low fence, as if everyone had animals or maybe just hoped to have them. But nothing was moving, just dust and tumbleweeds. It was as if the people huddled inside these shacks knew that something was coming. Not just the sunrise. Not just a New Year. Or the winter storm that had been predicted. Did they know something that he didn't?

Once again, he thought of Paula. What would it be like to be with a woman again? Then a man suddenly appeared, huddled in a blanket and outlined in the headlights of Carter's car. He seemed puzzled and lost so Carter gave him a ride to the highway, gave him a wad of one-dollar bills, and left him by a yonke a few kilometers closer to Juárez.

Now the sun was rising and the white, abandoned buildings scattered in the desert glowed like little stars. Sitting in the idling car with the dust swirling past, it felt as though everyone else had fled, like it was the end of the world and he was the only survivor. His jaw clenched; he gripped the steering wheel with all his strength to keep from crying.

The asylum was a long, rectangular, half-finished, cinderblock building that had "Albergue Para Discapacitados Mentales" painted along its north side. "Albergue" meant shelter but this was really an insane asylum. Or as Pantoja said, a "manicomio" or madhouse. There were about a hundred patients, roughly half men and half women. A number of them had jobs—helping in the kitchen, gathering firewood, boiling water in the huge barrels out behind the building, caring for the pigs, chickens, and turkeys, gathering up blankets and clothing to be washed, or preparing to serve the first meal of the day. Unlike so many Americans who had to have a boss watching them, Carter thought, laughing again, these "loquitos" simply woke up, went to work, and, to a large degree, ran the place. Crazy or not, they had responsibilities. It gave them a sense of purpose.

He parked near the large metal gate that opened onto the patio where the patients spent their days. To the left, they had painted flowers on the wall, using paints that Paula had given him for an earlier trip. He would take her a photograph.

Carter hadn't told Pantoja exactly when he was arriving. This "sunrise in the desert on New Year's Day" idea was his. He was here because he had fallen in love with his wife fifty-one years earlier, because on an anniversary like this, he couldn't bear the idea of being home and without her. But it wasn't something he would try to explain, especially to Pantoja, who would insist on praying for him.

He walked around to the rear of the building where two men named Memo and Alejandro were starting a fire in a big metal barrel to heat water to wash clothing and blankets. Every day here was a wash day. The wet clothing and blankets would be hung on clotheslines on the roof where, blowing in the wind, it would make the building seem like a great ship moving slowly through the desert.

Off in one corner of the sandy yard were two pens—one for a huge strutting turkey and several chickens and, next to it, a larger, rectangular one where seven pigs were rooting at trash. They would all be killed eventually. A number of the patients were killers so Carter figured it would be easy to find someone who was good with a knife.

"Señor Carter, Señor Carter." He recognized the voice of Becky, the woman who had killed another woman in an argument over a cigarette. Her hand reached out through a space between the cinder blocks that made up the rear wall of the room where most of the women slept. He couldn't see anything but her hand waving at him.

"Becky, I have cigarettes," he answered. He had brought enough cigarettes and candy for everyone, hoping to start their New Year with a moment of pleasure. A man dressed like a soldier appeared carrying a bucket. His name was Gaspar. "I was a paratrooper once," Carter had said to him on an earlier visit, but Gaspar had responded that he himself had never been a soldier. That didn't matter; as you got older, reality becomes less and less important. It's who you think you are that really counts, Carter realized, huddling against the wall out of the biting wind. He rubbed his hands together. With the death of his wife of more than fifty years, every part of his body seemed to be shrinking except his huge hands. He clenched them, suddenly glad to be here out of the wind but able to hear Becky's voice. Yes, his daughter and his friends insisted that Juárez was too dangerous, that he should give up these monthly trips, but, in reality, he didn't know where else he could go.

Carter had found a niche documenting people like Pantoja who continued their humanitarian work despite the terrible violence. People reading his articles were beginning to respond, bringing him clothing or sending checks, one from as far away as Japan, or contacting him as Paula had done. "Your camera is your scepter," Pantoja had said. "You have to tell the story of my loquitos." Gripping Carter by the shoulders, he had added, "Eres mensajero. Mensajero de Dios." "You're a messenger of God." Carter had laughed awkwardly; he had been an activist when he was younger, but now he felt like nothing more than an observer, back in the shadows with his camera. Besides, other than funerals, he hadn't been in a church in years. His wife's service had been a scattering of ashes in their backyard in Santa Fe. So, how could he be a messenger of God?

The long cinderblock building was coming alive now, as if rising out of the dust and wind. There was the wood fire, the hot water to wash the blankets, Becky still calling out to him, voices in the kitchen. Inside the patio, they were probably forming a chow line. Here the patients ate off their trays. No utensils because they could be used to stab someone.

Carter saw Pantoja's battered red Chevy pulling up next to the building. Hunched over and preoccupied, he hurried into the kitchen, not noticing either Carter or his car. Pantoja had been an addict, had been deported from the US and then lived on the streets of Juárez until, some fifteen years earlier, he had had a conversion, became a street preacher, earned enough with an evangelical radio show to start the asylum so that he could rescue others who were living on the streets or had been deported. He called them "tesoros humanos" or "human treasures." Combed straight back, his black hair contrasted with the pale, sharp features of his face. On Wednesdays, he would make a few extra pesos for the asylum by going to the municipal jail or "cereso" and praying. The jail administration thought that it was calming for the inmates, but several months earlier—just a day before Carter was scheduled to go with him—a shoot-out between two gangs left seventeen inmates dead. Although he never spoke of fear, Carter could see from his spare, honed face that it was working inside him like an acid.

When Carter joined him in the kitchen, Pantoja was huddled at a little table with Benito, the dark, burly patient who was in charge in Pantoja's absence.

"When?" Pantoja asked. "When will they bring this Marta? Why?" He waved his hands at Benito, but the big man just shrugged. They were huddled together as if to exclude him.

"You have to take her. You know that." Benito wore a cowboy hat adorned with an array of political pins. Obama, Sarah Palin, former governor Bill Richardson from New Mexico. Someone who had donated used clothing had thrown it in the mix. Now he was trying to calm Pantoja. "Pastor, you take the people the police want to get rid of; in turn, they leave you alone, don't ask you for money."

In the primitive kitchen, someone was chopping vegetables for the noon meal, the heavy knife making a "click-click-clicking" sound against the wooden table. Feeling the tension from Pantoja and Benito, Carter turned to Elvira the cook and Yeira, her thirteen-year-old granddaughter who lived with her and came to the asylum with her on the weekends. "Where else could she go?" he asked himself, imagining his own thirteen-year-old granddaughter with her private school and flute lessons but also knowing that Yeira's neighborhood was so dangerous that Elvira couldn't leave her home alone on weekends. With the slightest of smiles, Yeira pushed her long black hair back and handed him three sheets of white lined paper. Stunned, Carter realized that she had written out the full names, ages, and birthplaces of the patients he had photographed during his last visit. He was going to make a book of portraits as Pantoja had suggested, and now the little Yeira had become a part of the project.

Carter crossed into the patio. Half a dozen patients immediately rushed and hugged him. One held up his fingers as if he was taking a photo. This was a game, taking the photo, then showing it to them on the monitor of his digital camera, then bringing them a print on his next visit. Many of them were quite handsome—or at least striking looking—and he did what he could to accentuate that. He was careful, for example, to make sure that no one with bad teeth opened their mouth while he was photographing them.

Yeira followed him; seeing her dark, striking face had made him suddenly realize that he was going to call Paula as soon as he crossed back over the border. But first there was the portrait game. And then the candy and cigarettes. Yeira brought out two small plastic stools. Carter placed one next to the wall and sat on the other. Then she took Carter's notebook and ballpoint pen; she would write down the names. Gaspar came out of the kitchen, joined Becky, and the two of them began lining up other patients and moving them toward the stool. One by one, they sat and posed. Dominga, Blanca, El Cholo, Guadalupe, Yogi, Santiago, Juan Carlos, Leticia, Elia, Román, Petra, Cabrales, Victoriano, Juan from Cuba, Jesús . . . Soon he would know all their names. Carter was suddenly elated, prattling away as he tried to draw different expressions from them.

His first monthly visits had been just photography and note-taking for articles. In effect, projects where he was getting something for himself and his readers. Or for publicity for Pantoja. Now, bit by bit, he was giving back—the boxes of candy bars, the cigarettes, and now the game of the portraits. It was hard to explain how something as seeming inconsequential as a Mr. Goodbar could lift someone momentarily from the boredom of the patio or Elvira's ample but monotonous food. The cigarette smoke pluming in the air seemed to relax everyone, even those who probably never smoked before. Now the portraits with everyone jostling and joking, the laughter, the attention that he, Yeira, Becky, and Gaspar gave them. Before Pantoja found these loquitos, they had been living on the streets of Juárez, ragged, raving mad, eating garbage, targets for the police or the young "sicarios" or gunmen who killed them as a gang initiation. Carter's goal was to show that, despite all that had happened to them or that they themselves had done, they were still human beings or even "human treasures," as Pantoja called them. Sitting there with his camera, Carter felt a sudden moment of elation, a burst of happiness he had thought no longer existed.

Now he heard the rumbling sound of vehicles, car doors opening and then slamming, a heavy, reverberating sound that seemed to echo even inside the asylum. Men talking, harsh voices.

Then Pantoja, his voice oddly high-pitched. The patients suddenly went silent. Then Yeira grabbed his arm and pulled him up from his stool. Walking quickly—fiercely, it seemed—she pulled him toward the gate that led from the patio to the desert outside. He pushed it open as the patients gathered silently behind them.

Two dark police vehicles were idling in the sandy parking area. They made a rumbling sound as if they had some sort of oversized engines. Five officers had gotten out of the first car, carrying automatic rifles. Wearing dark blue uniforms, they looked more like soldiers than police. Three others were pulling a struggling woman out of the second car. She wore a stained blouse but no pants, just underwear. Her hair was a thick, dirty mat. She had powerful tattooed arms and appeared half frightened, half ready to attack. This was the Marta that Pantoja and Benito had been talking about.

One officer was holding paperwork out to Pantoja. Another had his pistol in his left hand. With his right, he removed the clip, then reinserted it. Again and again with a "click-click-click" sound. His face was impassive, his body motionless except for the movement of his right hand.

Carter picked out the officer who seemed to be the boss and commended him on the dangerous work of being a Juárez police officer. He wanted to get him to agree to a photo of the officers and their weapons with the desert in the background. It was an opportunity he couldn't pass up. Behind him, he could tell that Benito and some of the patients were taking Marta inside. Pantoja was saying something, but Carter was too focused on the officer to understand.

"I'm a writer from the US." He spoke slowly, his eyes focused on the officer. He realized that he was sweating despite the January cold. He was trying to make eye contact, but they all wore dark glasses.

"Carter, come inside," Pantoja said behind him.

Carter was watching the officer when Pantoja spoke again.

"Carter, it's time to go inside." Pantoja's voice had an even higher pitch. Carter waited as the officer stared impassively at him. Then the others began turning to get back in the cars. The moment was passing. Carter lifted his camera; that's what he was here for;

this was his scepter. He pointed it. "Click, click, click." Then another officer suddenly stepped around him and pressed his weapon against Carter's back.

"Our faces can't be recorded," he said, suddenly pushing Carter toward the second car. Carter reached out to the lead officer, but he just turned away.

"Carter!" It was Pantoja. Carter turned. Pantoja had his hands outstretched toward him, but other officers moved quickly and shoved him back with their rifles. Carter stumbled and almost fell as the officers pushed him toward the car. Two of them held his arms and a third opened the rear door of the car.

"No!" He heard a thin, high voice. The little Yeira ran toward them, the wind sweeping her hair across her face. Then the patients followed, Carter had no idea how many. They seemed to come flowing out the gate, silently crossing the sand as the officers shoved Carter into the second car. At first, he was too surprised to resist. Then Yeira darted between them and wedged herself between the door and the body of the car so that the officers couldn't close the door. She made a sharp, jerking motion with her head as if to say, "That's it. Now leave us alone." Looking at her from the backseat, Carter thought of the woman who had put up the sign along the highway, seeking revenge for her murdered daughter.

It was silent now, only the breathing of the fifty or sixty patients who were pressed around the two police cars. Then the wind started again with a shrill, whistling sound. Outside, Carter could see the clothing that was drying on the lines on the roof of the asylum suddenly lift, the wind ripping at it. The air was full of dust and something more. Snow! The pounding wind from the north was driving a snowstorm over the asylum and down onto them. A snowstorm in the Mexican desert. On New Year! He started laughing. The loquitos were laughing too, the hidden treasures. They were packed tightly around the two cars; no one could move.

He turned so that his face was just inches from the officer next to him. Fuck it, he thought, I am a messenger. His teeth bared and their faces almost touching, he slowly twisted his arm out of the officer's grasp and closed his hand on the back of his neck. "Me voy," he whispered. "I'm going." He forced the car door open and pushed his way out. Then he, Yeira, the loquitos all backed slowly toward the gate of the asylum, leaving the police cars isolated in the blinding snow. The officer was staring out of the car window, the snow pelting his stunned face. Carter waved; he laughed; he wanted to run at the officer, grab his neck again, choke him. Instead he knelt in the sand with his camera raised. Behind him, he could feel the loquitos were also kneeling. Did they think he was going to pray? He took picture after picture as the police slowly drove away.

NOW I CAN DO ANYTHING I HAVE TO DO

WILLIAM SNYDER

(WARNING: This work of literary art contains scatalogical references that some readers may find disturbing.)

On the Tripura Sundari Express, Varanasi-Delhi, October 2012

It is
India. It
is night. It is dark.
It is top bunk B
in a four bunk
curtained compartment.
It is a thin gray blanket
and a thin, flat
pillow in a cotton
case. It is
a fan switched off
when the switch was
found, but switched back on
by someone in the dark.
It is the train horn
blaring and hooting
at every road
or lane or path
in Uttar Pradesh.

It is jostle. It is sway.
It is track-thump, track-
click, track-hiss. It is the
aisle-way light switched
off for sleep. It is dozing. It is
trying to doze. It is worry about
sandals left on the floor—that
they might be stolen. It is worry
then, about Delhi, walking
the station in
stockinged feet.
It is the careful turning
away from top bunk A and peeing
into a collapsible canteen—
brought for peeing.
It is the very low ceiling
and a neck bent 90 degrees
in the knee-stoop necessary
to pee. It is peeing again.
It is 3 a.m. Or 3:30. Or 4.
It is an urge. An urge
as unwanted as
any urge has ever
been unwanted
in a world
of urges. It is
an urge
growing
stronger,
and insistent,
an urge
that
lying
straight
and squeezing
together the
buttox cheeks

cannot relieve.
It is resolve—
the pulling
on of trousers,
the contorting
on of a shirt.

It is opening the daypack
behind the pillow and rooting
inside for toilet paper,
a small, old roll
held rolled with a
rubber band.
It is slipping the roll
into the left
shirt pocket.
It is climbing over
the metal rail at the foot
of the bunk, laddering barefoot
down the metal bars and into
the aisle. It is being 66.
It is the coach's floor,
a floor where many, many
feet have stepped—in
shoes and sandals and with
calloused bare feet.
It is flashing a Maglite to locate
the sandals. It is
slipping them on. It is worry
about the rupees and camera
and passport in the daypack.
It is they are too
far to reach, and
the metal bars
are really really
hard.
It is the urge.

It is rumble.
It is sway and pitch
to the coach-end
toilet. It is knowing
it is western,
with commode
and seat.
It is—the door
is locked.
And no one answers
the knocking. It is, shit.
It is jolting sideways
and longways to
the next coach back
amongst the echoes
inside the vestibule—
the sizzle-screech
of steel on steel, wheel on
track. It is opening the
toilet door.
It is squat.
It is a
low watt
bulb above
the sink. It is—
Jesus—
water
sloshing
on the floor,
left, right, back
and forth and
around and rippling
with the coach's
bucks and
wanderings.

It is
not much
time.

It is closing
the door and locking
the lock. With
bare hands. It is planning.
It is removing sandals
and stepping back on top
of each. It is removing
trousers, holding cuffs
up and away from
the pooling water
and hooking
a belt loop
on a loose
screw on the wall
beneath the
louvered window.
It is knotting
shirt tails
at the sternum.
It is rolling
the #6 rubber band
from around
the toilet paper roll
and it is
congratulations
for packing
a small one.
It is
hoping
there are enough
squares.

It is backing
up and over
the hole and placing
the feet—on sandals—on
the raised-up foot-places
adjacent the hole.
It is squatting.

It is pain.

It is lurchinglist-
ingtottering
with the coach,
with the train,
with the tilting axis
of the world,
with the swirl and spin
of the universe. It is a
star out there
that's twirling like
a sonofabitch,
ready to explode.
It is holding tight to the pitted
rusty frame beneath the sink
with the free right hand.
It is water sloshing
onto a sandal,
onto a toe.

It is dejection.

It is the dump.

It is the loose, long string
 of curried turds
  jettisoned,
   ejected,
    jetting.
     No—
      rocketing,
       blasting,
        exploding in the tick
        of an eye-blink from
   a dark, smelly,
    putrid
     thrower of rectumy flame
      and rocketing down
       and through the bleak black
        shit-stained
         hole
       to spatter onto the night-time,
     shit-caked concrete ties
       whizzing away beneath
        the train, to

   ooze
  and drip
   and run
   and dry and cake
 there forever. It is letting go
  of the rusty frame
   with the right hand
        and using it.
  The right hand.

    It is pride.

And too, it is—
  there were
     enough
     squares
        on
       the
little
    roll.

PENELOPE FOR HIS THOUGHTS
LORRAINE DEVON WILKE

HE HADN'T NOTICED THE DEPTH OF HIS MALAISE, THE SHEER agony and grasp of it, until dawn rose that particular day. The day when his low-grade fever of boredom—expected response to retirement after decades of gainful, if uninspired, employment—slipped into despair.

Almost nine and a half months after vacating his desk at Mid-Town Auto Parts & Smog Tests of Murphysboro, Illinois, he felt the exact moment, 7:04 a.m., when whatever life force remained in his depleted, diminished self slowly seeped out like the last gasp of a withering balloon, leaving him empty. Bereft of anything even resembling life force. He could do nothing but slump in his worn recliner and note the sag of his soul.

With a deep, guttural sigh, he picked up his book—the tenth in a series of interchangeable spy yarns committee-written under a famous author's name—and commenced reading with dulled inattention.

Roland Caine was sixty-nine years old, an old sixty-nine at a time when even that age dangled the option of vitality. Not for Roland. He had little interest in vitality. Its required dedication to health, fitness, and personal composition was too exhausting to consider. He didn't want to work that hard. He'd already worked harder than he ever wanted to work again. He felt old, he saw himself as old, so he accepted his agedness with weary abdication.

For him this entailed painful knees and an oversized gut; scalp-crust behind both ears, and the total absence of sartorial vanity. He seldom combed his remaining strands, allowing them to stick haphazardly to his bald, greasy pate, and he found changing clothes to be pointless, sleeping in the same sweatpants and flannel shirt for days on end. Though he regularly watched the 5:00 news with his wife, Connie, their only predictable time together, he had little interest in politics and felt no responsibility to have an opinion. About anything. Even sports bored him.

"You're depressed," Connie announced upon entering the den to find him in the exact position he'd been in when she left for yoga. He may have moved at some point, surely to use the bathroom or grab the sandwich she'd left in the fridge, but it was also possible he hadn't. The room was dark, redolent with Roland's sourness. Connie flung the curtains back and slid the window open. "It reeks in here." She waved her hands around as if escorting Roland's odor to the outside world.

He ignored her.

"Did you eat?" she asked sharply. "I left a ham and cheese in the—"

"I ate. Thank you." He stayed focused on his book, annoyed that the interruption had him rereading an inane passage about the big-busted counterintelligence officer who was inexplicably naked in almost every scene in which she appeared. This sort of silliness used to thrill Roland, stir his libido in ways his wife hadn't for years, but now it did nothing but confirm the idiocy of gratuitous literary sex.

Connie plunked down on the arm of the sofa, eyebrows pinched, and pondered Roland's state. As an active sixty-five-year-old who'd stayed current and kept fit even while raising two girls and wrangling a career in food distribution (high schools, colleges, prisons), Connie was once again struck by her miscalculation. She had presumed, as wives often do, that Roland's retirement would inspire a resurgence of shared activity: increased travel, more frequent dinner parties, extended time with the grandkids; certainly, an uptick in the intimacy sadly lacking in recent years. Instead, as she bloomed, he faded. As she embraced her own retirement (commenced shortly after his), he shrank into the gray of obsolescence.

It left her resentful, but all she could say was, "You need to change that shirt. I can smell it from here."

He looked up and nodded, then went back to the naked spy.

AT ONE O'CLOCK in the afternoon, napping for the second time that day, Roland was startled awake when Connie burst back into the den, tittering with excitement. "There's a peacock in our front yard!"

He adjusted the chair to its full upright position. "A peacock? That can't be right."

"Well, it's out there. I just stood watching it for the last five minutes. It's got the little green crown, the whole thing."

He pushed himself out of the chair and walked to the window, looked out over the early-summer lawn, rough and sprouting. "There's nothing out there."

She dashed from the room, calling out from the front door, "Oh my goodness, Roland, it's up on the porch now!" The pitch in her voice was infectious; Roland felt a surprising jolt of energy. He slipped on his moccasins and, at a faster clip than usual, walked to the foyer.

Connie stood with the door cracked, eyes sparkling. "Look," she whispered. "It's still out there, just feet from the door. I'll go get something; maybe it's hungry."

As she rushed to the kitchen, Roland crept up to the door and peeked out.

There it was. A large, completely incongruous wild bird shuffling around the porch, nibbling whatever seeded things were retrievable from between the slats.

"It's a peahen," he corrected Connie when she returned with a bowl of crumbled Triscuits. "It doesn't have the big feathered tail like the male; that's the peacock. She's the female."

"Oh, I see." Connie, delighted to have something, anything, to talk to her husband about beyond the weather, leaned in closely. "Is she still out there?"

He opened the door wider and they both peered out. The peahen was strutting around their large wooden porch as if it were territory well known. Roland took the bowl from Connie's hand

and stepped cautiously from the foyer. As the hen focused on a small planter near the steps several feet away, Roland slid into a porch chair by the door and sprinkled a handful of cracker crumbs in a semicircle around his feet.

He waited.

Connie waited.

After a good long minute, the hen finally took note of Roland's offerings, and, intrigued by the unexpected bounty, inched closer with each peck. Roland found himself oddly anticipatory of her approach, pleased, in a way, that his presence wasn't judged an obstacle to her task. When she was within inches, he leaned down and placed a piece of cracker on the toe of his moccasin.

Connie shook her head, whispering, "Oh, she's not going to—"

The hen snatched the cracker from his foot and stood there, munching, looking around as birds are wont to do, until it finally glanced up at Roland. For a nanosecond he was convinced their eyes held.

"Well, how about that?" Connie chortled. "No fear at all. Let me try." She leaned through the door, grabbed a few bits from the bowl, and held out her hand. The bird, with neither move nor glance in Connie's direction, turned and sashayed down the steps.

"Well, guess I don't rate." She laughed. "Or maybe you're just the bird whisperer."

Roland flushed at the comment. Which was odd, since it really meant nothing. But he liked that he hadn't scared the bird off, that she'd chosen him over his wife. He liked that Connie noticed it and framed it as such. It made him feel special. Dogs and cats like anyone, but a peahen? That didn't happen every day.

As the bird made her way across the street, through another yard, and out to parts unknown, Connie looked at Roland wistfully. "That was unique. Wonder where she came from?"

"She must've broken out of an enclosure or something. Probably lives in that wetland area behind the school. Maybe she's one of their pet projects, who knows? Odds are good we'll never see her again."

He stood and flexed his aching knees. The excitement was over. He headed back in to his book and his boredom.

THE NEXT MORNING Roland settled into the den at 7:30 a.m., and though wide-awake when he got there, was sound asleep within thirty minutes. Three hours later, the abrupt scraping of the window being thrown open snapped him from slumber.

"I swear to God, Roland, it smells like a compost heap in here!" Connie's face conveyed authentic disgust. "I never thought I'd say this to my own husband, but if you insist on living like a hobo, I'd prefer you take it to the basement."

She wasn't kidding; that was clear.

He didn't appreciate her assaultive approach. He adjusted the chair until he was sitting up. He set his book aside and, huffing with indignation, snapped, "If a man can't be comfortable in his own home, what the hell's the point?"

"The point, Roland, is that you have to find a way to be comfortable without behaving like a bum. I work too hard making this home a lovely place to have you turn it into a freeway underpass."

She swept out to the kitchen to quickly return with a plate of food and a can of soda pop. "It's practically lunchtime so I made you a BLT with egg, your favorite. There's a bag of Ruffles, also your favorite, and I got cream sodas yesterday, your third favorite." She set everything down at his side table. "I'm doing everything I can to cheer you up, Roland, but if you're uncheerable, there's nothing more I can do. I'm going on with my life regardless."

"What does that mean?" he asked with genuine alarm.

"I've planned several short trips with friends, sightseeing kinds of things, and I'm taking a photography class at the university. I've always wanted to take better pictures. I'd hoped we might do some of those things together, but I guess not." She brushed her hands on her slacks and straightened her hair. "I'm headed to Carbondale right now. Afterwards I'm going to a movie and dinner with some of the girls, so I'll see you later."

When she got to the door, she stopped and looked back. "Please take a shower today, maybe walk around the block. Pretend you're alive for a minute or two. If nothing else it'll get your blood moving." Her head tilted with a sad smile and then she was gone.

Roland sat in a state of incomprehension. Photography? She'd never expressed one iota of interest in photography; how was he supposed to know it was something she wanted to do? He found himself irritated, thinking about the years of hard work he'd put in to afford the home she just accused him of sullying.

Then, of course, he remembered that her job paid nearly as much as his and provided the excellent health insurance they'd had throughout the years. He could hardly claim superiority on those grounds. He sighed again. There was no winning.

He briefly considered her admonition to take a walk. Maybe he should. These were still the cooler days of early summer, and if he was going to take a shower, may as well work up a bit of a sweat first. At least he'd feel like he accomplished something.

Then he thought about getting his shoes on, finding the right hat; deciding which blocks to avoid to avoid which neighbors, and it all became too much.

He leaned back in his chair and was overcome by the loss of his happiness. He had none. None. He'd never been a particularly jolly fellow, but he'd had some happiness, surely. Now he had nothing to be happy about: no job, no projects, no goals or aspirations; no deadlines, nothing anyone expected from him; nothing to do other than mindlessly walk and read banal books.

He didn't even like his grandkids at the moment. They were exceedingly messy, far too loud, and relentlessly in motion. He certainly loved his two daughters, but they were obsessive parent-types who felt everything about their children was noteworthy; their expectations of him to feel the same were oppressive. He tended to avoid them lately. The only thing he liked right now was Connie, and she didn't like him.

He closed his eyes and fell into the blackness of his gloom. It was a deep, dark place that appeared to have no bottom, and there was comfort in letting himself be swallowed up, further and further down until—

Tap-tap-tap.

An incongruous noise. Another sharp tap, then a scratching sound. At first, he thought he imagined it, but there it was again. He raised the chair and got up, flushed with inexplicable anticipation. He rushed to the front door and slowly, quietly, opened it a crack.

There she stood . . . the peahen.

She looked up at him as if she'd been waiting and was a tad annoyed. He smiled. "Hello there!"

Amidst subtle "clucks" of salutation, she immediately turned and began strutting around the porch, head jutting back occasionally as if inviting him to join her.

His breath quickened. This was no accident, no coincidence. It couldn't be. Peahens don't come to your door every day. If they do appear by chance, there can be no denying a second visit is by choice.

Roland hurried to the kitchen for something to share with his visitor. A small bag of sunflower seeds sat on the counter—clearly one of Connie's "healthy snacks." Whatever hesitation he felt about co-opting her provisions was lost in the urgency to get back quickly.

Ah! Still there, still clucking around the flowerpots to the left of the stairs, seemingly in no hurry to rush off. Roland stepped quietly out to the porch, and sat, once again, in the chair by the door, scattering sunflower seeds around his feet.

He waited. She ignored him. He tapped his toe. She ignored him. He whistled softly. She ignored him. Then, as if deciding she'd toyed with him long enough, she purposefully made her way to the treats and dove in.

Roland was charmed by her enthusiasm. "Better than that fertilizer stuff, isn't it?" He piled a few seeds on the toe of his moccasin and she didn't disappoint, striding close enough for him to touch. When he reached out ever so cautiously, his palm stacked with seeds, she balked only seconds before pecking right from his hand.

He felt triumphant. Which was absurd, he knew, but given the dearth of uplift in his life, her proximity was charming. As she stretched her long neck for the last morsel, she briefly brushed against his hand. He noted the softness of her feathers. In a quick turn, she strutted away, down the steps, across the yard, and off to wherever it was she went.

He took a deep breath and felt . . . something. He couldn't say what, exactly, but it held some harmonic of positive emotion. Which was also absurd. But he felt it nonetheless.

Penelope, he thought. *I'll call her Penelope.* He'd always liked the sound of that name but had never known a woman who bore it. It perfectly fit his new friend. Penelope the Peahen.

He would keep that to himself, naming her. Connie would find it ridiculous. But he didn't care. It made him happy.

CONNIE WAS STUNNED to walk into the den at ten o'clock the following morning to find Roland showered, shaved, and in clean clothes. She stopped and stared without a word, but he didn't look up from his book, aware that his status would be surprising and reluctant to make a fuss about it.

"Do you have a doctor appointment?" she finally asked.

"No. Why?"

"Just wondered." She began picking up random items from around the room, pretending nothing unusual was at hand. "You look like you're ready to go out."

He watched her and felt a stab of affection. "No. Decided you had a point."

She couldn't tell if the comment was sarcastic or conciliatory. Then he gave her a wan smile. "Well . . . good. I appreciate that."

"Thought you might." He seemed genuine. Which was odd.

"Did you eat?"

"Had a bowl of cereal."

"Do you have anything going on this afternoon?" Ludicrous question, they both knew, but it was her habit to ask.

"Just here. And you?"

"I start my class today. It's a pretty intense schedule: twelve to three, five days a week for two weeks, so I'll be—"

"Just enjoy it." He went back to reading.

She looked at him warily. He was definitely acting strange. "I'm sure I will." She picked up his cereal bowl from the side table. "Okay then . . . I'm going to yoga and then on to class, so I'll see you later this evening."

He glanced up from his book. "Yep. See you tonight."

She leaned in and kissed the top of his clean head. They so seldom touched these days it surprised him. He patted her cheek before she swept off.

As soon as he heard the front door click shut, he got up and rushed to the kitchen. From the lower cabinet where baking bowls and other seldom-used items were stashed, he retrieved the supplies he'd purchased from the corner market hours earlier: sunflower and sesame seeds, currants, and packs of various crackers. He pulled a cereal bowl from the shelf and filled it with a mix of everything, then tucked the bags back behind the Cuisinart. He went out to the front porch and settled in his usual chair.

To wait. For Penelope.

The street was quiet, traffic minimal, and he found himself enjoying the coolness of the early morning. He scattered the treats around his feet in typical fashion and leaned back to await his expected guest.

Glancing around at the houses that shared the neighborhood, Roland pondered the various people living there. Directly across were the Fairfields. They used to come over for barbecues on occasion, but with several kids now distributed at colleges around the country, they were seldom available. To the left of them were Mike and Sandy Cutter. They'd initially been frequent guests at the Caine household, but after too many Trivial Pursuit nights in which Mike's rabid competitiveness got aggressive, Roland decided the guy was an asshole.

There were others with whom they'd done this or that, but it was a different time now, a different era. That the neighborhood remained a decent place was enough. That people kept largely to themselves was his preference.

As if summoned by Roland's musings, Mike Cutter pulled from his garage and out to the street. When he noticed Roland on the porch, he stopped, opened the window, and leaned out. "Hey, Roland, haven't seen you in a while. How's retirement going?"

"Just fine." Roland nodded.

"Wish I could join you on that porch, but I gotta get going. Be careful, buddy; looks like you've packed on a few. Retirement will do that to ya!" He laughed and patted his relatively flat stomach, taking off with a wave.

"Asshole," Roland muttered.

Face hot with annoyance, hands clasped over his remarked-upon girth, he decided he wouldn't let Mike sour the morning. It was too nice a day and he had a guest to look forward to. He closed his eyes and drifted off.

At two thirty he jolted awake, stunned to realize he'd napped for so long. He quickly looked around. Nothing had been disturbed on the porch except for the few seeds scattered by fluttering sparrows.

His disappointment was palpable. Both Penelope's previous visits had been around one o'clock; it had been reasonable to expect the same today. At two thirty, it was reasonable to assume otherwise.

He felt the tugging urge to cry, which he knew was irrational. But he'd been so anticipatory of her visit it never occurred to him it was just as likely he'd never see her again, considering he never had prior.

How strange I am, he thought. He and Connie had never even owned a pet, and now he was mopey about a peahen?

Hungry, he snacked from Penelope's bowl and before long was once again slouched in sleep.

"OUCH!"

Yanked from rumbling dreams by a sharp pain in his toe, Roland awoke to find Penelope at his feet, happily partaking in the scattered feast. He had no idea how long he'd been out this time, but in a rush of elation he sat up, careful not to spook her. She clucked and flounced and ate and strutted, and he had the distinct feeling it was all for his benefit.

"So, Miss Penelope," he whispered with a smile, "guess you weren't ready to ditch old Roland after all." He felt warm and chosen.

He reached out his hand, filled with seeds and, again, Penelope got close enough to peck leisurely from his palm. Roland attempted to run his other hand down her feathered back, but she would have none of that, skittering away.

"Okay, okay." He laughed. "Too soon. I get it."

With a coy glance back in his direction, she hopped down the stairs and across the lawn.

"Glad you enjoyed the meal," he called out. "See you tomorrow!" She crossed the street, slowly disappearing from view.

Roland, energized by their brief encounter, went inside and did something he hadn't done in nearly a year: made a pot of spaghetti sauce for dinner. To say Connie was surprised later would be an understatement.

THOUGH IT WAS impossible to predict how long Penelope might continue her visitations, Roland decided to up the odds by providing irresistible grub to keep her enticed. He spent time in the local market scouring shelves for new seeds, new nuts, and different crackers, and every day that week, usually around one o'clock in the afternoon, Penelope did him the honor of stopping by for a shared meal. Roland considered it the peak of his social life. Which, of course, it was.

While Connie was off learning about apertures and depth of field, taking in movies and sharing dinners with friends, Roland begged off every invitation with claims of disinterest or lack of energy. He went nowhere and did nothing, so Connie had finally stopped asking. Now she couldn't help but notice the change in his demeanor.

Without prompting, he'd showered and shaved daily this week, sporting clean clothes as a matter of routine. She also detected a subtle skip to his step whenever he traversed the house, which flummoxed her. Given that he didn't appear to be getting any exercise, and didn't seem to have any friends or neighbors occupying his time and attention, the mood shift was confounding.

"Roland." She sat down on the den couch. "Can I talk to you?"

He put his book down and looked up. "Sure." There was no irritation in his face. That, too, was odd. He typically got peevish when she interrupted his reading.

"I'm taking off tomorrow for a field trip with the girls. We're driving up to Springfield to do the Lincoln tour I've always wanted to do."

His first thought was that he'd had no idea she wanted to do the Lincoln tour. The second was that it was a good, long drive.

"That's a good, long drive," he said.

"Just a bit over six hundred miles, but there's four of us, so we'll take turns. And we're giving ourselves the whole day to get there; the tour is scheduled for Saturday. Class was canceled on Monday, so I won't be back until that night. Now, I've left some prepared meals and—"

"I'll be fine, Connie. Just go have a good time."

His words were like a foreign tongue. She'd expected him to grumble about having to warm up his food, or being alone for four days, or not knowing where she kept this or that, so his benevolence was disorienting.

"Thank you, Roland," she said hesitantly, "I will." She also knew she'd be giving some hard thought to this new husband who'd appeared in recent days.

But for Roland her outing was a reprieve. He had been wondering how to juggle the weekend; how to be available for Penelope without getting Connie too involved. It wasn't that she wouldn't appreciate seeing the bird again; and it wasn't that Roland minded if she shared her visits. It was that he feared she'd see just how attached he'd become and judge him ridiculous. Think him crazy. Decide he'd finally lost his marbles.

He didn't want any suggestions of that nature to be triggered. Nor did he want to explain himself. He knew his enthusiasm tipped the scales a bit—naming her might seem eccentric to his wife—but he wasn't obsessed, surely. Not like those Tokyo businessmen with their life-sized "love dolls," or people who'd let their dogs lick their mouths.

He was just a regular guy who got a kick out of a wild peahen who seemed to get a kick out of him. He looked forward to the connection. He felt honored by her attraction to him and his snacks . . . and he was aware the snacks were the hook; he wasn't that delusional.

So, while Connie packed her weekend bag upstairs, Roland quietly prepped three bowls of seeds and crackers for the days ahead, eager to be able to just sit back, relax, and enjoy the time. He hummed as he wrapped plastic around each bowl and tucked them into the lower cabinet. He cleaned the counter, wiped his hands, and smiled. Both he and Connie were going to have really nice weekends.

* * *

BUT HE DID NOT.

Penelope never came. Not once. Not Friday, not Saturday, not Sunday. She was a complete no-show.

He was gut-sick. So frantic by Sunday night he eschewed the five o'clock news to roam the neighborhood in hopes of finding her, irked when Mike Cutter, out mowing his lawn in the remaining light of day, came on like an ambush.

"Well, howdy, Roland. Twice in one week, that's gotta be a record." He grinned.

Roland barely slowed his step. "Yeah, hi, Mike." He kept walking.

"Hey!" Mike quickly turned off the mower and moved to the fence. "Roland, hang on."

Roland reluctantly stopped. "What's up?"

"I feel like we haven't been very neighborly lately, what with everyone keeping to themselves. How are things going over there?"

"Fine. Connie's busy with all her stuff and I'm enjoying my retirement, like you said."

Mike laughed. "Lucky guy! I still got five more years, but let me tell ya, the minute I'm done, I set sail for the world and won't be back till I've seen the whole damn thing!"

Mike never failed to make clear he was younger, which irritated Roland, but there was likely another dig in there as well. Being the observant sort, Mike had to have noticed Roland and Connie didn't get out much. Sail the world.

Asshole.

Then Roland was struck by a thought: there might be some value in chatting up a guy who spent more time observing the neighborhood than he did. "Say, Mike, this might be a silly question, but have you seen a peahen around here lately, just wandering around the neighborhood?" He tried to keep the question as casual as he could.

"Hell, yes, I've seen that damn thing! Sandy found it ripping up her garden a few weeks ago so now we gotta make sure the gate's always latched, which is a pain."

"Yeah, they can be ... feisty!" Roland felt immediately defensive, but kept smiling. "Any idea where she came from?"

"Nah. Some idiot probably got it as a chick, threw it out when it got too big for the cage. All I know is, Sandy'll beat its head in with a shovel if it gets anywhere near her garden again. Peahen stew all around!" he guffawed.

Roland clenched his fist, tamping a sharp impulse to smash Mike's stupid face. "Okay, well—"

"Why do you ask?"

"No big deal. It's just been up on my porch a few times . . . kind of a hoot. Haven't seen it lately though."

"To each his own, buddy. It comes over here, it's stew."

Roland clenched again and, with a terse nod, hurried off. One more spin around the block and he headed home, bereft.

BY MONDAY EVENING and no Penelope, Roland moved beyond grief to metastasizing anger. Mike's cavalier threats openly suggested that neither he nor his wife would have any compunction about beating a living creature to death, and Roland's stomach knotted just thinking about it.

Connie was due home that night, giving him the distraction of cleaning the kitchen—which he'd allowed to sink into disarray—as well as get upstairs for a shower and shave. The last thing he needed was her questioning his regression to old behaviors.

But as he soaped and scrubbed away anxiety sweat and the dirt between his toes from forays around the neighborhood, his rage boiled unabated. He was not going to be passive about Penelope's imminent danger; it was absurd to think he would. He owed as much to that benign little being, whose only sin was being true to her nature.

He knew the gate to the Cutters' backyard had a flimsy drop latch; easy to open. A late-night visit to check trash bins and compost heaps was warranted; he had to be sure they hadn't already disposed of her. Not tonight, what with Connie arriving home, but if Penelope hadn't shown by tomorrow, his mission was fated.

THE HOMECOMING WAS pleasant, Connie was animated as she filled him in on the trip, but when she hadn't come into the den by ten the following morning, Roland was concerned enough to climb out of his recliner to go find her.

She was seated at the dining room table, face pale, lips dry, her eyes red and swollen. She didn't look up when he walked into the room.

"What's wrong?" Roland was suddenly terrified that something unexpected had happened to his beloved, if ignored, wife. She looked at him with such anguish his heart jumped. "What is it? What's going on?"

"Who's Penelope?"

It hit like a blow to the chest. "Penelope?" he queried weakly.

"Yes. Penelope."

"Oh, um—"

"I've been wondering what was behind your sudden change in hygiene, your uplifted mood, your unusual perkiness, but I didn't want to be the suspicious wife. Particularly since I couldn't imagine how you could possibly have met someone, given your general state of agoraphobia. But last night I was awakened by you thrashing around the bed mumbling 'Penelope' over and over, and there seemed little doubt. Be honest with me, Roland. Are you having an affair?"

"Good lord!" It was so absurd he almost laughed.

"Even an emotional one . . . online . . . through a porn site or with some phone sex operator? Or have you actually met someone?"

By now tears were streaming down her face and Roland felt, quite possibly, like the worst husband in the world. He went to her and put his arms around her in the first embrace he'd offered in months. She stiffened, but he blurted out his explanation:

"No, no, oh, my God, no, there's no woman. No woman at all. Penelope is the peahen."

Her reaction was so abrupt she snapped his arms away from her body. "The peahen? The peahen?" she yelped. "What the hell are you talking about, Roland?"

"It's crazy, I know, but yes, it's the peahen. I gave her the name Penelope, just something silly to call her . . . she's been visiting quite a bit."

He was so frantic to assuage Connie's fears he forgot how deranged he might sound. Which clearly he did, given the look on her face.

"I started making these little bowls of seeds and stuff, and every day she came, around one o'clock; she'd come right up to me and eat from my hand. I even felt her neck one time, she was that close. And it seemed like she remembered me, you know, like she came specifically to see me. The 'bird whisperer,' like you said, right? So, I got used to it, I looked forward to it. Then over the weekend she stopped coming. It's like she disappeared. It was so strange I went looking for her around the neighborhood but no luck. I even talked to Mike Cutter, but he got all weird about her eating up their garden or something, and I honestly suspect he might have done something to her—"

"ROLAND!" Connie snapped. "SHUT UP!"

He did.

She looked at him fiercely. "Why on earth would you be rolling around in bed calling out the name of a peahen? Do you know how insane that sounds?"

He did. It sounded completely insane. "But you have to understand, Con: she visited me every day, and then all of a sudden, poof, she's gone. Wouldn't you worry if someone you cared about just disappeared like that?" Beyond tempering his anxiety, he felt tears building.

Now it was Connie's turn to consider him with solicitude, adjusting her tone. "Oh, Roland," she said softly. "You need to see a therapist, sweetheart. You really do." She stood up, dried her eyes and rearranged her face, swinging swiftly from injured wife to concerned spouse. She patted his head tenderly. "I'm going to call your doctor and see if he can recommend someone. I think if you can talk about what you've been going through since your retirement—your loneliness, your isolation, your sense of irrelevance—it will go a long way toward alleviating your transference issues with this poor little peahen."

Before Roland could react or respond, she marched off on her mission, unwilling to give him a moment to debate the prescription.

He, of course, knew she was wrong. He did not need to speak to a therapist. He needed to find Penelope.

* * *

BUT SHE DIDN'T come. And that was it.

Later that night, as Connie snored softly beside him, Roland got up, slipped on his walking shoes, and snuck cautiously from the bedroom. Downstairs, he grabbed his camouflage hunting jacket from the closet and pulled a brimmed cap down to his eyebrows. The front door had a persistent squeak so he tiptoed to the kitchen, picked up a flashlight, and made his way out the back.

It was late enough, dark enough, to support clandestine maneuvers, but luckily the moon offered sufficient illumination to find his way to the Cutters' backyard gate. With shallow breath and heart beating like timpani, he was rewarded with a well-oiled latch. Opening it without a sound, he slid through the gate to their fastidiously landscaped backyard.

His hands were shaking and sweat rolled down his back. After perusing the garden—nary a stalk out of place—he moved to the shed in the southwest corner. He was convinced if any remains remained, they'd be in there, at least until garbage day, a thought that almost made him choke on his strangled breath.

When he got to the shed, he tested the door. Again, another drop latch, which he opened with ease. He found a small planter near the entrance to prop the door open, concerned the beam of his flashlight might be seen through the windows.

Three garbage bins were lined up to his right. He lifted the green lid and, with the handle of a nearby broomstick, rustled through the branches and leaves to see if anything more solid was contained. Didn't seem to be. He decided to forego the recycling bin; there was little likelihood they'd have thrown her body in there. But the trash container stood full and ominous. It might take him some time, but he was determined to get to the bottom of it.

Just as he angled to pull up the lid, a creak at the door startled him. His breath caught, but before he could turn, the barrel of a shotgun was shoved into his back.

"Move the fuck away from those bins," Mike growled, "or I'll blow your fucking head off." His voice sounded like a mix of gravel and razor blades.

Roland could have simply said, "Mike, it's me, Roland!" or put his hands up and pivoted so Mike could see his face, but for some inexplicable reason, and without a whit of wisdom or forethought, he was seized by combustible anger. In that perilous moment, he just knew this heinous man had killed his bird, he knew her shattered body had been discarded like so much trash, and he knew he was going to kick the living shit out of his arrogant, asshole neighbor.

With a roar that might have wakened the entire neighborhood, Roland swung around with little regard for the firearm at his back and came at Mike like a frenzied bear. Mike was so startled to see his former Trivial Pursuit opponent coming at him with teeth bared, eyes flashing, and rage propelling the charge, he stepped back, lost his footing, and crashed backward through the door of the shed, falling to the lawn outside. Roland leapt on top of him, arms flailing and fists pummeling with clear intent to inflict damage.

"You motherfucking murderer!!" Roland bellowed. "WHERE IS SHE? What did you do with her?"

Blood spurt from Mike's shattered nose, but even as he attempted to flip his body to a more defensive position, he was helpless in the flurry of blows. The back-porch light flipped on. Sandy came flying down the stairs, hair streaming, her mouth wide in a scream.

"ROLAND CAINE, GET OFF MY HUSBAND RIGHT NOW! I've called your wife, I've called the police, and they'll be here in minutes. GET OFF HIM NOW or I promise I will use that shotgun!!"

But Roland heard nothing. Every ounce of his anger, disappointment, rage, sorrow, loneliness, heartache, fear, and longing drove the onslaught. He'd lost control. His nose ran, his tears streamed; his anguish was raw and primal. All Mike could do was cover his head in hopes of mitigating further injury.

"ROLAND!" Connie's piercing shriek suddenly reverberated like a loudspeaker. Even in the din of internal chaos, Roland heard her. It shocked him. Connie? What was she doing here?

His mind went blank and he stopped moving, stopped howling, stopped flailing on his bloodied neighbor, and fell back on the lawn. Within moments, the just-arrived police swarmed on top of him, shouting commands and pinning him motionless, while Sandy administered to her battered husband and Connie stood in horrified silence.

As rights were read, handcuffs applied, first aid rendered, and order restored, Roland's eyes averted just long enough to see, in a moment of surreal irony, Penelope, strutting down the quiet street, blissfully unaware of all that had just transpired on her behalf.

Six Months Later

ONE DOESN'T NECESSARILY recover from a psychotic event of such magnitude. They simply get past it; hopefully heal the mental lesions that led to it, and gratefully accept the forgiveness and compassion of those who love them. That was Roland's assignment.

Initially Mike was unyielding in his intent to pursue aggravated assault charges; certainly the prosecutor was on board. But as wounds healed, and time was spent talking to both Connie and Sandy, gaining empathy for an "old guy who'd lost his mind in post-retirement depression" (as Connie so bluntly put it), he ultimately agreed to Roland's plea of "simple battery misdemeanor," which came with a $2,500 fine, two years' probation, no jail time, but a mandate of talk therapy and medical intervention for at least one full year. He was also required to pay Mike's related medical bills and refrain from proximity to the Cutters or their property.

Despite what had been settled legally, however, on a personal level, Sandy and Mike, along with several other neighbors, retreated behind an untraversable wall of sequestration. Connie felt deep embarrassment at their new role as the neighborhood pariahs, but her priority was getting Roland healthy. Over time, she presumed the neighbors would move on to other gossip-worthy spectacles.

Lastly, on advice from her own therapist, she got Roland a cat. A house cat of gentle demeanor, who seemed as devoted to Roland as he was to her. It was a good remedy. It didn't demand the engagement of a dog—walking neighborhood streets was not a good idea at this juncture—but did offer him companionship and attachment. He named her Lily.

They screened in the front porch so Roland could enjoy the space without fear of Lily bolting, and he was often out there, even on cold days, sipping his coffee, cuddling her on his lap, watching as life went by on a street that no longer felt like his own. He'd occasionally see Mike or Sandy emerge from their house or garage and, whenever he did, a pang of remorse was felt.

There was one time when he thought he saw Penelope strutting between the houses a few doors down from the Cutters'.

But he was probably wrong.

WHISTLE STOP
K.T. SPARKS

THE DAY BEFORE I LEFT THE COMPOUND FOR GOOD, CLAY
asked me to meet him at the barn on the steps up to the room
where we keep the chicken feed. I said sure, even though he's rude
and ugly. I thought he might want to kiss me. He's close to my age,
unlike Kenny and W.B., who are old enough to have gray in their
beards. Dad always joked he'd marry me off to one or the other of
them. Clay was twenty, and I was fourteen, but a mature fourteen.
Mom taught me, and I read at a college level. She used to work at
the best private high school in D.C., so I've learned about modern
art and astrophysics and real life. Not just Jesus and peach canning,
like you hear about with other homeschoolers.

I got down to the barn when Clay said, but he wasn't there. So,
I went in the feed room and fished a fresh-hatched baby duck out
of the bottom of the incubator and cupped it to my cheek to keep
us both warm. It was so soft and sunny. I thought maybe some of
that might reflect back and make me more kissable.

We stood out on the steps for a while, baby duck and me,
and I was just about to give up on the idea and go back to my
calculus when Clay came down the hill from Building #2. He
wore brown insulated coveralls, the ones he got from W.B. the
Christmas before, and no hat. His face was red, and his hair
stood up like bundled wheat. Watching him slip on the loose
gravel and stutter step and spin his arms made me reconsider the
kissing. I took the duckling back to the heat lamps, and when I
got out front again, Clay was standing there, his tomato face shiny
with sweat.

"Well, there you are," he said and grabbed my arm with one hand and halfway unzipped his top with the other. He handed me a magazine from under his suspenders. It was bent and limp and opened to what I thought was a picture of an underground cavern out West, slick red cave walls closing in on a creamy and ridged stalactite. But what it really was was a close-up of a man and a woman screwing. I turned the page to a shot of one naked woman, spread-eagle, and a lot of naked men. Kiss indeed. Before I could figure what was going on in that picture, my mom swooped in from wherever she had been hovering and snatched the magazine. She cuffed Clay into the frozen mud and kicked at him with her Carhartt winter boots until he screamed so loud Dad came out and pulled her off. She waved the magazine and spit at Dad and yelled, "This! This!" Clay lay flat back on the ground, eyes shut and legs open, kind of like the naked woman, but of course, he had on the snowsuit. Dad stood still too, like maybe if he was silent and calm, Mom would stop yelling and jumping.

She threw the magazine on the ground and stomped on it. The pages tore, and the naked woman's head stuck to the tip of her boot, like a mermaid on the front of a Viking ship. Clay remained flat but moaned, as if it were he and not the picture getting ripped to shreds.

"You keep them away from her, all of them," she said.

"She's not a baby," Dad said. "She's gonna have to learn to take care of herself. You know, for when you go off, with your boy."

The way he said "boy," two syllables, the first one as deep and echoed as a bullfrog's call, meant he was talking about a black man. I didn't know about Gideon yet, so I assumed Dad meant the substitute UPS driver, Lenny. He was the only black man I knew then.

"You shut up," Mom said. She stepped forward. A wind bit at my ears. It carried with it Sarabeth's distant chattering and the muffled baying of Dad's bear hounds.

Dad put his hand on his holstered 9 mm.

"Do it," she said and inched so close a strand of her kinky bronze hair caught in the stubble on his cheek.

I went up behind her and leaned against her back.

Dad stepped back once, twice, then shook his head and turned and walked down the drive. I put my arms around Mom's waist and moved with her breathing.

THAT NIGHT, DAD and Mom were in his office, fighting, and I was outside the door, listening.

"Jane, you're a fool, leaving me, for him."

"I'm just leaving you. Not for anyone."

"You're also a liar. Always have been. Not that I care, but you know, I can't keep you safe, if you leave."

Dad was obsessed with keeping us safe. Not just me and Mom. Also, Kenny and W.B. and old Mrs. Speck and her nephew Tiki, who couldn't drive a truck anymore after a guy at the dump put a ball peen hammer through his left temple. That was two years ago. A bunch of people Dad knew from high school: Eric, Bobby, Hercy, James Moore, Grail, and the women that sometimes went with them and sometimes didn't: Lottie, Brooke Jewell, Ann, Elestine, and Sarabeth Seamus. The twins Clay and Mitchell belonged to her. They used to live at the Compound until Sarabeth's sister was arrested, and Sarabeth admitted she couldn't handle them by herself and sent them to their uncle in Harrisonburg. They still visited a lot. Father John, a recovering heroin addict. And Juan, an illegal who stayed sometimes with us and sometimes in the shacks the Mennonites set up for the guys who help out in the turkey houses. He was a Mexican, but Dad said he was okay because he spoke good English and once killed a guy in the desert for raping an old woman.

At the Compound, Dad laid in enough ramen, canned beans, and venison jerky to last us all two years. One thousand pounds of coal. Four thousand liters of sterilized water. A base flock of thirty Black Australorps, twenty-eight broody hens and two roosters. And enough weapons and ammunition to repel those who had not similarly planned ahead.

It wasn't about end days or getting back to Mother Earth with Dad. It was about 9/11 and how they wouldn't let him join the Guard because of his feet. Mom and Dad were married two months before in D.C., where he built HOV lanes on I-66, and she worked at the school. That October, their mailman dropped dead from anthrax, and their letters came late and diverted through Cleveland, crispy and brown around the edges. The next October, on Mom's first day back after maternity leave, a sniper took a shot at a kid in her school's playground. The kid didn't die, but Dad moved us anyway, back to his great uncle's farm, halfway down the Shenandoah Valley. It's where he was from and where he'd always planned to build something like the Compound.

"Try and stop me. Try it," Mom said. She howled it, like one of the hounds hitting the electric fence.

A screech then a bump, which could have been a chair falling over or could have been Dad's fist hitting flesh.

"I don't need to stop you," Dad said. "You'll come back."

I pushed in the room. Dad was standing behind his desk, both hands on top, sunburn red from neck to brow. Mom was sitting on a wooden bench, knees tight together, looking like she was waiting for a bus she really didn't want to take. I ran to her and pressed my face into her lap. Her jeans smelled sour with sweat and musty with henhouse dirt.

"Don't leave, don't leave, don't leave," I cried.

"Take her with you," Dad said.

Mom didn't answer, stroked my hair lightly, like my scalp were a skittish cat.

"I want to go," I said, not daring to lift my head, not daring to see if her eyes were as indifferent as her touch.

"You don't want her either," Dad said. Still Mom didn't answer, not right away. I counted silently to ten and halfway back again before she spoke.

"Of course I want her. Alice, go get your things together."

I MOVED QUICK, in case she changed her mind. I didn't know when we were going, or where, or what to pack, which I guess didn't matter, because I didn't have a suitcase to pack in anyway. I went to the main pantry and found a plastic tub that used to hold onions. It didn't look like luggage, and, if you put your head full in it, it could make your eyes water with the smell of Vidalias gone soft. But it had handles and a lid and wasn't too big. I put in some jeans and

T-shirts and underwear and socks and my pink Adidas. I started
with three sweaters and a sweatshirt but pulled all but the sweatshirt
out again. There was hardly anymore room, and what if we were
going to someplace hot, like Florida? I took a faded flannel shirt of
Dad's I'd found in the rag pile. I tried to squeeze my pillow in, but
no go. I slid my math book, *Black Beauty*, a paperback about
vampires that Father John stole from the library, and two Archie
comic books down the sides. I set on top the burner phone my dad
got me for my thirteenth birthday, the sort all the adults on the
Compound carried. I wasn't even sure it worked. I'd never turned
it on. No one to call.

I decided to stay dressed and awake, in case Mom and I were
leaving tonight. I pulled back the blanket that covered the window
at the end of the bed. From there, I could see to where the gravel
driveway circled round the front of the barn. The wind was kicking
up, so all Dad's motion sensor lights had flicked on, and it was as
bright as the winter sun at three in the afternoon. Little streams of
cold air worked their way around the clear tape at the sides of the
window frame and tweaked my cheeks and the outsides of my ears.
Something metal clanged against the side of one of the tin
outbuildings. The Anatolian in Pasture #1 barked and barked.

Right after the roosters started crowing, so maybe around two
a.m., my mom came in and sat on the side of my bed. I might have
been a little asleep. I didn't turn toward her but let my shoulder fall
into her back. Her hair frizzed over the left side of my face, and it
felt like I was resting on a pillow made of a static cloud.

"We're not leaving until morning," she said, still not turning.
"You can go to sleep."

"That's okay," I said.

"Well, I'm going to," she said and skootched herself all the
way onto my bed. I swiveled. She lay on her back, eyes closed,
still dressed in her dirty work jeans and a black turtleneck. She'd
taken off her boots and socks. Her feet were long and narrow and
cracked and flaked with white skin tags all around the edges. I
pushed myself back a bit, put one hand on one of her feet. It
prickled, like stroking a splinter of old fence wood. I went back to
watching the driveway.

"Don't you want to know where we're going?" she said.

I did, but I said, "It's okay. I don't care."

"San Francisco," she said. "It's in California."

I knew that, so I didn't answer, just made a little noise, not happy, not sad. I sensed my part in all this was too new to be certain, so I was trying to make myself, my responses and expectations and baggage, as small as possible. Smaller is better when you're on the run. That's what Dad always said.

"A friend of mine's going to help us. His name is Gideon. He works for Amtrak," Mom said.

"Is he your boyfriend?" I asked before I could help myself.

"It'll be fine," she said. "You'll go to public school." This was an answer to a question I hadn't asked, but it satisfied me. Gideon might be a boyfriend. Maybe they were planning to get married. But I was still in the equation.

I'd only ever seen San Francisco on a Rice-A-Roni box and only ever gone to school at the black oak table in our kitchen. I'm glad she didn't ask me how I felt about San Francisco. I wouldn't have known what to say. I was like the first astronaut, the Russian guy. I don't suppose he could have told you truly how he felt about going into space. He probably would have said, I'll let you know when I get there. Of course, I would miss some things about the Compound. The barn cats. Sarabeth's coleslaw. Shooting the crossbow with Dad. But I would miss Mom more, if I stayed.

I DIDN'T SEE Dad again. He didn't even come out when Ed Aerhardt's car pulled up the drive the next morning. That was the first time I'd ever ridden in a taxi. Mom said there were all manner of them in San Francisco. Mr. Aerhardt dropped us at the train station in Staunton just as the sun finished rising, and the metal roof over the platform looked like it was painted with gold. Mom pulled her bag and mine next to a bench facing the track, sat, and started poking at her new iPhone. I stood for a minute smelling the frying bacon from the Depot Grill at the other end of the cobblestone road. Mom snuck me there once, for my tenth birthday. We had extra fries and free cake. Dad didn't believe in eating out.

I breathed one more breath of pork fat and joined Mom on the bench. I nudged her purse, really just a Food Lion tote, with my foot. I hoped she had brought some snacks.

"Live free or die," my mom said and looked up from *Angry Birds*. The quicksilver light beaming from her iPhone colored her face sterling.

"You have to survive to be free," I said, quoting Dad.

"Surviving almost killed us," said Mom. I knew she would have an answer. I didn't expect it to be serious.

"Freedom is just another word for nothing left to lose," I countered.

Mom rolled her eyes and looked down at her game. She lobbed a shedding canary into a pyramid of Corinthian columns and baby blue ice cubes and when it fell, pumped her fist. She flipped her head back and her hand-knitted watch cap dropped behind the bench, and her hair shot out all over like electricity.

"Freedom," she sang. "Freedom."

A young Mennonite couple dressed for the second sailing of the Mayflower backed away from our bench. They edged all the way to the other end of the platform, and the woman stared out at us through the tunnel of her black bonnet. Mom stuck out her tongue and returned her eyes to the phone.

I envied the Mennonites their religion sometimes. On their compounds, they had a rationale for keeping themselves shut away, something bigger and better than fear. Or maybe that's just what I wanted to believe. I wouldn't have liked having to wear long skirts. And even though the girls my age had skin like pink silk, most were missing a finger or two. Those old tools don't have safety guards.

I stretched my neck and leaned into Mom so our temples touched. She was all the faith I needed. I huddled closer to her and down into my parka.

Mom swiped the screen to the Amtrak app, showed me the train would come in twenty-one minutes, and swiped back to the game. She didn't offer me a turn, and that was okay. I was just as happy to watch. It was the first iPhone I'd seen up close, though I'd heard about them, of course. We kept up with technology at the Compound. Dad had a MacBook Pro with retina display, top-of-the-line ID-masking software, and one of the old unlimited data plans from Verizon.

"Twelve minutes," Mom said.

The train whistled from around the rock face of Sears Hill, and a light hit us smack in the face before turning onto the tracks. The silver cars hissed and groaned and settled and a high door opened with a puff and a black man as big as a bear hooked a brown hand on a steel bar and swung out.

"Jane," he called, and my mom pocketed the phone and stood up. He wore a conductor's suit, pressed as flat blue as midnight with gold buttons down his chest and gold braids around his wrists. His voice was as round as he was.

"And this is Alice," he said and jumped down to the platform and reached that big paw toward me and the bench. Mom stretched back and gripped my shoulder and whispered, "Here we go."

TWENTY-SIX HOURS after we left the Staunton station, Mom and I again sat thigh-to-thigh on a cold bench, this time facing the Calder sculpture in Chicago's Federal Plaza. It was called "Flamingo," according to the Amtrak informational brochure my mom had made me read at breakfast. It looked more like an enormous and ailing praying mantis in a color Dad, who loves Mustangs from the '70s, would have called "grabber orange."

"So, you just stay here and let me run my errands." Mom bounced her thighs off the cold concrete. "I'm not going to be long."

"Go on," I said, though I didn't really want to wait alone. Gideon had tried to talk Mom out of coming to this particular square. He said winos liked to shelter from the wind against the rectangular planters here, and flashers hung out around the bus stop. But Mom brought us anyway. She told Gideon she was sick and tired of taking precautions, of hunkering down, of sticking together. She left all that at the Compound, she said. And if we wanted to be with her, we had to too.

"Okay then," she said and stood. Her eyes popped to the street, the plaza, the orange bug, me, and the scent of roses pulsed off her. She'd never worn perfume before, that I knew of. What she smelled of mostly in Virginia was propane and wood smoke. She repeated my instructions. I was to sit and not worry about being kidnapped or raped. I was to think about what I would do if I could do anything.

I still felt the train rocking, and the winter-bright sky gave me a headache. "I'll be fine," I said. "Palm, knee, foot." That's the three ways you hit an assailant for maximum impact (palm to the nose, knee to the groin, foot to the top of the foot). She quit hopping and met my eye.

"Try not to put anybody in the hospital," she said, tapped the heel of her hand on my forehead, and jogged off to make the light.

I followed her flashing curls, bobbing above the ski caps and balaclava of the midmorning crowd, until her head disappeared. I didn't like her being where I couldn't reach her. For a long time, she never traveled out of hollering distance. Then around about a year ago, Sarabeth's sister got moved to the Alderson Federal Prison Camp, and Mom started going up there with Sarabeth for visits. Maybe twice a month, they would catch the train at three and come back the next day by two.

That's how Mom met Gideon. For fourteen years, he was a conductor on the Cardinal, New York City to Chicago by way of Washington, DC, Charlottesville, VA, Staunton, and Alderson Federal Prison Camp. Martha Stewart was jailed there. Gideon said no one fancy enough to stand out as her visitor ever showed up on the train. Mom laughed at that. She laughed at everything Gideon said.

Mom's head disappeared under the Walgreen's sign, and I burped up a bit of the Yankee Pot Roast ($24.75) I'd eaten in the train's dining room the night before. We were allowed to order anything we wanted from the menu. It was included in the price of the ticket. Gideon got to sit with us even though he was working, because it was his last run on the Cardinal, and we were his "special friends," according to the dining room attendant, Wylie. He was as white as Gideon was black and talked in the slow way of people from the way-south, like Kenny. All that deep breathing between words makes them sound dumb. But if you think they're slow, go ahead and turn your back for a minute. They're as fast as snakes. I know, because, besides Kenny and Sarabeth, we had, on and off, about ten others in the Compound from Alabama, and they all made me jumpy as hell.

Dad looked for people like that. Sluggish on the surface, but running quick and cold underneath, like Clay and Mitchell. Clay got in a fight with a guy with a hoe when he was twelve and ended up with a scar across his left cheek. Six months later, when it faded and opened up a bit, like a tiny valley, Mitchell cut his own cheek with a hunting knife. But he got the wrong cheek and nicked his eye, so now he wore plastic black-framed glasses, and that's how you told them apart.

Neither of the two boys skateboarding across the plaza had glasses, so they couldn't be the Seamus twins, despite their matching buzz cuts. That, and there was no reason they'd be in Chicago. Mom said paranoia can't be our second skin anymore. She said I should start worrying about normal things, like zits and prom dates and getting pregnant. Not Iraqi terrorists or whether the government was causing earthquakes through plate tectonics.

I chanted to myself: "Just a normal day. Just a normal day," but after a while, it stopped making sense. Twice I thought I saw W.B. in the swirls of people navigating around the sculpture and the office building behind it. Once I thought I spotted Dad. But when they got closer, I could see these men weren't a bit like W.B. or Dad or anyone from our part of Virginia. They wore shiny navy coats with team names, like BEARS, written on them in corn yellow block letters. They weren't bulky as much as they were puffy. Still, I couldn't help but stay on high alert for Compound members, and because of that, I missed the approach of the pervert.

He was an old man in a collarless beige sweatshirt and matching baggy track pants, and he plopped down next to me and placed a bare and red and swollen hand on my parka where it covered my thigh. He pressed down, as if he were flattening a grilled cheese. Both of us kept our eyes on sculpture.

"I just don't get it," he said. I didn't either, but knew better than to discuss it with him. I tried to inch away. He leaned down harder.

"Did you ever think about modeling?" he said, still not looking at me.

I wasn't entirely sure what my next move was. Palm-knee-foot seemed premature. He'd done nothing physical so far but smush my leg, and maybe that was a mistake. In any case, he was to my side, and we were both on our butts, which made any sort of self-defense problematic. No leverage.

I shifted out from under his hand and stood. He stood too, and he was much bigger than he looked hunched on the bench.

"I've got a car near here," he said, putting himself between me and my view of the street. "It wouldn't hurt to talk over your options." He sounded tired. I wondered if he did this a lot.

"Alice," I heard my mom.

"Mom," I yelled back.

She ran from across the street, ten-mile strides, swatting pedestrians with a white Walgreens bag. For a moment, I was sorry for the guy. I sidestepped right and moved to go to her. He grabbed my hood, and the parka's collar hit me in the throat like a hard swallow of hot tea.

Maybe I blacked out for a minute. I didn't see or hear Mom hit him. She must have clipped him at the back of the knees, because next I know, he let loose my hood and dropped his head to my level. Muscle memory kicked in, and I drove my palm up into his nostrils. The crust and hair tickled before the crunch of cartilage. It felt like smashing graham crackers for piecrust.

I pulled my arm back, ready to strike again.

"Wipe it," yelled Mom, "AIDS," and I noticed the blood on me, not too much. There was more on the guy's face and it spurted onto his sweatshirt. Mom grabbed my clean hand and pulled me away. Three policemen in uniform passed us on the left. They were carrying coffees in Styrofoam cups and ambling toward the wailing pervert, as if they were headed toward some sort of street performance in which they had very little interest.

I put my bloody hand in my pocket, and Mom gave me a tight smile. Nothing good came of involving cops. She gripped me tighter and jogged us into the middle of the crowd. When we got about a block away, she stopped dead and pulled me into a bear hug. My head bounced against her as her chest heaved. I assumed she was crying, because I was crying. But I was wrong. She was laughing.

She spun me out and away, like a swing dancer. She was having the time of her life. So I laughed back, what else could I do? We continued toward Union Station, hand in hand, swinging arms, laughing at my almost abduction, laughing at the wounded old man, laughing at our narrow escape.

That night at dinner, our first on the California Zephyr, the train that would take us all the way to San Francisco, she was still laughing when she told the story to a sparrow of a mother from the Chicago suburbs and her pale, silent son. Ten years old, according to the mother, eleven according to the boy, the only word he spoke all meal. She was terrified of my mom and falling in love at the same time. Mom made it sound like we were both superheroes. And maybe we were. The woman asked again, "You knocked him down?" Maybe I hadn't been in danger, real danger. Or maybe I had been in just enough danger to make it thrilling, like I imagined riding a roller coaster might be. I bet the boy wished he had my mom. If it had happened to him, he'd have been cut into a million pieces and stashed in the back of that creep's trunk. The thought made me sad, and I pushed the boy my dessert pudding parfait. He nodded and spooned a mouthful.

MOM AND I decided to sit after dinner and look out the window for a bit, even though it was so black you could only guess at what was out there: rutted and frozen dirt, bent and broken corn stalks, one white-board farmhouse and miles of empty driveway. We would ride through the plains all night.

I watched the scared mother and her boy wobble their way toward the sleeping cars. He was in front of her, leaning back, and her hands were on his shoulders, like she had to hold him up every step.

Mom stared out into the nothing. I tried to figure what she was looking at, but mostly all I could make out were the streaks on the window's Plexiglas from other peoples' hands and noses. Once in a while, a streetlight illuminated a crossing gate, with a beat-up car waiting there, exhaust settling like rain clouds around its tailpipe. The train whistle sounded like far-off crying, like it was coming from way underground and didn't have anything to do with this train at all.

Mom was looking at her own reflection.

Gideon showed up at the table just then, with an opened bottle of wine in one hand and plastic cups in the other. He wasn't in his conductor's outfit anymore. He wore a dark blue vest and matching pants with a summer sky shirt and tie.

"I made up your room," he said. "In case you're worn out, from all of the fighting." He laughed. Mom laughed. I even laughed a little, because of the way he said it, bobbing his head, holding the bottle and cups up in front of his face, a boxer ready to jab.

I wiggled myself out of the booth, and Gideon sat down next to Mom. I hung onto the edge of the table and watched him pour red wine. The smell of vinegar and sharp honey mixed with the sulfur emitting from the churning wall heaters.

"You want a Coke?" Gideon asked me.

"Why don't you get ready for bed?" Mom said.

"I don't drink Coke," I said to Gideon. "When are you coming?" to Mom.

"Soon," she said and toasted her smudgy reflection in the black window with her plastic cup.

"How long?" I wasn't ready to go back alone.

She pivoted and stared into me. Her hair mirrored behind her looked like a halo. She sipped her wine. She stared at me for a long time. Until the wine in her cup was almost gone. Gideon thrummed his fat fingers on the edge of the table, cleared throat twice.

"You wanted to come," she finally said.

I couldn't look at her so I looked at the reflection of the back of her head. The frantic chuck-chuck-chuck of wheels on rail began to slow in tempo and more streetlights clicked by. We were coming into a station. Mom waggled her cup, and Gideon poured her some more.

I staggered to the end of the car. I slapped the button that made the door open and straddled the shifting floor joints where the dining car met the sleeping car, riding it like a surfboard. Maybe I'd stand here until she came. Maybe I'd get off at the next station, make her come looking for me, if she could be bothered. The train's rocking slowed, then stopped. The engine wheezed and gasped. The car dropped and the doors to the outside opened.

Cold air jabbed at my nose with smells of frost and gravel and guns just shot. A couple stepped up to the train. They were bundled, so I couldn't see their faces. I stepped back to let them through.

I pretended the woman was me, but an older, taller me, holding hands with my own boyfriend. He'd be blond and thin as a reed and have white, white teeth. We'd be riding the Zephyr to San Francisco, or maybe away from it. I'd tell him that, when I was a child, I took Amtrak from the East to the West, and in Chicago, I fought off a kidnapper. He'd wind his arms around me and kiss my forehead. He'd believe me, because he'd know I'd seen things he hadn't, but still, he'd have to ask.

"Where was your mom?"

The cold air on my face felt like it was calling me closer. Steam formed where the inside crossed over to the outside; more steam rose from under the train. Past the lights on the platform was black and more black. I should have been scared, all that emptiness and not even the reflection of Mom to soften it. I wasn't though. In all of that space spread out forever behind the curtain of dark and cold, there had to be room somewhere for the possibility of love. I half-shut my eyes and leaned into the spitting snow and kicked one foot out into the whole wide world.

NEANDERTHALS
MICHAEL KEANE

WHEN FIRST CONTACT WAS MADE WITH ALIEN LIFE, ANYONE who wasn't off their head in bewilderment was busy browbeating the Neanderthals without the sense for proper confusion.

After all, anyone with even a passing opinion on man's first meeting with all things extraterrestrial had assumed that a frozen cabal of microorganisms, photographed by a rover on Mars or some equally sensible locale, would claim that historic pedestal. No one could have guessed it would go to the diplomatic attachés of the Sagittarian Star Collective, photographed not via rover on Mars, but via freelance photographer in bucolic Solvang, California, who fought tooth and nail to hold the locals at bay and keep the diplomats at the foot of their craft so that he alone could capture the moment in glorious 35 millimeter.

As for the aliens, most prospective xenoanthropologists were amused, if not professionally disappointed, to find that they looked quite like us. Aside from the garish unitards they called clothing, the only difference anyone could find was in a thin triplet of cosmetic forehead ridges, tickling even the most casual of *Star Trek* fans, and boring everyone else to death.

Sure, most people were "happy" the aliens could understand our language and mannerisms. Most people were "glad" they could share a laugh over a drink, let alone share a drink at all, but at the same time no one could deny that the whole affair felt rather . . . boring. It wasn't that anyone wanted to suffer thousands of years exchanging prime numbers with some insectian thing across the stars, but when the Sagittarians touched down among the quiet, timber-framed homes in Solvang's traditional Danish style and asked the locals, "If it wouldn't ruin your barbecue to direct us to some informed individual?" they couldn't help but confirm on a cosmic level one of the more sour truths to which humanity subscribes.

The anticipation of something is far better than the attainment of it.

MAYOR DOUGLAS "DOUG" Dougherty was nearing portly and forty the day he entered an unmarked, one-story building at the east end of Vandenberg Air Force Base. He wore a plain white button-up and his favorite tie, which was sky blue and speckled with little golden windmill vanes. He also brought a Tupperware bowl of jam-filled pancake balls, known by their Danish title of aebleskivers, but security was quick to confiscate them.

Walking with Mayor Dougherty were Secretary of State Helen Cope and Secretary of Defense Travis Toll. Secretary Toll came equipped with the dusky draw of a book safe made out of a bible, even if it had long depleted its stash of illicit cigars. He was fifty-eight, but his complexion was never clearer, and his jackknife jaw could run for hours quipping with the quickest of ground pounders, though most of their conversations wouldn't bare repeating. Secretary Cope was far more suited to civil discourse. She had lighted into age seventy "when she finally found the time," as she was fond of saying, but few noticed even that distinction. Her body was sinewy with decades of dawn calisthenics, and her mind could best the devil on a good day.

This day, however, was far from good. The secretaries were thrashed between a brain-swallowing exhaustion and a transatlantic, cross-continental jet lag. For the last forty-five hours they had been in constant contact with anyone who would have anything to do with the Earth's visitors. Now, in lieu of the president, they were tasked with ensuring the security of American interests during the only private meeting they would get before international pressure overwhelmed them all. No one marching up Vandenberg had found a moment's peace since First Contact. No one.

Save the mayor.

And so, it was little wonder that Secretary Cope and Secretary Toll looked with quizzical, bloodshot eyes upon the third member of their party and the plastic container of pastries he was so forlorn to surrender.

MAYOR DOUGHERTY WAS LUCKY.

Many in Solvang were lucky, it was true, but Dougherty was lucky in much the same way as a Mylar balloon that slips free of a child's grasp.

When the aliens first arrived, they arrived at his front door, backed by a marveling mob of Solvangites who watched as their mayor met the Sagittarian ambassador-at-large. Belgamin, or so the ambassador called himself, was finishing a cob of corn provided by the barbecue he had crashed, and, with a sheen of butter bright on his chin, asked in a voice made to sing tenor if the mayor had an hour or so to chat.

Naturally, Dougherty had the entire day. It was Sunday, and his wife, Maggie, preferred to spend this time reviewing case files, ironing her suits, and meal prepping for the coming week. They would have until six o'clock, the mayor explained, as he and Maggie preferred to wind down early and watch reruns of old sitcoms before bed.

Belgamin found these terms acceptable.

"Look, Mags," Dougherty had said when his wife emerged from her office. "Spacemen."

"Oh," she replied, her eyes scanning their dinner table. "Where from?"

"Far beyond the stars you see, ma'am," Belgamin said. "Lovely home."

"It's a mess," she sighed. "Let me know if you see a pocket square. Red. Like burgundy."

So began their afternoon.

As military personnel closed in on their location like starving bats on a mango tree, Doug and his guests glided through conversation, covering topics from the color of a supernova when viewed at 90 percent the speed of light to the preparation of Dougherty's traditional Sunday meatloaf of which everyone partook as a matter of course.

Maggie would pass by at idle junctures and listen for a bit before moving on, but through all the small talk, she heard nothing illuminating. Eventually, she decided to pose a few questions herself: What were the notable events in the Sagittarians' history? Why did they come to Earth?

Their answers were unsatisfying: They were animals once, and now they were something else. They were passing the Milky Way and noticed a people they hadn't met.

It was enough to spur Maggie to her attorney mentality—to passion, interrogation, and finally to green tea as Doug administered the only remedy for her compulsion to work weekends.

The Sagittarians made it clear that they wished the mayor would join them for the effort that would usher humanity into the Star Collective, but Maggie was unimpressed. After their guests departed with a federal escort in tow, she sat her husband down and begged him to keep a cool head. The meeting to come would require immense caution and unearthly tact.

Her husband reassured her. He was more than prepared.

DOUGHERTY THREW OPEN the doors to the conference room and bellowed, "Who have we here?"

The Sagittarians turned from the windows overlooking the nature reserve beyond to swell with delight at the sight of their old host.

"Ah! Mister Mayor!" Belgamin said, beaming a million-volt smile across the glass table. He crossed the room and shook the mayor's hand with both of his own. "So good to see you!" he said. "We've been all too eager to begin." His entourage harmonized encouragement.

Dougherty took note of the increase in number. There were easily four times as many than had graced his living room a few days prior.

"I must admit," Belgamin added quietly, "your welcoming committee is a bit prudish."

The mayor laughed. "Well, we're here now! Ready to go! I brought some of those aebleskivers I told you about, but there was a bit of a snag—"

"Mister Ambassador." Secretary of State Helen Cope appeared at his side.

"Secretary Cope!" Belgamin said through bright eyes. "Yes, we spoke over the landline, didn't we? Ah! And you must be Secretary Toll."

Secretary of Defense Travis Toll bundled his lips in an approximation of a smile. "Ambassador."

The word sounded strange directed toward an alien, regardless how normal said alien may have appeared. Which wasn't to say the Sagittarians looked entirely dull. Belgamin in particular had a lean, flexible form and a sunny nature that struck Toll as rather handsome.

Yes, he thought with some effort. Handsome. A blameless observation.

Belgamin gave him a once-over. "My, what an outfit." The medals on Toll's chest sent a dazzling spray of light across the ambassador's face. "Your style bears a certain rapture."

Toll had to clear his throat.

Cope interceded. "We'd hate to keep you waiting."

"Yes," Toll said, color filling his face. "How do we proceed?"

Belgamin smiled. "With crayons."

Several folders materialized out of thin air and settled in the ambassador's hands. The human assembly went wide-eyed and held their collective breath. Then, the folders opened, revealing a few pages of mere paperwork and a cluster of shiny new crayons in primary colors.

"It's really quite simple stuff to start."

Belgamin slid the first form to Cope. It read, "WELCOME," in big block letters at the top. Below were several questions in twenty-point font with four lines below each for handwritten answers: "What is your name?" "What would your name mean if it was an acronym?" "Do you have any questions about the Star Collective?" "Favorite food and why?"

This is a trap, was Cope's first thought. It manifested as a feeling before the words even came. It can't really be this simple, right? Right?

"Take all the time you need," Belgamin said, nestling into his seat.

A chair's length away, Secretary Toll had received a different form.

Its first question: "Have you ever flown a spaceship?"

He couldn't help but feel a little insulted. Though coming from Belgamin it felt less threatening. A touch mysterious, which, after all, was natural given the circumstances. Who knew what the alien wanted? What secrets lurked behind that alabaster smile and quixotic allure?

Remember your marriage counseling, he thought, and skipped to the next question: "If you haven't flown a spaceship, would you like to?"

He clenched his teeth. Don't tease me, you minx.

As for Dougherty, the mayor had neglected to read a single question on his own form, consumed with thoughts of his aebleskivers and how long they had been sitting out and how their raspberry jam filling was surely diffusing through the bread and how they were no doubt plummeting in quality by the second and—

Oh, forget it, he thought. He looked across the table to the Sagittarians, thinking he might ask for a reprieve to locate an icebox.

That was when he noticed a few new faces in the crowd.

It wasn't that he saw more faces than before. Rather, some seemed categorically different. About a quarter of the Sagittarians present had the same three forehead ridges he was familiar with. However, another quarter possessed only one forehead ridge and stood taller than the rest. The third quarter looked to have more bulbous craniums, and the final quarter had long simian arms and stood at the same height of his niece who was starting middle school in the fall.

He turned his attention to the document lying before him and began to read.

What are they? Helen Cope wondered. Are they clueless? Omniscient? Her caution strained against her opportunism. They asked her simple questions, and they gave her simple answers. They provided her with paper, yet they controlled space-time.

She snapped her crayon between her fingers. What is it you want?

"I'd like some help," Dougherty said. "I don't understand this question."

Cope and Toll blinked to attention. Belgamin leaned forward. A few of his aides peered across the room with wide, imploring eyes. Dougherty had a finger positioned below the fourth question on his form and was chewing the inside of his cheek trying to puzzle it out.

"It asks here, 'What species comprise your civilization?'"

"Yes?" Belgamin asked.

Dougherty looked to the secretaries, but their faces were as blank as his. "I mean, we've made use of many kinds of animals if that's what you mean."

"Oh!" Belgamin exhaled with a laugh. A few of his assembly smiled. "No, no. The question refers to the different sentient members of your civilization."

"Different . . . sentient members?"

Cope traded a sidelong glance with Toll.

"Come on, you know," Belgamin prompted. "I'm a type three." He spun around, pointing out a tall Sagittarian with only one forehead ridge. "That's my deputy ambassador. She's a type one." Then a short one with a bulbous head. "Type two." Then finally a small, long-armed individual. "Type four." He faced front. "See?"

Mayor Dougherty shrank back. "Are you talking about race?"

Belgamin pursed his lips. "Hmm." He sat up and folded his hands. "Here. You call yourself, what? As a classified species, I mean."

"Human?" Dougherty asked.

"Homo sapien," Cope answered.

"Right! Probably! I don't know for sure." He cleared his throat. "So! If, for example, I called myself a 'Homo sapien,' then I would likely call my deputy ambassador . . . "

There was a cold silence among the humans. A colder silence once they realized.

"Neanderthal," Cope breathed.

"Right! Probably! Again, I don't know." Belgamin tilted his head and squinted one eye as if to empty water from his ear. "Translator's a little rough around the edges." He tapped at his temple, then faced upright. "At any rate, this is the first time I've had to explain all this." He let out a warm laugh, but to Cope it felt less like a glowing hearth and more like the humid breath of a large animal.

"While we're on it," Belgamin continued, "we have been wondering about the others."

"The others. Yes." Cope turned to Toll and Dougherty with eyes the size of golf balls.

"As far as we can tell," he continued, "everyone we've met seems to be of the same species." The other Sagittarians nodded amongst themselves, mumbling courteous nothings as if to concede, on behalf of the room, that it was a fair point.

Toll's lip trembled. "Oh. That's. Weird." He felt like his lover had just appeared on his doorstep, and his husband was closer to the door.

The ambassador snapped his fingers. "Tell you what! Why don't we start there? List out all your species of humans. Tell us how you get along, mix your cultural dynamics, the whole deal! We'll listen."

The Sagittarians smiled. And waited.

The secretaries shot Dougherty a look.

He shot back—Help.

Cope turned to Belgamin and spoke with the hollow confidence of one given to the gallows. "Can we have a moment?"

THE THREE HUMAN dignitaries were already rounding the first corner of the hallway before the doors to the conference room shut.

Cope whirled on her heels. "What the hell is going on?!"

"Why are you asking me?" Dougherty squeaked.

"You talked to them on Sunday for three goddamn hours," Toll said. "If anyone should have any idea—"

"I don't know! We talked about a lot of things!"

"Should we call the president?" Toll asked.

Cope flinched. "Not yet. It's too early." She turned to Dougherty. "Now, talk."

"I just know what they told me," Dougherty said. "And they told me that aliens are pretty similar when you get down to it. I mean, really similar. I mean, out of all ten million species they even know of—"

Cope's breath left her in a wheeze. "Ten million?"

"—over ninety nine percent organically developed bubble tea. Bubble tea! All on their own!"

"What the hell is bubble tea?" Toll asked.

"Oh, come on, you've had bubble—"

"Shut up!" Cope was panting. "Are you trying to tell me—" she took a moment to breathe, "that there are ten million different aliens out there, and out of all of them—" she stopped to breathe again, "out of all of them, everyone developed multiple sentient species except us?"

"That's impossible," Toll sniffed. "If everyone else has multiple intelligent species, why don't we?"

Cope flailed like she was flying on broken wings. "They went extinct, you idiot! The question isn't why!"

"Then what's the question?!" he asked.

"What does it mean that we don't?"

A strangled sound came from Toll's throat. "Well, what does it mean?!"

"That's the question!"

Dougherty raised a finger. "I have a question."

"What?!"

"Why did the Neanderthals go extinct?"

They froze.

MAYOR DOUGHERTY WAS an accident.

His parents were young when they had him and seeking the most out of life, but not the kind of life that he provided, so they left him with his mother's family in Solvang. For all his grandparents' guilt over their daughter's abandonment, he grew up freer than his mother ever had. Yet he remained so comfortably wrapped in the Santa Ynez Valley that, to all who knew him, he seemed one of those few, blessed individuals whose very nature left him in want of nothing. In fact, he seemed in want of so much "nothing" that he eventually came to want all the "nothing" his small world had to offer, leading him to run for mayor of Solvang at eighteen years old.

His campaign was a resounding failure, of course. The harshest critics called him "a worthy competitor to white noise," with one local meme going so far as to compare his stocky form and blunt skull to that of man's Paleolithic ancestor. The winning candidate, however, noted Doug's love for his city and found a spot for him in good faith.

The same routine continued for thirty years, with Doug running—and losing—each race for mayor, all while moving slowly through the ranks of city government. He acquired his grandparents' home upon their passing, went steady with Maggie, who was a law student at the time, and, seven years later, accepted the marriage proposal she offered him after she came to the conclusion that her boyfriend was too blissfully unaware to think of asking her himself.

Then, the fateful election of 2050 arrived.

Standing in Doug's way to the position of mayor was the legendary Marcus Dowse, incumbent of incumbents, and, according to some, the perfect specimen. He stood six foot two at 225 pounds, owing to his Olympian, if sensibly adorned, musculature. His hair held a luster like a cloud against the moon, and his eyes were cool like stones in clear water. He was as golden-toned and oaken-souled a tech tycoon as there had ever been.

So, when he adopted a simple residence in Solvang to keep an eye on his aerospace ventures at Vandenberg it left the community in a starstruck daze.

To his own surprise, Marcus was a write-in for mayor on the next election, yet he shouldered the responsibility with such effortless grace that he became the most beloved mayor in all of Solvang's history. No one made a fuss over his unchanged corporate status, and not a single person sought to oppose him upon reelection, except for Dougherty, who saw the city of his birth like a shelter dog in perpetual need of adoption. Though he knew that any loving owner would do, he couldn't help but believe his love would make all the difference.

In the race that resulted, the comparisons made between Dougherty and early man spread far beyond Solvang. A short-lived but well-traveled meme, which compared Dougherty to a wax Neanderthal sculpture and Dowse to the godly, graphic novel character of Doctor Manhattan, whipped the capricious storm of internet attention to a thunderhead.

The race would take on a meaning of its own as the most absurd incarnation of Man versus Machine.

However, no one had expected Man to win.

* * *

ONLY ONE DEVICE in the lonely Vandenberg building had access to the internet, and the trio of human dignitaries commandeered it like a lifeboat. It was the computer at the front desk, and its operator had turned to see not three government suits approaching him, but polar bears bounding toward a seal. He slid from his chair and backed away.

The mayor filled his seat.

Before Dougherty could navigate to the internet, he noticed a list of on-base personnel residing on the computer monitor. A familiar name was highlighted in royal blue in a row all on its own.

"Marcus Dowse is on base?" the mayor asked.

Cope muscled in. "Internet Explorer. Internet Explorer!"

And soon they were online, reading an article about man's humble evolutionary cousin, Homo neanderthalensis, a being who, they were surprised to learn, was comparable in almost every capacity to the Homo sapien. A being with intelligence. A being with greater strength. Greater eyesight. Who most certainly possessed language. Who most certainly possessed tools. Who most certainly thought and felt like us, and who, by modern human standards, looked dumb as a box of rocks.

Toll squinted at an artist's rendering. "Kind of ugly, aren't they?"

"Let's put you in a loin cloth and see how you fair," Cope said.

Dougherty pointed out several illustrations. "Look. Others. Homo erectus, Homo flores— floresien— Um, that one."

Cope sighed. "This can't seriously be what they mean."

"Wait," Toll said. "Keep scrolling . . . There."

He pointed to a section titled "Extinction."

Dougherty read aloud. "'Several theories have been proposed as to why the Neanderthal went extinct, from climate catastrophe to interbreeding absorption, but most all acknowledge the arrival of . . . '"

Dougherty stopped. The others leaned in to read.

"Oh no," Toll whispered. He grabbed the monitor and yanked it to eye level. "Oh, you've got to be kidding me."

"This isn't possible," Cope wailed. She reread the line,

desperate to be wrong. "'Most theories acknowledge the arrival of, and conflict with, Homo sapiens.'"

Dougherty put a hand to his mouth. "We killed them."

Belgamin appeared out of thin air. "Hello!"

Toll dropped the monitor. It crashed with a punch of plastic and shattering electronics. Its cables ripped from their sockets and lashed into the air.

The ambassador recoiled, his mouth ajar.

"I didn't mean that!" Toll shouted. He reached out, but pulled his hand back, as if Belgamin might shatter at his touch. "Are you okay? I'm so sorry. This isn't like me, I swear. It's been such a day."

"I, uh," Belgamin stammered, staring at the broken screen. "It's just, you left so abruptly, and . . . " He unfurled Dougherty's questionnaire. "We just wanted to know if you needed help with the species question."

Dougherty's leg bounced of its own volition. "About that . . . "

Cope paled. She shook her head at him like a tremolo on violin.

"I mean," he continued, "How important is this, like, overall?"

"Pardon?" Belgamin asked.

Toll, to his credit, had become vaguely aware of the conversation passing through the space between himself and the ambassador. "Oh, it's just such a process," he said, patting Belgamin's shoulder. Belgamin, who was still a bit shaken, grabbed his arm to steady himself, and Toll's voice gave out.

"Yes!" Cope said. "Clerically! Just a . . . you know . . . just . . . " She rolled her hand in the air, searching for a word.

Toll's cheeks turned red. "Just, you know . . . There's . . . " He sent a look to Dougherty.

Dougherty shrank inward. Think! Think! Albert Einstein. Joan of Arc.

"There's a . . . "

George Washington. Marcus Dowse.

"There's, uh . . . "

What would they do? What do great people do? How would a smart person fix this?

He had no idea.

"There's three!" he blurted out.

"Three . . . human species?" asked Belgamin.

"Yep!"

Dougherty could hear himself talking, but he had no control. The secretaries looked on in shock, their tired faces hanging lower and lower, like they might slough to the floor at any moment.

"Three species," Dougherty confirmed.

"Ah, good." Belgamin flashed a meager smile and took to writing on the questionnaire with a blue crayon. "Homo sapien . . . Homo Neanderthal?"

"Uh-huh. Sure," Dougherty said. He blinked away the sweat invading his eye.

"And finally," Belgamin said, "I suppose, we have Homo . . . " He waved the crayon. Encouraging. Smiling.

Dougherty's brain puttered on like a mobility scooter off a cliff. "Homo sexual."

"Mister Mayor!" Cope latched onto Dougherty with such predatory speed that both Belgamin and Toll felt their hair stand on end. She lifted him to his feet. "I am so sorry! You brought a perishable food item and we didn't guarantee it was preserved. Ambassador, my apologies. Please excuse us. Just a minute. Would that be all right? Just a minute?"

Belgamin waggled his hands in surrender. "N-no problem. No problem at all."

Dougherty prayed with a barren desperation that she really did care about his aebleskivers. He prayed the way that fishermen pray for the mercy of storms at sea.

INDEED, MAYOR DOUGHERTY was a mistake.

His campaign against Marcus was a source of proxy embarrassment for anyone with but a hint of empathy. Even Maggie felt at odds watching him engage in a contest so dismissive of him as he willingly contested a wave with a ripple—the promise of himself against an icon.

Marcus Dowse, as a fact, was unbeatable. He was a man so popular that babies ceased crying at the sight of him—so popular that his lovers left their relationships open, believing a monogamous Marcus to be a loss unto the world—so popular that when no one found his name on the ballot that year, nearly every person in Solvang wrote him in despite mass déjà vu.

Marcus Dowse was so unassailably popular that everyone collectively ignored the fact that he had already completed two consecutive terms.

And so, was Dowse disqualified.

And so, had Dougherty won.

An election by default, and everyone knew it.

Every last citizen, tall to small, mourning the municipal loss of their savior while circulating memes of Dougherty's caveman visage, knew the truth. And, despite his self-assurances to the contrary, Doug Dougherty knew it too.

WHETHER SHE DID it to maintain the ruse or buy time to think, Helen Cope did retrieve Doug Dougherty's pancake balls. They walked in silence until they reached a small breakroom lit by fluorescents. At its center stood a card table well past its prime and four metal folding chairs. There were various particleboard cabinets with little in the way of contents, a sink, a microwave, and a mini-fridge.

Cope tore open the fridge and chucked Dougherty's balls inside. She backed against the wall and rooted a hand in her pale hair.

Toll closed the door and took a seat. He stared into his hands. "We're so fucked."

"Homo sexual," Cope muttered. "My God."

Dougherty landed at the table. "I admit that was ill-advised."

"Christ, Dougherty!" Toll threw his head back and cast his eyes to the lights above, searching in vain for the silhouette of an angel coming to take his soul. "So, now what? We call the president?"

Cope's eye twitched. "Is that your answer to everything?"

"And why are you so opposed, huh?" he responded. "Do you know what the hell this even is? A test? Torture? Some sick alien mind game?"

"Now, hold on." Dougherty straightened his tie. "They may be awfully powerful, but on the whole they're far nicer than anyone I've met in my whole—"

A light went on in Dougherty's brain. His limbs went slack. His mouth hung open.

"Goddamn Neanderthals," Cope growled. "So, what about them? Either we killed them or they starved to death or they vanished like any other obsolete animal. What does it matter?"

"It's a trick," Toll said. "They know we're lying. They're just making us sweat it out to prove a point. I know how this goes. But if they think—"

"They're nice," Dougherty said, quiet and plain, as if he were appraising a fallen ice cream cone. His strange tone wormed its way through the chaos and drew the secretaries into silence.

"They're nice," he said again. "They're just nice."

"Uh, yeah, we picked up on that." Toll said.

"No." He met their eyes. "They're all nice. Every last alien in the great beyond. They're just . . . nice by nature."

Cope knitted her brow into a delta of wrinkles.

Dougherty cupped his head in his hands. "Think. Think about how the Sagittarians behaved. What they've said. They even called the military, 'the welcoming committee.'"

"Crayons and paper. Simple questions. Travis?"

"Belgamin said my uniform was sparkly," Toll mumbled. "You don't think . . . "

"They told me they landed in Solvang because it looked nice," Dougherty said. "I thought they were being clever, but I think they actually landed here on a whim. Like they spotted a new restaurant and figured they'd check it out."

Cope shook her head. "They're like . . . children. All-powerful children with all of the innocence and none of the greed." She stared into what shallow middle distance the room could provide. "It doesn't matter how the Neanderthals died, because if we were like every other alien out there, we would have prevented their extinction out of some basic, empathic instinct." Her eyes darted back and forth. "We're literally the biggest assholes in the universe."

Dougherty pushed his chair out. "Well, I'm sure if we just explain, you know, it was a long time ago—"

"Are you kidding?" Cope asked. "The moment they go on the internet it's over!"

"It's not that bad."

"Dougherty," Toll placed his hands flat on the table, "last week I personally oversaw ten different drone strikes in a place I still can't remember the name of. Belgamin doesn't even know what soldiers are. It's bad."

Dougherty tugged at one of his fingers. "I'm sure they'd see—"

"Oh, God. Look at me!" Toll grabbed his suit, rattling his medals. "I'm, like, Cthulu or something!"

"Shut up!" Cope yelled. "Focus! Focus." She paced the room, though its size meant she had to turn around every three steps. "One thing at a time. If they have no reason to distrust any intelligent creature in the universe, then we already have the upper hand."

"You're not thinking of lying to them, are you?" Dougherty asked.

"Do you want to risk losing out on what they could offer?" Cope asked, her face framed in the jagged geometry of her fraying hair. "Because that's what will happen!"

Toll's eyes widened. "Do you think they'd take us out? Even for them, what's firing a meteor into the planet?"

"No. No, I can't see that," Cope said. "No. Not at all." She had gone from pacing the room to turning in circles. "But I'd bet anything they'd cock-block our development for the rest of forever. Keep us technologically stagnant. Planet-bound. Walled off. Running down our fossil fuels. Like animals. Like lions in a zoo!"

Four Sagittarians appeared.

"Holy—!" Toll tripped over Dougherty. Cope hit the wall.

A squeal resounded from the newcomers as they backed into a cluster.

Belgamin poked his head out from the middle, voice thick with fright. "Why do you keep screaming?"

"You have to understand, you can't just show up like this," Toll said, choking up. "People will talk," he whispered.

"What? But . . . but I . . . " Belgamin stammered. "I j-just thought, now might be a g-good time . . . " From the bundle of Sagittarians, a hand emerged holding Dougherty's questionnaire. "That is, if you saved the mayor's pastries."

Faster than the fearful Sagittarians could notice, Toll kicked at the mini-fridge's plug, snapping the electrodes off in the socket.

"Wouldn't you know?" he said with a wild shrug. "It's broken!"

Cope ripped the aebleskivers from their den, and Toll pushed Dougherty into the hall. As they left, Belgamin peeked out from the break room.

"Should we just come back another time?" the ambassador asked.

"No, no, no! Stay right here!" Cope called.

"Please!" Dougherty added.

He stumbled on, trying to keep up, watching the ambassador's trembling form recede as the secretaries forced him to gain ground, putting distance between them all.

ON THE DAY of First Contact, when Dougherty met the Sagittarians, he looked out into the crowd of Solvangites that had gathered at his doorstep—a haphazard collection of people who had abandoned their Sunday plans, picked up their lunches, dropped their shopping, left their jobs, and marched in a trepid, wonderstruck bacchanalia to his home.

At first, he thought they were looking at him, but he knew that couldn't be the case. Their eyes weren't glazing over or darting across his form. They weren't shuffling or otherwise moving somewhere else. Phones cropped up from the crowd like cattails, but the people holding them, weren't focused on the capture. No one was analyzing him, and yet no one was ignoring him.

Finally, no one was looking at Doug Dougherty.

They were looking to him.

Maggie had implored him to remain levelheaded, and, of course, he agreed with her in the moment, but he could not help the trembling sensation in his chest. He could not stop the feeling of transcendence that lifted him beyond the walls separating his heart from the world that called him a caveman.

After years of wanting, he finally had.

Now, he wanted to hold on.

THE SECRETARIES BUSTED out of the unmarked building with Dougherty trailing behind. Cope led them from concrete to asphalt to grass and then dirt, into the coastal winds tearing over the hills, whipping at their hair and the cuffs of their shirtsleeves, muffling their voices and throwing them off their balance.

"Where are we going?" Toll called over the wind.

"Somewhere without corners!" Cope yelled back.

"He can teleport, genius!"

"You have any better ideas?!"

Toll scanned the horizon like a castaway seeking rescue. "I want to call the president."

"We can't risk anyone listening in," Cope said.

Toll rolled his eyes. "No one will listen in."

"Do you know how many people are waiting to intercept a call like that?"

He pulled out a phone. "I'm calling her!"

Cope turned and marched back toward him. "We don't need her to fix this!"

"Can you drop the ego for five damn seconds—"

"Ego?!" Saliva frothed around Cope's mouth like pond foam on a sand bank. "I'm trying to do my job! I'm trying to keep this secret!"

Toll hammered in the number. "No one will find out!"

"Is that what you thought before the press found you with that twink?!"

Toll reared back in a horrified arch. "You . . . "

"What?!" She leaned toward him. "I what?"

"You bitch!"

He swung. The Tupperware bowl of aebleskivers flew out of Cope's hands and onto the ground, its pastel pink lid flying off on impact, its tiny, round contents spilling across the dust, tumbling away in the wind, indistinguishable from dirt clods and nascent tumble weeds.

Dougherty picked the bowl up off the ground, deaf to the argument unfolding before him. He stared at the meager remains—an enclave of pastries bleeding jam at a mortal rate.

A knot welled up in his throat. "Can we all calm down?"

Toll spun on him. "No, Mr. 'Homo sexual,' which, by the way, I did not appreciate—"

Cope grabbed Toll by his lapels. "We need to find an answer! Come on!"

"Answer to what?! Our innate evil?!"

"Just lay it out," she said. "Simplify it. They expect two things. Right? Two alternate species of humans. A Neanderthal and a 'Homo sexual.' Jesus Christ."

"But the Neanderthals are gone," Dougherty said.

Toll planted a finger on his chest. "How could they be when you're standing right here?!"

"No, you idiot!" Cope shrieked. "That's the kind of thinking that helped us kill all the Neanderthals!"

"Oh, come on! You take a look at this dumb bastard and tell me he doesn't look like a—"

Toll's voice caught in his throat.

Cope dropped her hands from the tangle of her hair.

They both turned to Dougherty, observing in a new light his flat head and barrel chest. Neither of them were privy to the local jokes regarding the mayor's appearance, but then again, the benchmark of absurdity had been demolished the moment Belgamin gave them crayons. In the kaleidoscope of their crumbling lucidity, anything less than that had as fair a shot at being normal as a blue sky in August.

"We couldn't." Toll dropped his brow in a line. "Could we?"

"Why not?" Cope rasped. "They're a bunch of boy scouts. They'll trust us. All we need is a different phenotype and we could do it." She turned to Dougherty. "You could, Mister Mayor."

Dougherty took tiny rabbit-sized breaths. "No," he heard himself say. "It won't work."

"It can," Cope said. "They're naïve by nature. They'll take our word for it."

"They could find out," Toll muttered.

Cope nodded. "They could. But not before we make progress. Not before they feel invested in us." She kept her eyes trained on Dougherty, advancing with an even stride. "We'll say we panicked and withheld the truth because we were embarrassed or ashamed or whatever else you can think of. Tug at their empathy. Lay on a guilt trip. It's easy." She grabbed him by the shoulders. "We need you, Mister Mayor."

For one who tended to puzzle at length over the order in which to return phone calls, Dougherty surprised himself with how clearly he could grasp the decision before him: lie and disparage himself but rescue the seminal event of human history, or refuse to lie, and, in doing so, resign alien negotiations, along with his soul, to the dungeon of peer disapproval.

He didn't want to lie. He didn't want to stand out. He thought he did, but for the life of him he had hoped it would be less dreadful. Now he was stuck in the middle, darn it all.

I'll never be more than what I am, he thought. And what I am is not up for this.

He was moments from folding. From taking his Tupperware and going home or, failing that, letting the secretaries figure it out on their own. At the very least, he would feel too rotten lying to Belgamin.

Belgamin.

He had looked so frightened when they left him. For all Dougherty knew, the poor ambassador was still waiting in the break room as they instructed. He seemed likely to shatter at the slightest conflict. A lie would do him no good in this moment.

But what would the truth do?

Distrust. Violence. Greed. Ambition. Telling your friend that you were using him for your own gain. Telling a child that their pet is dead. That Santa isn't real. That Santa is dead. That marriage ends in divorce. That mom and dad haven't come to see you, and— Yes, actions speak louder than words, but—No, of course they love you. And why wouldn't they? And you don't have to feel bad, because someday you'll grow up, and your life will change, and those feelings will go away. They will.

Someday.

Dougherty met Cope's eyes. "All right, then."

Her face broke with relief, and she clasped her hands.

"Great," Toll said. "We have a Neanderthal. What about the last one?"

"Actually," Dougherty sighed, "we may have that too."

He wiped his eyes of dust and wind and looked beyond his two accomplices. They followed his gaze to the rest of the base, and laid eyes on an empty launch pad.

WHEN THE TRIO reentered the conference room, Marcus Dowse entered ahead of them. A silence fell over the Sagittarians in the manner of all creatures inclined to sunsets and string quartets as, in that moment, Marcus Dowse was proven universally appealing. To the Sagittarians, however, he was one more thing: "Homo sexual." The third and, evidently, most exquisite of all humanity's recently devised species.

Cope and Toll reintroduced themselves as Homo sapiens proper, and Dougherty, with his own take on grace, admitted to being a Neanderthal. He delivered the line so well that Toll, who had worried he might crack up, scarcely had time to process the event as anything other than ordinary. For when the mayor announced in front of all in attendance that he was something less than the modern man, he believed it as much as Belgamin, who accepted the secretaries' explanation for their prior distress when they claimed the Sagittarian arrival had sent them spiraling with emotion. After all, even the sweetest people aren't perfect.

Except for Marcus, perhaps.

From the moment he entered, the room was remade under his egalitarian distribution of charm. The minefield within the alien questionnaires diffused, leaving an air of cathartic freestyle that Cope and Toll had not felt since they were children performing cutesy classroom activities on the last day of school.

Myriad discussions filled the room. Laughter peeled in proximity to the tech tycoon. Cope embraced relaxation with the awkward determination of a newborn fawn attempting to walk, and Toll hovered near Belgamin's aides asking if their ambassador was at all reciprocal to platonic coffee dates.

As for Belgamin himself, his eyes landed on Dougherty.

The mayor was tucked at the end of the table, away from the mingling species, where he had resigned his attentions to the bowl of surviving aebleskivers in his arms. Belgamin approached, his hands clasped behind his back in mild-mannered curiosity.

"You seem perplexed," he said.

Dougherty glanced up. His eyes were swelled red. "I'm just a little tired, you see."

Belgamin took a seat beside him. "My friend," he said with a hush. "You're hurt."

Dougherty stared at Belgamin. His shoulders went slack and sloped away, leaving his head wavering like a radio mast in the wind, a receiver and transmitter, transparent to the human eye. Belgamin was not human, however, and could not differentiate between a false face and a true one. So, the moment passed, and Dougherty reclaimed his composure.

"It was very windy outside," he said. "Lots of dust."

"Oh. We should get you some water, then."

Dougherty raised a hand. "No, I should be fine without water."

Belgamin gasped. "Goodness. What happened?"

Dougherty traced the ambassador's sight to the bowl in his hand. He had revealed the dusty pastries, red-stained, like wounded chipmunks in a cardboard box.

He bit his lip. "Oh. An accident. We were, um, outside, and I, well . . . " He took a breath but nothing came. Instead, he mustered a smile and shrugged.

"Oh," Belgamin echoed. He looked deep into the ruined dish, as if trying to make out an unfamiliar shape. Then he turned his big, blank gaze upon the secretaries and Marcus Dowse. Smiling. Conversing. The happiest they had been all day.

"Didn't they see?" Belgamin asked.

Dougherty placed the lid on the container and rapped it a few times. "It's fine, Belgamin. I'm fine."

The ambassador turned back to Dougherty, eyes bulging, cheekbones stretching against a tense expression that Dougherty had never seen him adopt even once before.

The mayor locked up. His mind shut off, and he said the first words that found their way to his mouth.

"Don't worry about me."

Belgamin curled his fingers over his lips. "Excuse me," he whispered.

He stood, turned to the assembly, and cleared his throat with a forced effort. The Sagittarians faced him, smiles dropping like bright red apples into a worm-ridden undergrowth. It lasted about a second, and it caught the humans unprepared. They had no time to process.

Then, Belgamin nodded.

And the Sagittarians disappeared.

From the corners of the room, a breeze rushed in to fill the void they left, then rebounded with enough force to rob a single lock of hair from the divine, obsidian forest on Marcus's head. The questionnaires were gone. The crayons were gone. The room—or the world—felt colder. As if time and space itself had been folded inside out. As if every shred of alien DNA on Earth, down to the tiniest lipid from the tiniest skin cell, flying rogue in the ocean wind, had vanished.

All was silent.

Cope passed a hand through the space where one of the tallest Sagittarians had been. It landed on the backrest of one of the chairs.

"Okay," she said, her face falling vacant. "Call the president."

WHEN LAST CONTACT was made with alien life, anyone who wasn't off their head in bewilderment was busy browbeating the Neanderthals without the sense for proper confusion.

After all, anyone with even a passing opinion on man's first meeting with extraterrestrial life had assumed that any and all foibles over miscommunication and culture shock would be mere bumps in the road to a grander future. No one could have guessed that the default species of the cosmos was so pure that even the notion of a little characteristic callousness would send them hurtling away without so much as a dialogue.

As for the aliens, the only explanation they left was a short message that appeared in digital form on every server in the world. Aside from the signatures of the Sagittarian delegation, the message read, "We apologize for leaving, but it has come to our attention that our relationship may prove unhealthy in both the short and long term. Best wishes to you."

Sure, most people could imagine alien appall at some of humanity's moral blunders. Most people could even conceive of a reality in which this very event occurred in one form or another, but at the same time, no one really believed it would. It wasn't that anyone wanted to ignore humanity's faults in favor of a narrative championing human exceptionalism, but when the Sagittarians left with no implication that alien contact would ever recur, they couldn't help but confirm on a cosmic level one of the more sour truths to which humanity thought they no longer subscribed.

No matter what you anticipate and no matter what you attain, the life you live and the person you are will never truly change.

DOUGHERTY LAY IN bed for a week. The city called, but he didn't pick up, and when his wife bridged from inquiry to interrogation, he mumbled something about green tea and wrapped a pillow around his head. She brought him doctors, family, and even a friend's golden retriever. Nothing worked.

When the mayor finally did leave his bed it was to buy a gallon of whole milk from the nearest gas station, but he didn't stop driving when he reached the store, and he didn't stop driving when he hit the freeway, and he didn't stop driving when he left the Valley, until only the dry California countryside stretched before him.

He hadn't told a soul what he did to push the aliens away. It was a secret wrapped in the corpse of a confidential meeting that wouldn't be made known for over a century. There were no crowds to haunt his waking hours, no national think pieces to pick him apart, no looks of disappointment from those he knew, and no one to talk to about any of it.

I wonder where I'll end up if I just keep driving, he thought, expecting to feel the same anxious pull for the land behind him that he felt whenever leaving Solvang for long.

But the pull wasn't there.

He felt no tether, no churn in his stomach, telling him he should turn his old VW Bug around and sputter home. It scared him, and yet, he felt as if it was a long time coming. As if the city would be free of their carnival attraction, and his wife free of . . . Well, just free.

His heart raced at this potential, and he pulled off the freeway to catch his breath. He parked on the shoulder of a dusty road and stepped outside. Yellow tufts of grass crunched beneath his sandals as he walked, their coarse blades whipping at his ankles with every footfall.

Oh Maggie, he thought. Look who you married.

He watched as the sun fell closer to twilight and scanned the horizon below it. For something. For anything. An answer in nature. A greater truth he had missed in forty years. A remedy to a feeling he had always had and hoped wasn't meant to be.

But the earth bore him no secrets, and the grass sent him no sign. The wind passed without whispers, and the hills called to no one. The clouds didn't part, and the sun didn't stop.

But, for what it was worth, the sky spoke.

"Hello?" came a voice like wind chimes.

"Belgamin?" Dougherty asked, spinning about. He saw no one, but the ambassador sounded as if he was standing right in front of him. "Belgamin, is that you?"

"Y-yes. You probably can't see me."

"I can't. Where are you?"

"Nowhere in particular," Belgamin hummed. "Somewhere outside your observable universe. Riding a singularity. As you do."

"Ah," Dougherty said. He didn't understand, but he was too lost for questions. "Nice of you to call, I suppose."

"Oh, I don't know. I don't know a lot anymore. Not after our visit."

Dougherty raked his hair. "I'll say. I left to go get milk and now I'm standing in the desert."

"Heavens, why?" Belgamin's voice was like a light-bath for the mind. It bore concern without fear, and interest without judgment. It ran off of Dougherty's brain like a cool summer shower and roused him to respond.

But how could he put it to a being such as this? How could he explain to Belgamin what he couldn't decipher for himself?

"Belgamin, I . . . " He moved his mouth in hopes a sentence would appear. "I never thought I would get married."

A lilting, "Hmm," trickled from the ambassador.

"I never even tried," Dougherty said. "That is, I never thought it was in the cards for me. I went steady with Maggie for a while. Figured one day she'd move on, what with the firm and all. But then she asked me to marry her, and all I could think was, 'What lie have I been acting out that made this poor girl want a life with me?'"

Belgamin took a deep breath. "Wow. That is way over my head."

"Yeah. Huh," Dougherty said, leaning against his car. "You're all too perfect for stuff like this."

"Perfect? Us? Stars, I wish. Maybe then we wouldn't have waltzed onto your planet with so many assumptions. Maybe we would have taken our differences in stride as opposed to hightailing it out of your galaxy."

Dougherty felt his heart skip, and he looked skyward. "So, you're coming back?"

"Oh, no. Not at all."

"Ah. Well." He tisked.

"Yes," Belgamin said, "we've done plenty of research since we left, and there's no way it'll happen. It would be quite detrimental in all likelihood."

"I suppose I'd have to agree with you there," Dougherty sighed.

Belgamin was quiet for a long moment.

"See, that's what I can't figure out," he said at last. "I can't even tell if you mean that or if you secretly want us to come back."

"Well, of course I mean it," Dougherty said, "but that doesn't mean I wouldn't want you back. If anything I would love that the most. So would anyone."

"But that's what confounds me. You've been on your own for as long as you've ever been around. Why do you need us when you already have yourselves?"

Dougherty tugged at the fabric of his shirt. The same shirt he had been wearing for days. For disappointing himself and others. For want of something. "For feelings," he said, rubbing his arms. "We have desires. It's who we are."

"In that case, I was right to call," Belgamin said. "I have a gift for you."

An electric crackle played at the edges of Dougherty's ears. In the time it took him to blink, a small, round container appeared at his feet. It was a plastic bowl of sorts, white as the milk he was starting to crave with a blue and gold lid fastened by a latch the size of his own thumb.

"What is this?" he asked, lifting it off the ground. It rose with ease, bereft of gravity.

"Something to keep your pastries cool," Belgamin said.

Dougherty pressed the latch. It slid without friction beneath his touch, and the lid opened, revealing a smooth, empty interior.

Dougherty put his hand inside and found that the air within remained cold, unchanged by the environment.

"I made it myself," Belgamin said. "You can alter the temperature by running a finger around the lid. It acts as a dial."

"Belgamin," Dougherty breathed.

"Do you like it?"

He squinted, shaking his head in disbelief. "Why?" he asked.

"Because it's something for the little things, my friend. And you so love the little things."

"The little things," Dougherty repeated, staring into the bowl. "And I thought I could be mayor."

"But you already are."

"Oh, for goodness sake, Belgamin," Dougherty moaned. He wanted to drop his hands in frustration, but he was holding the bowl, so he settled for letting his arms sink with a huff. "I'm not like you," he said. "We're not like you."

"You don't love your wife?" Belgamin asked.

"Of course I love my wife!"

"And what about where you live?"

"Yes! I love that too."

"And aebleskivers?"

"A little less after last week," he mumbled.

"Then what else do you love?" Belgamin asked.

Dougherty closed the lid on the bowl. "I'd love a nice, tall glass of milk right now."

"And?"

Dougherty tapped a foot against one of the front tires of his Bug. "In better times," he said, "I loved going on nice, long drives." He stared off to the inland reaches, where the first trace of night was folding over the hills. "I love my memories of my grandparents. They gave me so much advice that I can't remember, yet I can't forget the taste of their homemade sausages." He flipped a rock with his sandal. "Who am I kidding? I still love aebleskivers."

Belgamin chuckled. "Now, Doug—"

"And I love how city hall smells. Namely on Fridays."

"Mm-hm."

"And fireworks on the—"

"Doug?"

"Sorry. Yes?"

"Everything you listed?" Belgamin said. "That's you."

Dougherty blinked. "But that's just my—"

A buzz riddled his leg. He checked his phone and found Maggie had texted him. She was asking where he went and if he was okay.

"Yes," Belgamin mused. "Yes, it is."

Another crackle danced at Dougherty's periphery, stronger than the one before.

"I'll have to hang up now," Belgamin said. "Things get wonky outside black holes."

"Belgamin," the mayor called. He hesitated, trying not to scare him any further, hoping to say what needed saying in the Sagittarian way.

He looked to the sky. "Thank you for the cooler."

A smile filled Belgamin's voice as he replied. "Thank you for the lovely afternoon."

And with a POP, the line was out. Belgamin was gone.

Mayor Dougherty climbed back inside his car and placed the alien cooler in the passenger seat. Overhead, the sky was deepening into a midnight blue. Laid before Dougherty was a path to the bright horizon, where the sun might never set if he could only travel fast enough, but his car was old and tired, and he was just as well. He figured he had a few more wakeful hours in him, provided the radio was on. So, he texted his wife, and she called him back, happy to hear he was alive if anything, and confident that in time he would also be well. She talked out her stressors, and so did he. The weeks had been brutal, and such brutality called for a traditional Sunday meatloaf of nontraditional immensity.

As Dougherty pulled back onto the freeway, he realized he was smiling, and that, in itself, yielded a second, softer smile that rested on him without effort. He made the turn away from the edge of dusk and embraced the widening blanket of starlight wrapping the world that he called home.

ASK AND YE SHALL RECEIVE
MICHELE E. REISINGER

IT'S A PUZZLE, AIN'T IT? HOW SOMETIMES LIFE GIVES YOU ALL the pieces but their edges are rough and the colors are blurry and it ain't till you step a ways back and rearrange that you see the patterns. You know? You asked what brought me here and I'll tell you, but first I got to tell you something else. Since Pa died, I barely spoke, but after the ruckus in church a few weeks back my words is like a fountain. You don't mind, ma'am, do you? We got time.

Anyhow, Ma and me live a ways out of town, near where the river bends like an elbow. You can see it from the train bridge, over there. Our house's the one made of two squares, a big one and a little one, plus a shed out back where Pa kept things like hoes and threshing rakes for Ma's garden. The big square is where we done our eating and sleeping, Pa and Ma in a nook off the kitchen and us four children in the loft. Evenings, Pa'd tell stories and Ma'd rock by the fire knitting or sewing up the holes in Brother's shirt. Sometimes I sat in Pa's lap, sometimes on the floor. That was my spot, Ma tells me. Near Pa.

The time I'm needing to tell you was one of those days can't make up its mind to be spring or winter. Ice melting and muddy, but the sun shining like a promise ring. I remember Ma and Pa both was in a tizzy, though I did not know why. I's fourteen now. Then I's only six. Anyhow, we hadn't a real preacher for longer than I'd been alive, the last one an itinerant came through for the christenings and deaths. Sometimes weddings. So, Pa and the other men would do the preaching, telling stories that I thought were Pa's stories but turns out belonged to Jesus and his own pa, which a course I thought was the same thing. That day we was supposed to get a new preacher and someone, Ma can't remember, decided Pa should do the welcoming.

Me, I remember the kittens. Kitty had them in the shed in a little soft hole in the corner where Pa told me I could look but not touch, at least until they was weaned or their eyes opened. Which for me was the same thing. He told me I could have one when they's grown, so I picked the runty one 'cause she's little like me but I didn't tell no one. I'd study them for hours and tell Pa's stories to help them grow like Pa's stories helped me. That day, four a them had their eyes open but my runty one didn't. I knew I shouldn't touch but I did 'cause the littlest one wasn't moving and I wanted to get it to move. It was dead, which I knew but didn't want to know. I remember running for Pa. He'd told us 'bout Jesus resurrecting from the dead and I thought Pa could bring Kitty's runty kitten back alive like he done Jesus. I remember the mud squishing my toes and slowing me down like fingers grabbing at my ankles. I didn't think I'd ever find Pa, but when I circled the house, I heard Pa and Ma telling my sisters and Joe our brother to settle, and then another voice I didn't reckon. Both low and loud at the same time, like how thunder starts quiet then blows like a wave through the clouds. I thought, or maybe heard, I don't remember exactly, that somehow Pa had knew and asked Jesus direct about Kitty's kitten.

Well, I burst into the house babbling like Ma tells me I used to do and I seen a man who wasn't Jesus at all but a man in black with a frown like Pa's scythe and he's helping himself to the last of Ma's turnips. Children should be seen, not heard, he says, nodding at Ma to scoop another turnip on his plate. The only plate on the table.

I threw a tizzy, Ma says. I's so mad 'cause Pa always told me I should ask when I need something, and here I was asking and he ain't doing nothing but minding some stranger without manners enough to share. I must of said as much 'cause Pa said I's being disrespectful and to wait outside till I find my own manners. I should be ashamed, he said, scampering all over Ma's clean floor with my muddy feet and interrupting Preacher. Mind you, I did not know Preacher was Preacher until Pa's service and then it's too late to hush.

The day after Preacher came, Pa died and I stopped talking to most everybody 'cept Ma and sometimes Schoolteacher. Miss Sophie's the one what taught me to write my stories if I couldn't see fit to talk them. She came year before last, after the measles took the last one. That ain't how Pa died, though. Him and the other Pas was plowing the big farm in the hollow over there when one a the draft horses got spooked. No one seen why, least that's what they told Ma, who's left with four children to raise, me being the youngest. Joe quit school and hired himself out in Pa's place. Our sisters wasn't much for schooling, not like me a tall. They stayed long enough to cipher and tally bills at the mercantile. First for us and Ma, then for they own husbands and children. Janie has two and Sarah has one, a little girl with green eyes like mine. I love her especially. She is three and fierce like a lion. Which I ain't never seen but imagine from the books Miss Sophie let me borrow 'cause I take care of them and bring them back to school on Mondays and after planting and harvest. Preacher has the running of the school in between harvesting souls. The wheat from the chaff, he says, though he can't tell a spade from a shovel if you catch my meaning. Miss chuckled when I told her on my slate. Then she told me to tell her out loud and I did. And then I told her about Pa.

Last month, I heard Preacher and Miss talking in the schoolhouse while I's outside reading and the other children was playing marbles or some such so's Preacher could have his word. I'd been feeling poorly, like I'd swallowed a bag of rocks, 'cause Miss said she'd done taught me everything she could and it was time for me to graduate. She's planning a whole ceremony, she said. A commencement. I never heard that word before so I looked it up in the fat dictionary Miss keeps longside her desk. She'd got it wrong, I read. I wasn't beginning something, I's ending. There ain't no secondary school anywhere near here and besides, Ma said it's time I got a job like Joe and our sisters when they's my age. I even wrote another story about it, trying to keep my innards steady, but every time I thought about leaving school, I swallowed another rock.

Anyhow, my breath got hitchy when I heard my name 'cause I thought I was in trouble even though I hadn't done anything wrong that I could remember. Mind you, I was not eavesdropping. Preacher is loud and forgets I can hear just fine. Miss's voice was happy like sugar and she's telling Preacher I's the smartest she ever seen, like a dry riverbed drinking up the rain. She told Preacher she put some a my stories in the post and some school up north wants me to study there, the same school Miss told me she'd gone to. Can you believe it? Tuition included, plus a place to stay. I'd just need travel money and a few extras, which I could get working in the school kitchen once I got there, and Miss asked a course could the church help?

Preacher, he just laughed. Mind you, there's all kinds a laughs and you can read them like you read a book. Ever notice? Least I can, and Preacher's laugh was like someone showed him a porcupine and told him he could magic it to a squirrel. He said there had to be some mistake, surely one of the boys'd be a better candidate than a half-wit girl and he'd see to fix it. Well, Miss's voice went from sugar to fire, like each word's a match, till Preacher said something about contracts and options and how St. Paul certainly had it figured when he told Timothy's womenfolk to hush. After all, if it ain't been for Eve talking to that snake we'd all still be in Paradise stead a this Podunk town. Miss got real hushed then. I waited till Preacher left and I seen Miss sitting at her desk with her head in her hands and her face grim like . . . Well, I don't rightly know. But she straightened right up when she saw me, she knew I heard. We'll figure something she said, I shouldn't worry.

But a course I worried. All Miss done was try to help me, I didn't mean for Preacher to trouble her. It was like Kitty's kittens when I's little. After I interrupted Preacher's supper, Pa and Ma shared a frown and Pa told me to get along outside, he'd be along after a bit. But the words in my throat was rushing and I did not listen. I hollered something ugly and ran to the shed for Pa's shovel and some rocks 'cause I remembered the part about the angels rolling the rock away. Pa's stories was all jumbled in my thinking, and a course I's too little to figure the shovel. I cut up my feet something fierce and started wailing at the gush a blood. Pa and Ma both came running, Preacher a ways behind with his napkin tucked in his collar like some flag. Next day, Pa tucked one a the boss's spare kitties in his pocket meaning to walk home noon hour to give it to me, 'cept it got loose and spooked the horse.

I ain't supposed to know that but I do. I told you Preacher talks too loud.

Anyhow, try as we might, Miss and me couldn't figure a way to raise the money. Ma had a little extra but it weren't near enough, and Miss needs her extra for her own ma and pa back home. Miss even wrote to the school but they's sorry they couldn't do anything else but hold my spot a while if need be. You're right, ma'am, times is tough everywhere. Ma said it's for the best but her eyes was contradicting her mouth. All this is yammering in my head in church last month when Preacher's preaching bout prayer. He's saying how God is good to His children like our papas is good to us and that got me thinking about my own Pa. I closed my eyes so's I could remember better. I's thinking he could a figured a way, Ma said Pa could fix most anything. I missed him a course, but not as hurtful as it used to be. Mostly I missed how he used to explain things sweet and easy so's I could understand. Pa's why I loved school so much, least after Miss came, 'cause Miss learned us with stories like he done. Meanwhile, Preacher's preaching about asking and receiving and I recollected how Pa used to tell me all I had to do was ask and Pa'd see what he could do. I also couldn't sit on my behind, Pa said. I had to do some a the work. He said it's kinda like when you lose something. The asking kinda quiets the yammering that keeps you from seeing what needs seeing. The rest is like walking through an unlocked door.

But as I'm thinking this, I'm hearing Preacher and he's telling it all wrong. Like he's the only one can see who's asking proper. That got me so mad, let me tell you. Ain't no one more proper than Pa and Miss, and Preacher got no right saying otherwise. I scrabbled across Ma for a prayer book and turned to where Preacher's railing and there it is. Matthew's story, same as my own Pa's name. Ask and ye shall receive, seek and ye shall find, knock and it shall be opened to you. Can't be any more clear than that. Anyhow, I don't even know what I's thinking. I just stand up and tell Preacher he got it all wrong. He's gone around telling me and Miss and near half the congregation we oughtta hush when it says right there we gotta open up our mouths what God gave us. Ain't no way He'd of ever wanted us to hush. I said I tried hushing after Pa died, figuring keeping quiet'd fix the mess I made killing my Pa in the first place, even though I ain't mean to cause I's little. I told everybody I ain't no half-wit like Preacher says, I's smart and so's Miss. Miss is the one what figured out my mess when nobody else seen it. She told me Pa wouldn't of wanted me to feel bad about his accident. She told me Pa was a teacher like Preacher oughtta be, telling stories and showing me the right a things. I told everybody about Miss' school and how I's gone write and tell them to hold my spot, even if I got to work till next year for the money. Everybody's looking between me and Preacher then me again, till one of the pas Pa used to work with marches up to the altar and grabs the collection basket. Everybody starts filling it with pennies and nickels, even a silver dollar, and one a the elders says they needs a meeting bout Preacher's contract. Ma, she starts crying and hugging me and Miss. Miss just smiles big as a rainbow. Told you, she tells Preacher. She's the smartest I have ever seen.

A course I cried too and then I hollered a thank you so loud it woke the babies, but the mamas, they just let 'em cry.

Which is why I'm waiting on the train like you, ma'am, I got a ticket right here gone take me to my new school. Everybody chipped in, even Preacher. Though I could of swore he done it with a bellyful a rocks. Anyhow, Miss says if I study real hard and practice my speaking, soon enough I'll be even smarter. I will a course, 'cause telling you this I figured the last piece a my puzzle. I'm gone write me a schoolful a books, bigger even than the one Miss says is at my new school, and I ain't never gone hush again.

A MIX TAPE ODYSSEY
DOUG BOST

Side A

MIX TAPES ARE CREATED TO CONVINCE SOMEONE TO SLEEP with you.

They do not always work. Sometimes they work, and it's very important not to forget that. Sometimes they work. But the great thing about a mix tape is that if it doesn't work, you still have a great tape with good music, arranged in an order that means something to you. In contrast, a perfectly worded love letter where you put all your deepest feelings of longing and lust down on specially chosen paper seems great, but if it doesn't lead at least to making out in somebody's dorm room, it's garbage. Unless you're William Shakespeare or Evan Dando, it is actual garbage.

I say mix tapes are created, present tense, because although a plastic Maxell High Bias Type 2 Gold cassette tape is a relic of years gone by, the idea of the mix tape lives on even today as a romantically shared Spotify playlist or as a Soundcloud file uploaded before the girl you love goes to Colorado for Christmas. Sharing a mix of perfect songs has been, for generations, a cornerstone of bedroom access.

That afternoon, in 1988, I had finished this particular tape, the one I would take to see Julie. The Ann Arbor Mix.

And at 11 p.m., I was in the Port Authority in a line of students and slackers and desperate lovers and deadbeat dads, all of us with big destinations and little money, going from New York to points west on an overnight bus.

If you buy a bus ticket, you're essentially saying you don't have to be anywhere, anytime soon. This particular Greyhound did not disappoint.

I settled in next to a guy who seemed to be already asleep, and put on side A. The art of the mix tape is to pack as much onto each side as possible, and to orchestrate the flow from one track to the next. A second song should seem inevitable once you hear it. The song after that should make the listener nod and smile and lean forward, whether the song is familiar or not. Of course, you should say. Of course "Wonderful World" by Sam Cooke is followed by "I Scare Myself" by Thomas Dolby. Of course the final falsetto notes of "Smalltown Boy" by Bronski Beat lead directly to the crisp opening drums of "The Letter" by The Box Tops. Of course.

The bus creaked and lurched around the diesel curves of the Port Authority sublevels and spit us out on the other side of the Hudson lumbering into New Jersey and I closed my eyes.

"Naïve Melody" by Talking Heads, the Stop Making Sense version. "Domino" by Van Morrison, the radio edit. "I Just Wasn't Made for These Times" by the Beach Boys with a deliberately jarring transition into "Something I Learned Today" by Husker Du and a softening of that alt rock message by leading from there into the one-hit-wonder of "Drivers Seat" by Sniff n the Tears. It was all about pop music, and making the listener a little amazed to hear these great songs together in this way for the first time. A mix that can go along with you anywhere but also transitions into something you can play at home while you talk about the day. A mix that becomes a bed on which you can lie down, and the maker of this tape lies down with you.

Of course this amazing person would create a mix just like this. And now that I've heard it—of course I love him.

Julie had never been my girlfriend. We'd met at NYU and I had become smitten with her early on. She was beautiful. Blonde. Funny. She had a huge laugh. She'd read all my favorite books. And she was completely out of what I considered to be my league. But she never acted like it and maybe that's what rewired my brain. She was the type of girl I'd never had any kind of flirtation with, but now, here, look at this craziness—this girl seems to really like me. How—This isn't—Really? And once I got rewired for this new sunshine possibility, I couldn't get out from under it.

She'd call and then she wouldn't call. She had transient boyfriends who were inevitably drummers. She would disappear for a week. We'd kiss in the ballet studio. My friends all said she was bad news for me. We'd go to a play and laugh like I'd never laughed before, and then I saw her sitting on the steps of a brownstone doing coke from a little glass sniffer, sitting with five guys who were either The Jesus and Mary Chain or an improv troupe and she waved me on as if I shouldn't be seen knowing her. No matter how much writing there was on the wall, I read it all as "Come save me."

She gave me my first joint in her apartment, and when we smoked it together, with Julie curled up in my lap like a cat, nothing happened; the pot must've been some useless herb. And then I took the book of matches we were using to light and relight that joint, and I looked at the little quiz printed on the book of matches, and read it out loud to Julie, and the question on the outside said, "Who won the first Super Bowl in 1967?" and I opened it up and the answer said, "Eleanor Roosevelt." And suddenly the room expanded like an accordion and we realized we were so wonderfully, hilariously, deeply stoned. And it was just a misprint on the matchbook, but it turned one night smoking a joint into a journey, and that turned Julie into the person I wanted to take every journey with.

And then, rather suddenly, she left New York. Moved back to Ann Arbor, Michigan. Wrote me. Called me. Missed me. Hated it there. But she was stuck. So, I decided I had to take a bus out there and make this thing real once and for all. I would be the guy from back East with all the weight of a new character in a play who's been discussed for the whole first act, finally entering with a kicked-open door and a gasp from the audience.

But, y'know, I needed all my firepower. So, that's why I made the mix tape. I would give it to her, leave it behind. It was hers. By breakfast tomorrow, Julie and I would be face to face again.

I flipped over to side B—side B started out with "New Coat of Paint" by Tom Waits—and then played side A again, and I fell asleep somewhere in Pennsylvania, at around three in the morning. And when I fell asleep, I was leaning back in my seat but when I woke up, I was in the air halfway over the seat in front of me.

I was in the air because the bus had gone off the highway.

This crowded Greyhound bus had slammed into a ditch, which chucked all of us forward, and then threw everybody back into their seats as it went up the other side of the ditch and over some scrub brush and through a wood and wire fence into a cow pasture.

People were too stunned to scream at first. There was a lot of grunting and vocalizing as everyone got jarred back down. Out the window it was all dark grass. I strained up to get a look at the driver and I caught him leaning way out and around to see back down the aisle, presumably to check if all of us were okay. But without another word he cranked the bus into reverse, and we humped back into the ditch toward Interstate 80, and he did it with a lot of speed, as if he could kind of muscle this giant cracker box back onto the highway. But we hit the far side of the ditch and that's where we stayed. Front wheels up in the air. Back of the bus jammed into the mud near Youngstown, Ohio. Done.

There was total confusion on the bus then, everything we had was up at a 30 degree angle, and when we got off we were standing in this swampy pasture just at dawn, maybe forty strangers, people coming up to me and saying, "He was trying to avoid a deer, right?" and an elderly woman saying, "Little driver man fell asleep," and when my original seat-mate got a whiff of that rumor, he started rubbing his neck like he felt a lawsuit coming on.

How bad was this? I'd been on my way, and now I wasn't. Maybe I just had to wait this out. Calm down. I could still get to Ann Arbor this weekend. The cows were staring at us.

I noticed the bus driver was staying apart from everybody else, waiting for someone from Greyhound to arrive, and when they did, an hour or so later with a state police escort, he got into a car with them and we were all told that a Peter Pan bus would be along soon that could take us to Fort Wayne, of all places, and we would have an opportunity to find our way from there.

I could feel my weekend with Julie slipping away in the hands of Greyhound bureaucrats. I had done one thing smart, in hindsight. I had put my duffel bag in the space above my seat, because it had all my other tapes in it. I didn't have to wait for my bag to be retrieved from the luggage compartments under the bus, like everybody else.

I was free to go, actually. So, I grabbed my bag and waited until the state police cruiser had pulled away, and I walked to I-80, stuck out my thumb, and put on my headphones.

"State Farm" by Yaz. "Hold On I'm Coming" by Sam & Dave. "Walk Through the Fire" by Peter Gabriel, which was a B-side from the soundtrack to *Against All Odds*—not a good movie but that song should've been a hit. Just play it all loud.

Eleven hours later I was dropped off by a nice family in a Suburban at Julie's address in Ann Arbor. Here I was, a guy with a purpose, a story. An odyssey. And a mix tape. How could I lose?

Side B

IMMEDIATELY, IT WAS wrong. It was midday and Julie wasn't home. The house she lived in was a big old thing with a sprawling, creaky porch and airy spaces inside, and you could see it had once belonged to some wealthy family of the industrial revolution but now it was occupied by at least seven women who went to various colleges in the area and who parked on the lawn and left set pieces from last fall's production of *Vanities*.

I was welcomed in by Julie's roommates, I have no idea now what their names were. Not-Julie 1 and Not-Julie 2. They seemed to know about me, and they knew I was coming; that made me feel better. I told them how the bus had crashed last night, and how I'd hitched, and how it had taken a half dozen rides to get me here, and how one of the rides was with a guy who said he was searching for underground UFO bases in his van. And y'know when you tell a story to somebody and you can tell they don't give a shit? Because only at the end when you get to a detail like underground UFO bases do they stop and look you in the eye and they say, "Wait—where was this?" and you realize they weren't listening at all and you'll never really get them to listen because they have a base-level of don't-give-a-shit that you'll never overcome. That's what was happening here.

Not-Julie 1 asked if I wanted to get some sleep, and I was led into Julie's heavily curtained room. I dropped onto a bed that smelled like talcum powder and clove cigarettes and I didn't think I was that tired, but before I could even put on my headphones and find a Brian Eno tape, I was asleep.

Julie got home an hour or so later. She snuck into her own bedroom, giggling, and jumped on the bed and rolled around hugging me with that raspy smoker-voice laugh saying she couldn't believe I was there and wasn't it great I was actually in Michigan, wasn't it incredible, was I sleeping, did she wake me? She wanted to know every detail of my trip. So, I sat up and told her. She loved hearing it, she yelled and bounced up and down with each new character in the saga. And when I was done, she put on some music, Crowded House, which was interesting because I don't know why I hadn't included any Crowded House on the Ann Arbor Mix. Shit, that was kind of a miss.

It was so great to see her. She was wearing the earrings I got her, and did I like them? I did. But she didn't kiss me. I noticed that. Instead, we lay back and she took a breath. And she said, "I have to tell you something."

Goddammit, I thought. "Go ahead," I said.

"I'm seeing this guy. He lives here in town. It's kind of serious." She looked at me. I looked at her and nodded. "And that doesn't affect this weekend, we'll still hang out, but I gotta be at his house tonight. I just want you to know."

"Okay," I said with my face probably getting red. "Totally cool, great for you. You like him?"

"He's a lot." She laughed.

"What does he do? You're in class with him?"

"Yeah, but he's not—he's really a drummer."

Unbelievable, I thought. But totally believable.

"His name is Marcus." Also believable.

"Okay," I said. "Do you want me to stay in a hotel? I can."

"No, no!" she yelled. "I want to introduce you. To everybody. Are you pissed at me? Are you? It's okay if you are."

"I'm not," I said. "I didn't know, that's all."

We lay there on the bed in the dark, and she held my hand, which I thought was really weird in a way, but I didn't let go. And we lay there listening to Crowded House for the rest of that side of the album. Just lying there and listening.

I started thinking about leaving. I had a plan. The plan was this: I was staying here tonight, which was Saturday night, and then

Sunday night, and Monday morning I'd arranged that my friend
Scott would pick me up on his way from Los Angeles back to New
York; he was gonna swing through and drive me home.

I had anticipated regaling Scott with stories of wild you-came-
all-the-way-out-here-to-see-me   sex   and   smug   I-told-you-this-
obsession-would-become-true-love monologues, my feet on the
dashboard, fresh off a weekend of fulfilled desires.

But that was not happening. And now, lying here, I didn't want
to say it to Julie but suddenly I couldn't wait for Scott to arrive. Scott
was my buddy. Scott would understand. I could tell Scott
everything. But I had to get through the rest of the goddamn
weekend first.

I killed time at a movie that night, the seven p.m. show of *Who
Framed Roger Rabbit.*

And then Sunday morning sometime after nine Julie pulled up
in her sister's car. She seemed giddy about the day of driving we
had ahead of us. Her happy Sunday morning mood was hard to
resist and out on the lawn, packing the car, she got us laughing at
the other girls, laughing at the way Julie was basically living with the
cast of the *Golden Girls* if there were seven Golden Girls, and if
they were all in their twenties, and if most of them were Rue
McClanahan. She was funny, right?

"Bring some music," Julie said. So, I brought all my tapes and
as soon as we'd gotten on the road I put the Ann Arbor Mix in the
stereo.

The mix played. We talked and listened and drove.

Julie liked it. Sam Cooke. Thomas Dolby. The Box Tops. She
pounded on the steering wheel during "I Will Dare" by The
Replacements. But out on the highway, when I involuntarily sang
along with "Something So Right" by Paul Simon, she made a
surprised face like she'd just realized something and she said, "Aw,
it's a love mix."

There was nothing I could say to that.

We drove to a lake she knew and took roadside pictures in
front of a sign for a town called Climax ("Hilarious!") but by the
time we got back to her house, I couldn't remember much about
that day. "It's a love mix."

Pulling up in front, Julie said she had to return the car and I knew she was gone for the night. Before she left, she asked was I gonna be okay with all the Rue McClanahans having a party at the house tonight? A lot of people were gonna come over, it was somebody's birthday, was that okay with me?

Of course. Of course it was.

The party started early and loud. There was some live music planned, everybody said, but I never saw it. Up until about eleven, it was just the stereo blaring songs that lived in a dreadful middle-ground of party music: you couldn't dance to them, you couldn't nod your head to a groove, they didn't have words you wanted to sing, but at the same time they reminded you of songs that did all those things.

The stereo was in the living room, and the party radiated out from there. I sat right in the middle of it, drinking a beer off the coffee table in a circle of empty couches. And on the coffee table, along with a couple of pizzas and six-packs, was a kitty. A mason jar with a label on it that said, "IF YOU EAT OR DRINK, YOU PAY." People would come by and grab a slice and for the most part they were diligent about putting some money into the kitty.

A few of the guests were dicks. There were three or four guys who apparently lived down the road, and they came and accidentally broke something, but nobody paid much attention, and after a half hour or so they left.

The music just got worse. From Starship to John Parr. And the kitty just kept growing. A second round of pizza and beer came out and more guests cycled through the house, so that by midnight, when I just wanted to go to bed but I knew I'd never sleep, I was sitting in front of maybe three hundred bucks in fives and ones, listening to, I kid you not, Whitesnake.

That was when the guys from the other house came back.

Two of them stood by the door, and one of the others walked right over to the coffee table where I was and started loudly talking about how all these girls were teases, and that he loved them but this was the worst party they'd ever thrown.

This is a type of low-wattage prick I'd seen before.

Without looking at me, he reached down and scooped up the mason jar and tucked it in the crook of his arm like a football player and kept walking forward as if he hadn't just done that.

I was on my feet without thinking. Something about seeing this brazen grab tripped my Zorro gene. If I'd had a cape and a mask, I would've put them on.

I got in his way and grabbed the jar under his arm and we were both kind of straddling the couch and I put on my deepest voice and said something like, "That's not yours!" I could smell his sweat as he hung onto the jar and, in fact, dug his hand into it, clutching as much of the cash as he could and then suddenly swinging it toward me like a club. The jar caught me on the shoulder and knocked me back, and all his friends were laughing by the door as he pulled back and headed for the exit.

A couple of the Not-Julies had come out by then and were yelling at both of us as I rushed back at him and shoved him down onto a couch and grabbed at the jar again. I was standing over him and he kicked at me lamely and the money started flying out of the jar and all over the couch and we were both yelling at each other and his friends started yelling, too, "Leave him alone," as if I had provoked this asshole.

It was the weirdest fight I've ever been in. He spit at me. I guess I flinched when he did it but I didn't let go of the jar, and we kept wrestling as more of the cash spilled out and the music was deafening and the yelling was getting more pitched and somebody was pulling on my shirt so it was becoming shapeless.

And I suddenly had this overwhelming thought: What the fuck am I doing?

What possible reason did I have for trying to fight these total strangers over a couple hundred bucks belonging to some other total strangers, when all I really should be doing is going outside, calling a cab, and finding a hotel until my friend could come get me tomorrow?

What was wrong with me?

So, I whipped my shoulders back and forth and got off the guy on the couch and let go of the jar and he got up fast and swore at me and threw the jar across the room and made a big show of dropping the rest of the cash on the rug. He said some stupid thing nobody cared about, and he kicked the coffee table, but it was bolted down so it sounded like he probably really hurt his foot, and he and his friends left.

Somebody closed the door after them. Nobody was yelling anymore. That was a relief. I went over to the stereo and turned off the goddamn Whitesnake.

Not-Julie 2 said, "I'm really sorry." I said it was okay. Over and done now. And she told me again she was sorry.

Back up in Julie's room, I sat on the bed.

Jesus. Jesus H Christ.

I shook my head, thinking whether I could get a shower in the morning, and I noticed Julie's milk crates full of LPs and 45s. It was a collection that I hadn't really even thought about since I got here, for some reason. Her turntable was perched on top of her receiver and a really nice Crosley dual cassette.

There must be a lot of great music in Julie's records. Music that I could tape tonight, and if I did that, I'd have a fresh mix for the road tomorrow. There was always something exciting and a little bit criminal about plundering another person's music collection to make your own tape.

I dug out the Ann Arbor Mix and looked it over. I'd removed the plastic tabs on the top of the cassette, which meant you couldn't record over it unless you covered the holes with scotch tape. But Julie had some scotch tape right on her bookshelf.

It made sense. I wasn't leaving this mix for her anymore. No. I could tape over it. Symbolically erase the obsessive planning I'd done for this ridiculous trip to nowhere, wipe it out. Tape over the tape.

But who was I kidding?

The Ann Arbor Mix was too good to tape over. And Julie had a whole stack of fresh tapes she'd never even opened.

So, I got started.

She had "O Superman" by Laurie Anderson. "Do It Again" by the Beach Boys. "Ain't That Peculiar" by Marvin Gaye. "Mayor of Simpleton" by XTC—she had a lot of XTC. "Consider Me Gone" by Sting, which was a live version and ended with applause that blended perfectly with the applause at the start of Lou Rawls' "I'd Rather Drink Muddy Water," so it sounded like one continuous track. I think I may have given Julie that record, *Lou Rawls Live*, wasn't that mine originally? It's really a shame Lou Rawls wound up with a reputation for elevator jazz, because that live 1966 album is amazing. And I had room on side B for three songs by The Zombies. I'd always heard how great The Zombies were but I'd never really listened to them.

Two sides. A full ninety minutes of music on a brand new tape.

I knew that when I got back to New York, I'd thank Julie for spending as much of the weekend with me as she could, and thank her for actually telling me honestly about her brand new drummer boyfriend. In a way it was the best thing she could have done in the situation. I would send her a perfectly worded letter on specially chosen paper.

For now, I wrote "Let's Go" on the outside of the cassette box and, while I waited for my ride to show up, I put on some Steely Dan.

MY BODY IS 2 BODIES

JAY EDDY

M y
body is 2
bodies, girl
and fish. I
am 6 years
old. In

the summer, on the weekends, I stay with my
grandmother whose house is full of mermaid
dolls and
prints. We
go to the
beach, and
my grandma
says that I'm
a mermaid, too.
I am B I G and
strong, and I can
swim the crawl, the
breaststroke, and the
backstroke. I can al-
most swim the fly. One
day, I dig myself neck-
deep in sand—my mother
washes my hair for h o u r s
and h o u r s and h o u r s and
grandma laughs. My mother who
   is dark and
   slender like
    a stalk of
   rhubarb. My
   grandmother
    who is pale
    and round
     like an
      Opal
      Apple.

M y
body is 2
bodies, 1
belongs to
me and
1 to

everybody else. I am 10 years old. My new
pants are too small already, and I don't want
to be big
and strong.
I have hips
and tits—I
don't know
if I like them.
I've grown into
my mom's old
bathing suits, and
my favorite is the
navy blue Miracle-
suit with the sheer
mesh w a v e across
the front. One night, a
man's hands touch me
when I'm half-asleep—he's
a boy, but he's a man to me—
or maybe it was only a dream.
   I tell myself
    it was a
    d r e a m.
    I wish I
    were flat. I
    wear the
     Miracle-
     suit un-
     der my
     clothes.

M y
body is 2
bodies, 1 I
have and
1 I want.
I am

16 years old. I stop eating. I can make a
cup of applesauce last a w h o l e day.
I listen
to The
Carpen-
ters. Karen
died hungry
at thirty-two
(I wanna be
like you)—I love
feeling h u n g r y,
I study, study her
b i o g r a p h y like
a How To. I drive
to   the   beach   in
w i n t e r t i m e and
sit o u t s i d e on the
hood of my sensible car
or walk across the frosted
sand. I dip my b a r e feet in
the water.
It stings my
s k i n like
sticking my
finger in an
e l e c t r i c
s o c k e t
I love
feeling
cold.

M y
body is 2
bodies, flesh
s t u c k on
bone but
some-

thing else, too, I cannot name. I'm twenty-two
years old. BA honors, MA with
distinction
(cue sar-
castic ooh)—I
move back in
with my parents.
H e y , I h e a r
ev'rybody's doing
it. Waves of panic
(daily) c r a c k and
c r a c k down on
my head, and my ears
and eyes and lungs fill
up with w a t e r. In
dreams, I swim the crawl
across the sky. I like my
therapist—number four—
because she asks, "Are you
still anorexic?" then corrects
    herself and
    says, "Not
    t h a t i t
    e v e r goes
    away." She
    tells me
    I have
    P T S D.
    Crack.
    Crack.

M y
body is 2
bodies, 1 I
had and 1
I have—
a n d

h a t e, h a t e, h a t e, h a t e—now. I am
twenty-six years old, and I am always sick
with some
thing I can't
n a m e. My
intestines are
twisted, stomach
h a r d and dis-
t e n d e d, h e a d
heavy and listing like
a boat weighed down
with stones. Too dizzy
to stand, too nauseous to
eat, and a c h i n g and
a c h i n g all over, I curl up
like a question mark in bed in
the dark. I want to unzip my
spine, shake off my skin, and
float like a feather away on the air.
"I don't want to be s i c k ."
    Like a chant,
    I don't want
    to be s i c k.
    I don't want
    to be s i c k.
    I don't want
    to be s i c k.
        I don't
        want
        to be—

—
Then
I meet A r l o. He's a 1
year old mutt, a scruffy little
nothing born on Dead Dog
Beach. He l e a p s into my
arms and stays there. I
take him home.
I know, I know
we all make fun when
someone says, "My dog
rescued me," but he does,
that skin-and-bone sato saves
my life. I watch his fur grow in and
his flesh f i l l out. For him, I am a
a warm, soft body. A bed. A scratch.
A bowl of food. For me he is a levy.
My body is 2 bodies, g i r l
and d o g. M e a n d A r l o.
I am twenty-seven years old. I
live in Brooklyn,   but I
think I may   move
up north. Somewhere   on the
water water water   water.

ASSISTED LIVING
BENJAMIN KEYWORTH

THEY CALLED IT ASSISTED LIVING, BUT IN TRUTH IT WAS MORE like postponed dying.

That was the point of places like Shady Pines. It wasn't about you. It was about whoever put you there not feeling guilty about letting you die. They—the amorphous "they," your children, your relatives, the state—didn't want to have to lie in bed at night and feel bad, so they paid for your shuffle to the grave to be lengthened. The same way people bought freezers and filled them with leftovers that they'd still eventually throw out.

At least, that's how it felt to Jez.

At twenty-four, he was the youngest person that should've been dead in Shady Pines by at least half a century. Not that age mattered—he still required the same amount of care as any of the other walking corpses. Feeding, dressing, the daily changing of the colostomy bag. The break in his spinal cord had come beneath his C4 vertebrae, so thankfully he could still breathe on his own, but the rest was pretty much out. Still, at least he was alive. If the very kind and talented rescuers who'd extracted him from the wreckage had been just a little bit slower in delivering him to the very kind and talented surgeons to operate, maybe things would have gone just a little bit less worse and he would've died without ever waking up. Died without ever knowing, like his parents and sister. Imagine how terrible that would've been. If he'd just been dead instead of stuck in a motorized chair for the next few decades in the constant process of shitting his pants.

Some might have called Jez bitter, but it'd been six months now and he was past that stage of grief. Besides, how could anyone be unhappy when they had canasta?

"It doesn't have to be canasta," Susan said kindly. She indicated a semi-manicured hand back at the trolley. "There's checkers or dominos. How about backgammon? Monopoly?"

"Big poo bum fart," said Dennis.

The common room was the same as it was every day. Soft and ugly carpet the color of vomit; old chairs as worn as their residents. The musty, grassy, greasy smell of the old and aging, as pervading and innocuous as it was unpleasant. Slippered feet shuffled on the carpet. Walkers ached, recliners creaked. The muffled voices of the residents mumbled in the same pitch and cadence as the daytime television playing inoffensively in the background, the lull only occasionally spiked through with the younger tones of a nurse.

Thursday afternoons at the nursing home were game days. In reality, those same games were available to play on any day at any time, but management had long since found that giving old people a predictable routine kept them docile. Stopped them thinking too hard about their quasi-imprisonment and the looming specter of death.

"Whatever it is, make it quick," snapped Violet. Thinner than almost everyone there, with thin lines of white hair hanging limp behind her skull, she resembled nothing so much as a heron afflicted with mange. She clutched at her pink woolen shawl and glanced around the common room anxiously, scanning over the other residents and their tables. "My Thomas is coming to pick me up soon and I can't be in the middle of something."

"Cock dick penis," replied Dennis. He was in his mid-eighties and bald, with only singular wisps of hair circling his skin spots like cobwebs tangled on a broom. There was a chunk the size of a spam steak missing from one side of his neck where a skin cancer used to be. He'd been a war veteran, apparently.

"Oh, I'd like to play canasta," said Ethyl. Plump and rosy-cheeked with curly hair a bottled gray, she beamed up at Susan through tortoise-shell glasses. "I think that would be just lovely."

"Fuck dicks mangy cunt."

Aging, it turned out, affected people in different ways. Dennis had been afflicted quite distinctly—the language centers in his brain having rotted to the point where he could only say curse words. Violet on the other hand had been stricken less markedly, but no less severely, with the implacable conviction that her husband was always coming to visit. And then you had Ethyl, upon whom age had inflicted no interesting condition but instead just turned into an incredibly basic old person, which was in a way more cruel.

"Well, Ethyl," smiled Susan. Some of the thick foundation she always wore had rubbed off onto the blue collar of her nurse's uniform. "Unfortunately, it's Jeffrey's turn to pick a game this week. We all have to take turns. What game would you like to play, Jeffrey?"

Jez made no move toward any game, still being paralyzed from the neck down.

"I said Jeffrey, it's your turn to pick a game this week, which game would you like to—"

"Dungeons and Dragons."

For a moment, the only sound was the soft, indifferent shuffling of the other tables and the distant phlegming of Mr. Johnson's hacking cough.

"Jeffrey, I don't think—"

"I know you have it." Jez kept his gaze resolute, which was quite easy to do when you didn't have to worry about your body going anywhere. "I know the game shop donated a set last year."

"Jeffrey . . ." Susan sighed and looked at him with the expression of an exasperated mother. "I think it's really important to think about those around you. I know you're bored. But we all need to try really hard to be considerate of other people."

"Faggot vagina," said Dennis.

Jez was resolute. "I'd like to give it a go."

"I think it would be difficult for—"

"Why are we still talking?" Violent barked. "Why isn't the game happening? I told you, Thomas is coming to pick me up soon and if I'm not ready he'll—"

"Are we playing canasta?" asked Ethyl, looking confused.

"No, Ethyl," said Jez, rotating his neck to look at her. "We're trying something new."

"Oh, dear. I hope it isn't too difficult."

"Piss."

"It's not," he replied, turning back to Susan pointedly. "It's just like playing make-believe."

Susan's forehead crinkled, but ultimately it was difficult to say no to a quadriplegic.

"Give me a moment." She sighed and walked toward the office.

"SO, YOU HAVE to pick your class," said Jez. He double-flicked his eyes at the A4 sheets with premade characters on them, which was the cue for Susan, who was acting as his hands, to pass them around. "You choose who you want to pretend to be."

"Thomas and I were in the class of '52," Violet said, glancing at the others around the table with the smug air of a particularly well-fed cat. "Head boy and head girl. He can tell you all about it when he gets here."

"You can be an elven wizard," Jez said, rolling his eyes, which counted as his exercise for the day.

"I'm not a wizard, I'm a woman."

"Elven wizard woman."

"Hmpf." Violet turned her head away disdainfully. "Thomas hates magic tricks."

"Shitting penis asshole."

"You're going to be a paladin," Jez said, turning to Dennis. "A noble knight cursed by a witch to never speak a single word. Is that all right with you?"

Dennis considered for a moment. "Ass-face testicle."

"Glad to hear it."

"Oh, dear, Jeffrey, I don't know about this," said Ethyl. Her liver-spotted hands trembled as they shuffled through the character sheets. "This looks very difficult."

"You'll be fine, Ethyl."

"I don't know what half these words mean."

"Just choose what you want to be and I'll help you."

"Oh, dear, I don't know, there're so many choices." She squinted through her reading glasses. "Con-sti-tu-ti-"

"Just pick. Warrior, cleric, barbarian—"

"Oh, I could be a barber," Ethyl said suddenly, perking up. "I used to love cutting my sister's hair."

"Barbarian it is," said Jez. His eyes turned back to Susan. "Set us up."

The young nurse hesitated for a second, then gave a small shrug as if to say "it's your funeral."

"AS YOU WALK up to the bodies of the dead horses with black-feathered arrows sticking out of them, four goblins leap out from the thickets on either side." Jez paused and looked around the table. "What do you do?"

The group was silent. On the table in front of them a plastic chessboard Susan had drawn on with whiteboard marker stood as a silent representation of Violet's, Ethyl's, and Dennis's characters and the made-up place they were pretending to be. In college the guys Jez had played with had had model terrain and painted miniatures to fuel their imaginations. Here their wizard, paladin, and barbarian were a pepper shaker, a white chess bishop, and the little dog from Monopoly.

At his word, Susan laid out four red checkers to represent the four goblins, then returned to sitting silently beside him, her chin resting glumly on one hand. Violet was glancing around at the other tables to see if Thomas had sat down at one of them by mistake. Ethyl was gazing up at him with the blissfully sunny expression of someone who hadn't heard a single word he'd just said. Only Dennis, situated at the opposite end of the table, was peering down at the chessboard, his eyes narrowed and his fingers pursed in front of his lips like a grandmaster planning his next move.

"Fuck ass ballsack," he said with grave finality. Jez and Susan just looked at him. After a couple of seconds, Dennis reached out a wrinkly hand and moved his bishop next to one of the checker-goblins. "Cock."

"Um." Jez frowned. He gazed directly into the old man's gray eyes, which were surprisingly sharp. "Attack? Do you want to attack?"

This was how the game worked. One person said what they were pretending was happening, and then everyone pretended what their particular character would do. Then you rolled dice to see what happened.

"Bastard," Dennis confirmed with a nod.

"Right." Jez had Susan roll a normal square dice and a bigger, twenty-sided one. "You hit the goblin. 6 damage. Well done."

"Cunt." Dennis smiled.

"This is ridiculous," Violet hissed. She wriggled in her seat, her agitated fingers unknitting threads from her shawl. "Where is he? He should be here by now."

"Violet," Susan chided kindly, "look here, please. We're playing a game now."

Violet kept looking behind her. Jez followed her eyes.

"He won't come until we finish the game," he assured her. Violet's white-haired head spun back around, and she fixed him with a piercing gaze. "You don't need to worry. Nobody's coming until we're finished."

Violet hesitated. Then she twisted back to face the table, straightening herself up. "Well, why didn't you say so?" she snapped. "Let's finish then. Quickly, get it over with. I want to see my husband."

"It's your turn."

"Well, I don't know what I'm doing," she said haughtily, gesturing at the board. "I don't understand this silly game."

"You have to defeat the goblins."

"What goblins?"

"The little red checkers."

"And how do I do that quickly?"

"You use spells on them."

"Fine." She scowled. "I want to use the quickest, most powerful spell and kill them all until they're dead."

There was a moment's silence. If Jez's shoulders had worked, he would've shrugged.

"You cast Magic Missile," he said. "Three glowing darts of magical force hit the goblins." He had Susan roll more dice. "The goblin closest to Dennis is dead."

"Oh, dear," said Ethyl, looking gravely concerned. "I hope he's okay."

"No, Ethyl, he's dead. It's your turn."

"Oh, dear." She looked down at her Monopoly dog. "What should I do?"

"Well, you're a barbarian. I'd suggest you Rage."

"What does that mean?"

"You can get angry. Your character is a very big man and he gets stronger when he's angry."

Ethyl shook her head, her face aghast. "Oh, no, I couldn't do that. I'm not an angry person."

"Ethyl, it's just make-believe."

"Oh, no," she said, still shaking her head, quite adamant. "You shouldn't get angry. Do unto others as you would like them to do unto you. I would like to check if that gobbin fellow is all right."

Jez sighed. Technically, the mark of a good dungeon master—the person who ran the game—was allowing their players the freedom to do what they wanted.

"You walk over to the goblin," he said. "And you check how it's doing."

"Is he okay?"

"The goblin is still dead."

"Oh, dear," Ethyl lamented. "Can we call an ambulance?"

"Fart ass dick fuck."

Susan's head sunk lower into her hands.

THE AFTERNOON ENDED with the battle complete and Ethyl's placid barbarian having checked each dead goblin individually and given them a blanket. Susan wiped the whiteboard marker off the chessboard, and Jez was wheeled back into his room by another nurse to be fed and watered and put into bed to stare at the ceiling for another empty night. Morning came around like it always did, and Jez got his half an hour out in the garden to photosynthesize with the rest of the plants. Lunch was spaghetti Bolognese, the Friday afternoon movie was *Casablanca*, and by the time Humphrey Bogart thought he spied the beginning of a beautiful friendship the memory of the game had already diminished into a small blip of abnormality in Jez's mind. An off-colored bauble, hanging on the sad branches of his life to mark the passage of time.

Until Violet sought him out.

He was positioned to sit alone and stare out the common-room window when she stormed, as furiously as any eighty-five-year-old woman could storm, to stand, hands on her hips, in front of his chair.

"Now listen here," she demanded and Jez, unable to really go anywhere, did indeed listen from the very spot he was in. "That ridiculous game we were playing. Did we finish it?"

The question took Jez somewhat by surprise, but he nevertheless tried to answer honestly. "Well, no, not really. We finished one battle. But the whole game can go on for much longer."

Violet looked to her left, her eyes narrowing. "I knew it," she hissed. "That explains it. Thomas said he'd pick me up after the game was over, and he hasn't arrived yet. He must be waiting for me, you know. Blasted man. Too polite by half."

"I don't think—" began Jez, but Violet interrupted him with a snap of her fingers.

"Come on then. Let's go. I haven't got all day. My husband is a very patient man, but I won't keep him waiting. We need to keep playing. Chop chop."

It took Jez's brain a few seconds to process what was going on, but he didn't resist when he got there. That was another thing about being quadriplegic—you sort of got used to going where people took you.

"Well, see if you can find the others," he suggested. "We'll need more than just you if we want to play."

"Others?" frowned Violet.

"Dennis and Ethyl. And probably a nurse."

"Obviously," Violet said with a snark, and strode off—as determinedly as any eighty-five-year-old woman could stride—to gather up their party.

"THE TOWN CONSISTS of forty or fifty simple log buildings, some built on old fieldstone foundations. More old ruins—crumbling stone walls covered in ivy and briars—surround the newer houses and shops, showing how this must have been a much larger town in centuries past." Jez paused. "As you approach, you see children playing on the town green and townsfolk tending to chores or running errands at shops."

"Oh, I do love children," said Ethyl. She smiled a heartfelt smile at Jez, and the needles in her lap clicked through with the steady rhythm of weaving yarn. "They're simply marvelous, absolutely grand. What game are they playing?"

"Thomas and I never had children," sniffed Violet. "For the best really. Oh, we considered it. But he had his career to think about, and I—" She stopped abruptly and her face hardened. "I . . . never mind."

"Shit-breath cocksucker."

"I beg your pardon, dear?" frowned Ethyl, craning to hear.

"Asshole."

"As you enter the town, you're approached by four human ruffians in grimy scarlet cloaks," Jez continued. "They look at you menacingly and draw their weapons. 'Listen up strangers,' they say, 'Give us everything you've got and get out of here.'" He paused and looked between the three seniors. "What do you do?"

There was silence at the table as Violet fretted distractedly in her seat, Dennis silently studied the layout of the town Susan had drawn on the chessboard, and Ethyl peered shrewdly at Jez.

"Do they look very nice?" she asked slowly, as though the question was both profound and of paramount importance.

"No, Ethyl, they look like thieves."

"Oh, dear," Ethyl said sadly, looking back down at the board. "Well, better do as they say. Oh my, this is unfortunate." She turned to Dennis. "I don't think this is a very safe neighborhood."

"Fuck bum smelly shit." Dennis reached over and moved his bishop next to the closest bandit, staring gravely at Jez, then raised his hand and made a firm motion of hitting someone over the head.

"Roll to attack," said Jez.

"Rolling to attack." Susan sighed, scooping up the appropriate dice.

"Are we fighting?" barked Violet. She gripped either side of the table and glared down at the board. "Vermin. Vagabonds. Vile cutthroats. Kill them all, get this over with. I'm sick of waiting, Thomas."

"Gonna take that as another Magic Missile."

"I would like to know," said Ethyl, placing her knitting down cautiously and folding her hands in front of her, "if it would be possible to ask, very politely, if we could resolve this all without violence."

Jez frowned at her. "Ethyl, again, your character is a barbarian. You're a big, tall muscly man who likes fighting things."

"Oh, no, I don't think so, dear. That would be most terribly rude."

"Fucking fucking cock fuck."

"Well, I suppose you can always ask," said Jez.

"Do I have to roll something to see if she convinces them?" asked Susan.

"Yep," replied Jez, flicking his eyes twice to point. "The twenty-sided one."

"Hurry up," snapped Violet—though she made no movement to leave. "Hurry up."

"YOU STEP INTO the evil wizard's room."

They'd been playing for almost four hours. After every battle and encounter Jez expected it to end, that the group of seniors would become tired or distracted or wander off—but they never did. With only a quick break for afternoon tea and biscuits, the three geriatrics continued to move their little pieces around the made-up world that Susan drew and redrew, growing, if anything, ever more animated as they did. They defeated the bandits and some skeletons, an ugly monster with one eye, and then some hairy things called "Bugbears," which, Jez explained, kind of looked like very hairy people or maybe a little like brown abominable snowmen.

And now they'd reached the bad guy.

"Cock," said Dennis.

"Not wrong," said Jez, then continued. "The walls of his bedchamber are covered with drapes of scarlet cloth. A short, dark-bearded man in robes sits at the desk with a beautiful glass staff leaning against his chair."

"Oh, I love glasswork," said Ethyl, leaning back in contentment. So far she'd declined to actually participate in any of the fighting, but seemed to be having fun nonetheless. "I would like to check," she paused and smiled knowingly at Jez, having now learned that an important part of the game was asking to check things, "if he made it himself."

"Magic Missile," Violet interjected through gritted teeth. "Absolutely absurd. Sorcery. Games for children. I cannot believe Thomas is forcing me to finish this nonsense."

"Violet," Susan began kindly, placing a hand on her arm, "if you don't want to play, you—"

"Hush up. Don't you talk about my husband. Magic Missile. Let's get this over with."

"You're out of Magic Missiles," said Jez. "You've done that one too many times. You need to use something else."

Without prompting Dennis passed her the *Player's Handbook*. "Fucking cock fart."

"Absolutely outrageous," complained Violet, but nevertheless began reading through the pages on additional spells.

While they were all momentarily distracted Jez continued his description.

"The man sees you and rises to his feet. Before you can do anything he steps back and points the staff at you with one hand and with the other drags out a hostage, a little girl, who he holds in front of himself as a human shield. 'Stay back!' he snarls. 'Foolish do-gooders! Take one step closer and this sniveling brat gets it! Her soul is mine!'"

"Cocksucker," growled Dennis.

"I don't understand what he's doing with their souls," complained Susan, "Is he like eating them or something?"

"He's evil," explained Jez. "He's an evil wizard. He's doing evil."

"Wizards and magic. Ridiculous."

"Motherfucking dickbag cock ass."

"He's . . . he's got a girl?"

The chatter stopped. Everyone, with the exception of Violet, looked across the table at Ethyl, who was sitting, silent, her knitting seemingly forgotten, staring at the little makeshift objects on the little made-up board. The words had slipped out of her mouth like sewing pins, small and sharp and pricked with pain.

"He's got a little girl," she whispered. Her hands trembled in her lap. Susan shot a panicked glance at Jez before turning back to the old lady.

"Ethyl, it's fine," the nurse reassured her. "It's just a game. You don't—"

"No!" cried Ethyl. The word cracked her voice. She rose unsteadily to her feet, her shaking hands clutching the table. "You leave her alone!" For a wild moment Jez thought she was talking to him, but then he followed her gaze as it burned into the solitary figure of the black king, standing in the center of the board.

"You vile, evil man." Her finger quivered as it pointed, as the accusation fell. "You do not touch her! You listen to me. You do not touch little girls!"

"Ethyl—" Jez began, stunned, but before he could think of what to say the old woman gave a soft wail and collapsed back into her chair, hunched over, her chest heaving. Her thin hands grasped at her shoulders, clutching herself as if cold.

Nobody spoke. After a few moments, Violet reached across from her book and without looking took Ethyl's hand. The old woman sniffed. The table was silent.

"It's not real," Jez said softly. But Ethyl shook her head.

"It's not right," she whimpered. Her eyes brimmed with tears. "He shouldn't do that. He can't get away with it. He can't—he can't hurt little girls."

She turned to Jez, pleading. "She needs to run away."

Jez could do little more than shake his head. "She can't."

"Someone needs to help her."

"They can't, Ethyl. There's no one here but you."

Silence. Ethyl gazed up at him, her eyes swimming and red. Words seemed to choke in her throat—but eventually, they crawled free.

"Can I stop him?" she whispered.

The chest Jez couldn't feel felt tight.

"Yes," he said simply. "You can."

"You are Ragnar the Mighty. You are proud and you are brave. You are stronger than a lion and taller than a tree. You are not afraid of bad guys. Bad guys are afraid of you."

Ethyl's chest heaved. She bowed her head and her lips quavered. For the longest time, she said nothing.

Then finally, in a hoarse whisper—

"I attack."

THE NEXT DAY it rained, and Jez's time outside was canceled. He resigned himself to being inside and being warm and hating every minute of it. He took lunch in his room and tried his hardest to move his mouth the right way so as not to drip any on the nurse. He spent hours tracing raindrops down the window with his eyes and wondering what it would be like to fall.

And then, to his surprise, he had a guest.

Violet was both unapologetic and impatient, citing a conversation they'd never had and the absolute necessity of her husband's arrival. Hunched over her walker, her heated tirade about the game and its subject carried nothing but scorn, but when he was wheeled from his room the other two were already waiting.

AND SO IT went, on and on, like Jez had never expected. Every afternoon the group met, and every afternoon he guided them. Through caves and castles, across mountains and seas—fighting demons and dragons and genies and giants and a hundred other creatures living only in his words.

They had their impediments, but they adapted. Ethyl crocheted a small scarlet beret and put it on whenever her character needed to be angry. Dennis bought himself a deck of spell cards off the newfangled computer, and by holding them up and pointing could fairly indicate what he wished his righteous knight to do. Often Susan acted as Jez's hands, but if neither she nor another nurse were available then Violet took charge—muttering the whole time about how her Thomas hated "incompetent layabouts" but nevertheless doing Jez's bidding without missing a beat.

The days rolled into weeks. Jez's voice grew stronger. And the party journeyed ever onward.

"AS THE SMOKE clears the necromancer stands aghast. His hands clutch to his chest as his power drains out of him in thick, silky waves, and all around him his undead minions fall to the ground. Behind you, the great dragon roars, and the dark shackles of magic that bound him crumble to dust. He spreads his golden wings and lets loose a mighty bellow, then turns toward you to offer thanks."

"Oh, see." Ethyl smiled. "I knew he was nice."

"Shitty cock anus," agreed Dennis.

Jez tried not to grin. "The magnificent beast lowers his head and affixes you with eyes the size of cellar doors. 'You have freed me,' it rumbles, in a voice that shakes the air. 'I am forever in your debt. Name one thing you each desire, and if it is in my power, I will grant it.'"

A lull descended over the table as the three players frowned and considered their options.

"I think," Ethyl said slowly, "I'd like . . . a cup of tea." She smiled warmly at everyone and got to her feet. "I'll put the kettle on."

"Fucking cunt shit dog," said Dennis. He mimed hitting someone over the head, then a lengthening. Jez frowned.

"Big sword?" he asked. Dennis made a face. Jez tried again. "Better sword?" This time Dennis's face split into a toothy grin. Jez smiled. "You got it, boss."

"Excuse me," sniffed Violet. Jez rotated his head toward her as Susan rubbed clear the chessboard. She cleared her throat and sat up a little straighter. "I know what I want."

"Sure," said Jez. "What is it?"

"I'd like to speak to Thomas."

"All right." He sighed. "We know that. But what would you—"

"I'D LIKE TO SPEAK TO THOMAS!"

Everybody froze. Around the common room, a dozen heads with hearing aids turned toward them.

Jez blinked. "Violet, you—"

But the old woman cut him off. "No," she told him. Underneath her knitted shawl her thin frame trembled with anger. "I've had about enough of this. Every day I play this absurd game, and every day he leaves me waiting. No more. I will not be stood up like a . . . like a common . . . " Her weathered face crinkled into lines of rage. "I WANT TO SPEAK TO THOMAS!"

For a moment the room was silent.

"Violet." Susan reached over to take the old woman's hand, her voice honey and placation. "You need to calm down, okay? Why don't I take you for a little lay down and—"

"Quiet, wench," Violet snapped, and the nurse physically recoiled at the acid in her tone. "I don't need your idiotic dithering. I am not a child. You!" She pointed directly at Jez. "You seem to be in charge here. Where is my husband? Why won't he come to see me?"

A heaviness settled around Jez's heart.

"Violet—" began Susan, but Jez spoke over her.

"Thomas is dead," he said simply.

The silence scrapped around them like a knife. Violet glared at him, her eyes narrowed to points.

"Dead?" Her voice was cold. Jez quietly met her gaze.

"Yes," he replied. "For some time now."

Silence.

Across the table, something flickered in Violet's eyes. Her thin knuckles twisted on either side of her shawl, and her lips pursed as though sucking on something sour. For a moment, her shoulders hunched. Then she took a long, deep breath, as deep as her small form could carry, and straightened up, looking down on Jez with an imperious gaze. She gave a single, curt nod.

"Be that as it may," she said stiffly, "I'd still like to speak to him."

Jez's face was blank. "How?"

"What do you mean how?" Violet replied irritably. She waved toward the board with a single bony hand. "Magic, that's how. Clean out your ears, boy, that man was commanding the dead. If he can do it, why can't I? I have spells, don't I? Well what's the point of all this magic nonsense if I can't use it to speak to Thomas?"

She lifted her chin and stared at him straight on. Jez said nothing. To his right, he could feel Susan looking at him, but he ignored her. It was his game. It was his choice.

"Okay," he said softly. He took a deep breath; his mouth was dry. "The dragon hears your request. It draws upon the magic deep inside it, and with a rush of power casts Speak with Dead." Jez closed his eyes, and the world around him disappeared. "The connection is made. Thomas can hear you."

For a few moments there was no sound, no light—only the swirling darkness beneath his eyelids. Jez waited and waited, though for what he wasn't entirely sure. Then finally, tentatively, Violet's voice extended from beyond the black.

"Thomas?" she whispered. Then a second later he heard her click her tongue. "No, don't answer. You were never one for talking. I'll just—you just listen, dear one."

Violet let out a long, heavy sigh. "It's so nice to talk to you again. It's been so long, I . . . I hear you're dead." She drew a deep, shuddering breath, and her words wavered. "I'm so . . . sorry that I missed that, Thomas. I'm so sorry I couldn't be there. I should've been there. I'm sorry, I . . . " She gave a weak, hiccupping laugh. "I suppose I'm sorry for a lot of things.

"I'm sorry for being such a miserable cow. I'm sorry for making you put up with me. I'm sorry for Peter. And I'm sorry for the baby." Thick tears leaked into her voice. "I'm so, so sorry about the baby."

The table was silent. Behind them, the low mumble of the common room shuffled on, oblivious. Rain pattered on the windows. Jez blinked back tears—then drew his voice as deep as he could.

"There is nothing to forgive." He opened his eyes and looked at her.

Violet blinked quickly, looking away. "Good," she murmured. She sniffed, and in that single breath pulled away any semblance of trembling in her speaking. "Of course not." Her back straightened. "Now get out of here, you daft man," she commanded. "Leave me be. I won't have you moping about. This place is dull as dishwater and not worth your time." Her voice wavered, just a crack. "I'll see you when I'm good and ready."

The group fell silent. Beside him, Susan gave a wet sniff. Dennis bowed his head. Ethyl was still off getting tea. After a moment or two, Violet glanced between them.

"Well," she said impatiently, "what're we all sitting around for? Get on with the game. I haven't got all day."

"THE DEMON RISES."

Violet sat at attention. Dennis anxiously thumbed his spell cards. Ethyl had her red beanie on. In front of them, Susan adjusted

the porcelain Hummel figurine—a whistling boy with an umbrella—
which represented the towering infernal beast of twisting horn and
flame.

"Its footsteps shake the cavern. Cracks zigzag through the roof
and lava seeps up from the floor. Its burning eyes turn upon you
and the rescued captives. It roars."

"I think now would be a good time to leave," Ethyl suggested
mildly. There was a general mumbling of agreement. The party
moved their characters toward the door.

"Suddenly you are overwhelmed by the smell of sulfur.
Nimble, spiny demons materialize nearby, their ravenous fangs
gleaming in the lava-light. They swarm toward you, inhumanly fast."
Wordlessly, Susan scattered a bunch of red checkers. "The captives
are too slow. The creatures are gaining."

"Leave them to die," said Violet.

"Oh, don't be so horrible," chided Ethyl. "These are people,
just like us. We have to rescue them."

"We can't rescue them if we're dead."

The descent to the demon's lair had been treacherous. The
party were bloodied and weary. The odds looked grim.

"We are supposed to be doing the right thing."

"We're supposed to win."

The argument went back and forth as the demons advanced.
Jez looked between Ethyl and Violet seated on either side of him,
and then at Dennis, sitting alone at the other end.

"Dennis?" he asked him, "what would you like to do?"

But the old man said nothing. He simply rocked, back and
forth in his chair, his hands twisting over and over in his lap. His
lips twitched soundlessly, his eyes staring unblinking, burning into
the board.

"Dennis?" asked Jez.

There was a moment of silence. And then, to his amazement,
the old man spoke.

"Go."

A single word. A whisper, strained and malformed through
jerking lips.

"Go."

Dennis rose to his feet, and as his whole body trembled he reached out and moved his lonely white bishop between the demons and the door.

"Go."

He bent his head, and to Jez's shock fat tears leaked out from the corners of his eyes. He reached out his gnarled hands to either side of him and, wordlessly, Violet and Ethyl took one each. Violet's face remained stony. Ethyl smiled and gently patted his wrist.

"You face the demons alone," said Jez. "As the world around you crumbles and burns. The people you swore to protect go behind you. Everyone is safe."

In a world that did not exist, a lone, silent knight raised his sword and stood firmly, a proud soldier in shining armor, against the rising tide of evil, and died valiantly for his friends.

ETHYL DIED IN her sleep eleven months after Jez moved in.

It was unexpected, the nurses said, or as unexpected as it could be at ninety-two. She went to bed one night feeling unusually tired, and in the morning didn't wake. The doctor pronounced it natural causes and the family visited to mourn. A service was arranged—the shuttle bus would take any resident who would like to attend. Few did. A death in a nursing home was like a disaster far away, too expected to stir empathy, only a tragedy in the technical sense.

Jez, Violet, Dennis, and Susan all made the trip.

It was a nice church and a calm, cloudy day. Ethyl's daughters said kind things about her, and the priest led them all in peaceful song. The family said their goodbyes. Dennis held on to her knitted red hat. Violet placed the little Monopoly dog on her coffin. The four of them sat there, quietly, and didn't say a single word all the way home.

"ALL RIGHT," SAID Susan. She sounded nervous. "Why don't— why don't we go along and introduce ourselves?"

It was two weeks later. The four of them sat in their usual positions around the table, along with three newcomers who blinked like owls at the whole situation. From her seat at the head of her table, Susan cleared her throat. It was her first time as dungeon master.

"Kindergarten nonsense," huffed Violet, clutching tightly at her shawl. "Bah. I'm Violet. My room is 13C. I am pretending to be a magician. Her name is Elyndari the Elder. She is an elf from the forest. She had a husband and she lost him. But she is okay." The old woman raised her chin. "She loved him dearly and will join him in time."

"Cock bum shit fuck asshole," said Dennis, which took some of the new residents around the table slightly aback. Susan, however, smiled and read out the messy, painstakingly drawn words on his character sheet.

"Flynn the Bard. The most charismatic speaker the land has ever known. Famed throughout the kingdom for his charming songs and his silver tongue. You cheeky bastard." She sighed, looking up. Dennis grinned. Then they all turned to Jez.

The young man cleared his throat. "My name is Jeremy. I've been here almost a year. I'm going to be Valerian, a dragon-born cleric. He looks like a giant golden lizard, who walks upright like a man. He's got wings. He can fly wherever he wants."

Jez paused and looked around the room.

"He is a cleric of life."

TOURISTS
LYLE STILES

The Tourists have arrived!

In this crazy Place we live, the Tourists welcome us.

They fly in, draped in their clothes of confusion, barely making time to unpack, before unloading on our Native bodies with shock.

Instead of us greeting them, they greet us.

"How could something like this happen?" They cry.
"This is not the Country I know." They yell.

Most of our Native mouths open but hesitate to respond.

Some hopeful ones do though, and soon it's all too clear—the Tourists know this Place of Pain, better than those who live here.

Now, fewer of us speak. But the one or two that do, those that offer their personal energies to give guided Tours, are met with no-ledge about their own land.

"I saw this Place's map, designed by Cartographer Mr. Know-It-All (or was it Ms. One-of-You?), who is very articulate when it comes to using legends I can understand," proclaims one of the Tourists. "Based on their summary of the topography, that fit my 30,000 ft perspective during the flight, I am pretty sure this Place exists because of Not-the-Point or Something-I-Don't-Want-to-Admit."

Us Natives stand with mouths agape. All surrounded by silence, trying to find the right time to speak, but really seeking the space to be heard. As we wait, the Tourists shove their items and souvenirs in barely opened luggage, zipping them tight once again.

There is little opportunity for responses, guided tours, or even reminders of our historical sites. The Tourists' backs quickly fade into the distance, still stained with the sweat of well-meaning ignorance, as we point to several signs, including the one hanging above the entrance. "The Problem has been here all along."

Our Native necks strain with stress. Our hearts are heavy with [insert-condition-here]. And Our bodies wear the other physical manifestations, developing from being here too long. The strain grows, watching the Tourists fly upward and away from this Place.

Before we can tame the tightness building in our throats or lower our gazes to see each other, another Place related event is promoted, and a new set of Tourists fly in.

The time on our shorter clocks ticks faster.

And instead of us greeting them, they greet us.

OLD TIME RELIGION

MARK CHESNUT

Where he leads me I will follow,
I'll go with him, with him all the way.

THE LYRICS BY SALVATION ARMY OFFICER ERNEST W. BLANDY
dated to 1890, but the pull was very much in the present as we sang.
In between verses, the pink-faced preacher—who all the grownups
called Brother Eustace—raised his hand from the blond wood
pulpit and the singing would stop, even as the organ kept playing.

"Isn't it time that you accepted Jesus Christ as your personal
lord and savior?" he asked, scanning the room with wide eyes. "Or
perhaps you accepted him a very long time ago, but you have let
your faith lapse. Now is the time to come back."

I looked around at the sea of people, clad in the candy colors
of summer. Some were cooling themselves with promotional fans
from the nearby funeral home. Two women in brightly patterned
blouses and a man wearing a pastel tie started to cry. My mother
and grandfather stood silently on either side of me, waiting for an
indication to sing the next line.

I had witnessed this call to salvation many times at the First
Missionary Baptist Church in Benton, Kentucky. I lived in the north,
but my mother and I visited my grandparents down south at least
three times a year. And every week during every visit, my grandfather
(who we all called Pop) and I would go to our respective, age-
appropriate Sunday school classes (he taught the one for older men,
and always carried a big yellow note pad with his lesson plan). For

some reason my mother didn't go to Sunday school, even though there was one for grown-up ladies or middle-aged ladies or mothers or whatever category she was in. But she'd usually join us for the church service. My grandmother was always kind of sickly—something about her heart being too big or something—so she stayed home and watched a bunch of ministers on TV.

The organ music rose again, and we all started singing.

"I'll go with him through the garden, I'll go with him through the garden . . . "

One of the crying women gently pushed her husband aside, one hand to her face as she walked toward the front of the sanctuary, sobbing. The minister smiled and spread his arms wide, like one of those guys at the airport who tells the planes where to park. Well, that lady sure did understand runway language, because she picked up the pace of her steps and went right to him, giving him a hug before stepping back and facing the audience, her eyes overflowing and her body shaking.

"We welcome you back, sister Lena," Brother Eustace said. "Now, who else would like to come and renew themselves in front of our lord and be born again?"

My mind started churning.

Should I go up there?

I knew the preacher would be leading us through this routine for at least fifteen or twenty minutes, like he always did, at least once a month. This wasn't going to end soon.

The music, the emotion, the tears, the repeated verses urging us to follow. It was hypnotizing, like a tractor beam. Or a sales talk.

It makes sense, doesn't it? We should all confess our sins and be reborn so we can be good people and go on with our lives.

No one in my family had ever gone up to the front of the church crying. We'd all been baptized, of course, like you're supposed to do when you're around age twelve (I loved getting baptized, because it gave me a chance to stand in a big pool of water in the front of my church up north). I had done that just a couple years ago, actually.

So, did I need to renew myself at age fourteen? No family member ever talked about being saved again; that was a topic usually discussed from a distance—like when my grandmother watched Oral Roberts or Billy Graham and praised the missionaries who saved people in Africa and Asia. But not even Gran had ever told me to run up to the front of the church bawling my eyes out. My mother never talked about religion at all, even though we basically went to church every single Sunday, whether we were in New York or Kentucky.

Still, the music was pulling me. And the preacher kept talking.

I really need to do this. I need to start my life over, from scratch. Things will be better then; I will know what to do in my life and things will be good.

My mother stood between me and the aisle. I'd have to push past her and then walk all the way up to the stage. And everyone would be looking at me.

What if I go up but I don't cry? Will people think I'm weird if I'm not crying? And what am I supposed to say to people after I accept the lord again? Is it like a job interview? I don't know what I'm supposed to say. I didn't really feel like I accepted any lord after my real baptism. I honestly didn't feel any different. So, what's this supposed to feel like now?

"Sister Lena, do you accept Jesus Christ as your personal lord and savior?" the minister asked.

"I do, I do," said Lena, whose face was so wet and red now it looked like she'd just gone swimming.

"There is room for more," he said, turning to the audience. The organ swelled.

"I'll go with him to dark Calv'ry, I'll go with him to dark Calv'ry . . . "

I really need to do this.

I bunched up the green polyester of my leisure suit pants with one hand and wrapped the other around the hymnal. My mother's soft singing voice rang in my left ear, and Pop's enthusiastically loud voice—which sometimes sounded more like yelling than singing—vibrated from the right.

But maybe I can wait until I get back to Brockport. They don't do these calls to salvation at the First Baptist Church, so I can just talk to Mr. Deichler and make a special request. He's a cool kind of minister; he won't do anything overly dramatic in front of everyone. He's a former FBI agent, not a missionary like this guy in Kentucky is. He never talks too much about his former job, but he also never pushes religion on people, especially if he knows they aren't interested or don't feel comfortable.

Even my own friends didn't seem to get that there was more than one type of Baptist religion. In the south, our church was a member of the Southern Baptist Convention. They always talked about being saved. They called people to the front of the sanctuary, to make sure that salvation stuck. They raised a lot of money to send missionaries around the globe, to give food to poor people in poor countries—but even more importantly to convert those people to the Baptist faith. In the north, our church was part of the American Baptist Association. It's not the same thing. They did some missionary work, but not as much, and they didn't encourage public salvation. And our northern minister didn't talk about religion in personal conversations, unless you really wanted to.

In the south, we had to call the minister "Reverend so-and-so" or "Brother so-and-so." In the north, it was just "Mr. Deichler." With his modern suits, tall frame and shaded glasses—he never wore a formal robe, unless it was for a special occasion, like a baptism—Mr. Deichler looked like a normal guy. So, of course you'd call him mister.

I can just make an appointment to be saved privately, and I know Mr. Deichler will be cool about it. That's what I'll do.

So, I stayed put there with my mother and grandfather until the last person was reborn, and then rode home in Pop's maroon Ford LTD to pick up Gran and head out for chicken and dumplings at the Iron Kettle.

For the next couple of weeks, my usual Kentucky activities distracted me from thoughts of salvation. I stayed busy visiting various great-uncles and aunts, driving to the wild buffalo range at Land Between the Lakes and riding bikes with my Kentucky best friend Neal. I didn't need to feel safe with the lord, because I felt safe enough when—after a few hours hanging out with Neal at the gas station where he worked after school—a giant, mentally challenged man I knew only as Bird Dog would walk me back to

Pop and Gran's house. "Y'all have a big time?" he would ask every single night he walked me home, and his immense arm draped over my skinny shoulder made me feel like nothing bad could ever happen on those otherwise scary dark streets (I knew I was too old to have felt scared in the first place, and only Bird Dog seemed to recognize that I didn't like to walk alone at night).

Even going back to church—albeit a different one—didn't reawaken my curiosity about being saved. The following Sunday, we went to the Briensburg Baptist Church, where our extended family of great-uncles, great-aunts, and cousins were all members. Benton's First Missionary Baptist Church was big-city sophisticated compared to the lively country ambiance at Briensburg. I loved going there. The congregation favored bouncier gospel music, with lots of hand clapping and harmonizing. It was harder to get bored during their services, and I loved the warm welcome we'd get from all those family members who I barely knew. It was like we were foreign dignitaries. And there was no call for salvation on the Sunday we visited, so I didn't have to deal with the tractor beam pulling me in.

And at my grandparents' house, I continued to volunteer to recite a prayer before meals, at least occasionally. Pop liked when I did that, and I always said the same quick verses that he did:

Our father in heaven, accept our thanks for this food, forgive our sins, we ask in Jesus's name, amen.

As the summer weeks came to a close, it was time to start loading my mother's Ford Galaxie 500 for the two-day trip back to Brockport. I'd have plenty of time to think about everything. We hugged my grandparents and pulled out of their circular driveway, watching them pop up into the family room window to wave yet again. And then we were gone, on our way back to life up north.

When I was younger, I might have started a conversation at this point by reaching over to jiggle the flabby lower part of my mother's upper arm, now chilled by the extra-strong air conditioning, and singing "Convenient FatsoMommy, open seven days 'til FatsoMommy," my cruel and nonsensical version of a radio jingle for Convenient Food Mart. But I was older now. I had better things to do with my time than torture my mother.

"So, what do you think about those people who go up to the front of the church to get reborn?" I asked as she steered the car up the Western Kentucky Parkway toward Louisville.

"I think it's wonderful that people find comfort in their religion. For some people, that's all they have, and it's what gets them through hard times. Sometimes I wish I could have faith like that."

"But do you think that people really get saved, and if they do that they'll go to heaven? Do you think there's a heaven and hell?"

"I think the church provides help and support to a lot of people in need. The church can do a lot of good work."

"But what about heaven and hell and being saved and all that stuff?"

"I don't think all of those details are necessarily true."

"But what about the stuff in the Bible?"

"The Bible is an important book. It provides comfort to people who need it. But I don't know that it's one hundred percent based on facts."

BACK IN BROCKPORT, I fell into my Sunday morning tradition of sitting in a hard wooden pew at the First Baptist Church, bored out of my wits. My eyes scanned the sanctuary for anything that might be more interesting than the sermon: the older woman sitting near us, whose outdated clothing made her look like a witch, the travel agent lady in the choir with long blonde hair who I wished would share the secrets of the airline industry with me, the colorful stained glass windows that were framed by what appeared like weird, faceless human figures with upstretched arms.

Sometimes I'd pretend I had to go to the bathroom during church service and wander the building, exploring a parlor I called God's Living Room because it was furnished with couches and comfy chairs where I imagined God and Jesus might hang out, reading magazines and entertaining visitors.

After every service, Mr. Deichler would always engage me in a polite conversation about school or pop culture. He knew I liked airlines so he would bring that up sometime. He even knew about *Star Wars*.

I never asked him for that appointment to be saved. I guess I knew I wouldn't, even when I was feeling the pull at First Missionary.

* * *

THE NEXT SUMMER, Mr. Deichler and his wife (who also happened to be my Sunday school teacher) took their annual month-long vacation. Laypeople took over the services while he was out. And for some reason, my mother signed us up to lead an entire Sunday. The whole hour, from start to finish. She wanted me to write and present the main sermon. She liked to be in front of an audience, and so did I. Even though neither of us really paid much attention to religious stuff and she had told me the Bible wasn't very factual.

But we did go to church every Sunday, so I guess we were as qualified as anyone.

I loved the idea of performing, but I was too lazy and uninspired to actually sit down and write a sermon. I didn't have a clue what to write.

Finally, when the service was only three days away, my mother started losing patience.

"Do I have to write this god-damned sermon for you?" she asked.

Well, as usual, I put off a chore, she yelled, and then she ended up doing some of the work herself. She wrote the whole sermon, and titled it "All I Have Seen." She had me talking about how, in spite of my young age and being nothing more than a humble high schooler, I had already witnessed the bountiful goodness of people's hearts and good deeds, or something like that.

My mother's words and my presentation were sufficiently impressive that, when Mr. Deichler heard about it, he sent me a congratulatory note.

"If you feel the calling, I would be very pleased to write you a letter of recommendation to study at the Colgate Rochester Divinity School," he said.

I thanked Mr. Deichler the next time I saw him in person, but ignored his suggestion. And he never followed up about it. He just kept being a cool kind of minister who was ready to talk about *Star Wars* if I wanted to. It would be several years before we actually had a meaningful interaction with Brother Eustace. But it wasn't the kind of experience he would have hoped for, I'm sure.

Benton, Kentucky, 1988

MY GREAT-AUNT Rhea Nelle was perplexed. I could hear her talking with my mother as they sat on the upholstered chairs near my grandfather's casket. "Is that how all the kids in New York cut their hair nowadays?" she asked, pointing at me. I was engaged in another conversation, so I pretended not to hear the question. "It looks like someone just put a bowl on top of his head and cut right around it."

I had to admit she was kind of right about my hairstyle. I was still trying to be New Wave, and some of my style experiments worked better than others.

I smiled to myself and turned back to my great-aunt Myrtie, who was regaling me with tales of her trips to the slaughterhouse to pick up suet, the hard beef fat. "The birds in our yard love it," she explained. "They could really eat it all day, I can tell you that much."

"I bet you never fell in your yard, have you?" Rhea Nelle interjected. She'd somehow jumped up and toddled her way over to us, brushing loose curls from her forehead as if she'd just run a race. Her tongue swirled with excitement as she spoke. "I fell real bad one day. Real bad. I went out to the henhouse to get me some eggs and I fell backwards. Well, no sooner'n I got back up, the dog raced in and ate all the chickens. We lost all our chickens that day!"

Death in the family inspires a lot of interesting conversations.

Pop—as everyone in the family called my grandfather—died at age eighty-nine, in March 1988. He passed away in the hospital where I was born and where my father died, in my western New York hometown of Brockport. But my mother shipped his body to Benton for the funeral, since he'd only been living up north for a couple of years, and all his friends and extended family were in Kentucky. My grandmother was already buried there too, and Pop had a space reserved right next to her.

I was in my early twenties and living in New York City, so I flew to Rochester and then accompanied my mother and aunt to Louisville, where we hopped in a rental car for the four-hour drive to Benton.

My grandfather's body arrived, in a box, on the same day that we did. But we didn't see it until a couple days later, when we entered the funeral home for the calling hours.

The building's muted décor was designed not to shock, offend, or distract grieving visitors. Nondescript wallpaper, which might have hung in your grandparents' dining room if they were rich, lined the walls, with soothing pinstripes that ran down to the padded, wall-to-wall carpeting, coating the hallway in comfort. The hall led to the visitation room, where the thick carpet was marked with four indents, beneath the wheels of a big stand draped in tan fabric. On top of that stand was Pop.

He was lying in an open, metallic casket that reflected the sickeningly weak yellow glow of the floor lamps. He didn't look like himself. His skin seemed powdered and glazed. His nose looked larger and hawk-like, since he wasn't wearing his glasses. And he wasn't smiling or laughing like he usually did.

"Oh," my mother said when she saw him. "Well, they did do some work on him, didn't they?"

My mother had put some effort into her look too; she was wearing a light peach skirt and jacket and had actually put on a bit of lipstick and makeup. But her father was definitely wearing more than she was.

The calling hours—that's the term we used in the south; I'd only recently learned that Catholics and some other people call it a wake—took place at Filbeck and Cann, a small funeral home on Benton's town square, across from the town hall and within view of the Rexall drug store where I used to order vanilla Coke and vanilla phosphate when I was a kid.

My mother and I took turns standing next to the casket and greeting visitors; a flurry of minted breath, hairspray, and soft, ancient hands as a steady stream of kinfolk and friends made their way to the front of the room to offer their condolences. Rhea Nelle and Aunt Myrtie were among the most interesting.

Several people asked if I was married yet. I politely responded in the negative and changed the subject, skillfully shifting to questions about their families, about the town's most recent last Tater Day and Big Singin' celebrations, or perhaps about the First Missionary Baptist Church. And wow, I marveled, it's true, I just couldn't believe how time had flown and how long it had been since my last visit to Benton.

At one point, my mother and I were both standing near the casket. My grandparents' Southern Baptist minister, Brother Eustace, had cornered her. He touched the sleeve of her peach jacket and smiled, his thick glasses shining like they'd just been polished.

"Eunice, it is a joyous thing that we will all be reunited with our loved ones in heaven when we pass away. Your father is blessed."

"Thank you very much for saying that," my mother replied, smiling back.

"You understand that, don't you, Eunice? Your father has been reunited with your mother. And you will be together with him again too, someday."

"Well, it gives us comfort to know that our father believed that," my mother said diplomatically, nodding and smiling in an effort to speedily end the conversation. Even though she'd never fully renounced her religious beliefs and had taken me to church nearly every Sunday when I was growing up, my mother had pretty much raised me as an agnostic northern Baptist. She taught me that churches provide valuable social support and services, but that all those religious details in the bible—and all the judgmental things that ministers might say—were not necessarily true or correct. And while she envied people who did have faith, she couldn't bring herself to believe in heaven or hell.

Still, these were the calling hours before her father's funeral. He was an active member of the church. She wanted to be respectful. It's what her parents had taught her to do.

But the minister wouldn't accept my mother's attempt to avoid a deep-dive religious discussion. His brows came together as his smile became more purposeful. He was entering full-on missionary mode. "But . . . Eunice . . . you do believe that we will all be reunited when we join Jesus Christ, don't you? Heaven is waiting for us."

My mother shifted in her open-toed shoes. Her eyebrows raised as she smiled even more purposefully.

"Well," she said, "I can tell you one thing. If I die, go to heaven, and see my husband who hasn't been around since 1969, the first thing he's going to say to me is 'how'd you get so fat?'"

The minister's eyes widened. For a split second, his mouth opened with the beginnings of a confused smile that quickly evaporated, as he stood, wide-eyed, for a heartbeat more, before walking way.

My mother turned to an elderly woman who was standing a few feet away. She smiled warmly and extended her hand. "Hello, how are you? Thank you so much for coming. Pop would be so happy to know that you're here."

MY MOTHER'S LESSON
KAREN GREGORY

I GOT THE FIRST HINT THAT SOMETHING WAS WRONG WHEN I was sitting in Mr. Hughes's high school history class. I always liked Mr. Hughes. He could be boring and dry and wore the same tan/brown suit a lot, but he was one of the understanding teachers, like Mrs. Robey, who made me feel like I was worth something . . . that I could succeed in my life.

I was a farm girl in Iowa, a teenager going to high school in a small town, doing my best. I loved school, and usually I was an A student. Except for algebra and chemistry, which both of the male teachers told me (when I desperately asked for help after class) are subjects "girls don't really need to know about." In other words, I'm not worth your time, I thought. I felt ashamed to be a girl when they said that, and that in itself made me angry. I never told my mom and dad about those incidents. I probably should have.

It was mid-December, just ten days after my mom's birthday. It had turned frigid early that year, back at the end of October. We had dry snow and it was really cold. Then, suddenly, it turned warmer and wet—ugly, rainy wet—and the snow melted and froze into sheets of ice. Now, mid-month, the air snapped and crackled again with the dry snow, and the smell of it was in the air every day. It fell on the ice that had accumulated. But any snow was okay, we thought, because it was going to be Christmas soon, and snow was always neat at Christmas. (At least when you're still sort of a kid.)

Suddenly the intercom blasted over Mr. Hughes's lesson. "Karen Schmidt, report to the principal's office immediately." A chill went through me. The entire class, as one, commented,

"Ooohhh . . . you're in trouble!" What? I'd never been called to the principal's office. I was an introvert. I was a good kid. How could I possibly be in trouble?

My teacher nodded "go on," so I collected my books and stuffed them in my bag and went out the door, shaking a little. I heard comments from classmates, like "I hope they go easy on you!" I left the room, wondering what my fate would be.

As I rounded the quiet corner and looked to the right, I could see all the way down the empty linoleum-floored main hallway, lined with most of the students' lockers. At the very end, before the main entry/exit doors to the school and where the principal's and administration staff's offices were located, I saw my dad standing in front of the sliding glass window.

Dad?

Why was Dad there in the middle of the afternoon? I could see he was in his farm clothing: work shoes covered in mud, worn jeans, a dirty blue denim work shirt—but no jacket, and it was damn cold outside. I felt a stab of shame. Why did you come to my school in your dirty farm clothes? Then I thought, What am I thinking? Something is definitely wrong. As I hurried toward him, he turned and looked down the hall at me. I'll never forget what I saw. He had blood all over the front of his shirt, and he was crying.

My heart lurched, and I could hear my heart pounding in my ears. I'd never seen my dad cry. His shockingly blue eyes had always been clear and usually happy, although at times, they were filled with worry about the farm or anger at something stupid one of us kids had done.

When I reached him, he didn't even let me say anything. "I might have killed your mother," he blurted out. The tears coursed down his cheeks. "I took her to the emergency room. I need to take you kids to her now." When he talked, it felt like I was far away, that I wasn't experiencing this at all. Kind of like an echo in the universe.

Oh, God, what had happened?

Then I rallied; I didn't hesitate. "I'll get Kevin," I said. I knew my older brother was in physics class—with one of the teachers who told me I wasn't worth his extra time. "Just stay here," I told Dad. I ran down the side hallway, burst into Kevin's class, and told him to come with me, now. He could see it was serious and grabbed his things and followed me. Surprisingly, the teacher didn't stop us. I guess he saw the "this is no bullshit, so leave us alone" look on my face.

Dad had composed himself a little bit by the time we got back up the hallway and told us to get our books and coats from our lockers. He was trying to be stoic, I could tell. He had parked the old yellow pickup truck right outside the front of the school in the no-park zone. Now we're going to find out what happened, I thought—what horrible thing happened. Once we opened the door to the cab, we saw blood everywhere. Mom's blood.

Dad tried to tell us about Mom's accident. That he'd taken her to the hospital as quick as he could. He still couldn't really tell us much; he was so distressed, but he drove the truck. "We have to stop at the junior high and get the other children," he insisted. So, Kevin went in and had Steve and Susan paged out of class, the same abrupt and rude awakening that life will never be the same as I had experienced. They came out, as confused as we had been. Now, we four kids and Dad were crammed in the pickup truck cab, and we were all getting blood on us. We were very quiet. All I could think of was, is Mom still alive? I'm sure we were all thinking the same thing.

As we drove on to the hospital emergency room, Dad finally, haltingly, explained what had happened. He and Mom were going to sell a load of hogs that day. They were up at the barn. Dad was backing up the pickup, and Mom was outside directing him back to the barn door so he could get close enough to load the pigs up without any gaps for them to escape. Dad was looking in his rear-view mirror, then his side view, to watch Mom's signals and see how close he was getting to the barn.

Suddenly, he felt the truck bump up against the barn. This was wrong . . . he knew he had at least six inches or more before he'd get to the barn door. He looked out and couldn't see Mom. "She just disappeared," he moaned. "She'd been there a second before; then she was gone." He thought, where was Katherine? He threw the truck into park and got out.

Then he saw the blood, already starting to pool under the truck, running down the slope of ice, and Mom caught hanging there, her head stuck between the truck bumper and the barn door. At the very moment he'd been backing up, somehow she'd slipped on that dry snow that coated the ice beneath it. At the exact moment she fell, her head was caught and crushed between the truck and the barn.

Dad panicked. "This is my lovely wife! And I've killed her!" He pulled off his jacket, put it on the cement stoop under Mom's head, ran back to the truck cab, put the truck in drive, and pulled away.

Mom fell, bleeding profusely. When Dad got back to her, he saw she was still breathing, and he could only think of one thing: getting her help as fast as he could. So, he swaddled her bleeding head with his jacket, picked her up in his arms, put her in the cab of the truck, and drove like a madman to the nearest hospital, praying, "Dear God, don't take my Katherine," the whole way.

Once she was in the emergency room doctor's care and he was assured Mom wasn't going to die while he was gone, he came to get us kids, speeding to the high school first. But we know now that he feared the worst, and really didn't know if Mom would still be alive when we returned. He told us all that the ER doctor said her injuries were life-threatening. But he said Mom was conscious and talking. Dad had actually said his goodbyes, but Mom didn't understand why he was so concerned.

When we pulled into the emergency room parking lot, we knew this would be very hard for all of us. Our lives would be forever changed. The hospital smelled of pine cleaner and disinfectant when we pushed through the door of the emergency room area. They let Dad in first; then we were allowed in. Amazingly, Mom seemed very calm and alert, lying (it seemed) high up on an examining table. She was still covered in blood except where they had cleaned her up a little; there was still some on her face and head and arms and down the front of her sky-blue jacket. And her face was skewed in a strange way. She turned to us and tried to talk, and it sounded all crazy, slurred, like we'd heard on TV from people that had strokes. She tried to smile and said, "I'm going to be just fine." Then she wanted to know how school was that day and she felt terrible that she'd slipped and fell, because now Susan was going to miss out on Christmas caroling that evening. She wondered aloud why her head hurt. It was so scary. Now the doctor was wrapping up our visit, quickly. So, we said our goodbyes. Is this our last goodbye? I thought. Please, God, no . . .

After the doctor shooed us kids out, he pulled Dad aside to tell him the plan. Dad came out moments later, and said, "We're going by ambulance to Gunderson Hospital in La Crosse. That's the only place that can save Mom. I'm going with her. You kids go back to the farm. Kevin and Steve, take care of the livestock. Karen, call Grandma Sutton and Grandpa and Grandma Schmidt, and call Pastor Urlaub and tell them what happened." It's really bad, I thought, if he wants our Pastor to come. With that, he went back into the emergency triage area, and we kids were on our own.

I let Kevin drive the bloodstained pickup home. He was the oldest and seemed the calmest. Inside, I was freaking out. Outside, I was trying to put on a brave face. Later, I found out he was in the same state, but for him, driving was a good way to concentrate on something other than "Mom might die." He told me later that he put all his feelings inside and didn't let them surface for years. He just didn't know how to deal with it . . . and he was angry. He knew the setup for loading the pigs was flawed and had talked to Dad about it. He blamed Dad for not getting it fixed up right.

Steven and Susan were, I think, also in shock. They were so much younger. And we still had to worry about Karl, our youngest sibling, coming home on the bus like normal from Waterville Elementary School, and then finding out what had happened—he had no idea. So, we drove in silence.

When we got to the farm, it felt so strange. Empty without our parents. Dark. Foreboding. Too quiet. I called Grandpa and Grandma Schmidt first, and immediately regretted it when I hung up the phone. What was I thinking? I should have called Grandma Sutton: my mom's mother, Ruth. After all, it was her daughter being carried off in an ambulance with her life on the line to a hospital in Wisconsin. But the phone call was done. They said they'd immediately call Ruth and then the pastor, and they did. What a way to find out your daughter could be dying, I thought. Thanks to me.

After the phone call I knew I had to set aside the guilt and make supper for everyone. Mom would want me to. Kevin and Steven had gone out to do the chores that needed to be done. A farm never sleeps. The livestock didn't know we'd had a tragedy; they expected to be fed. So did the people in the family. We have to have our strength, I thought. I don't remember what I cooked up, but I'm sure it was something like sandwiches and milk or macaroni and cheese. That part is all a blur. Karl arrived home. I had to tell him what had happened. It wasn't easy.

Dad called late in the evening. They'd arrived in La Crosse. Mom was still alive, but she was in critical condition in the ICU. He asked for Kevin and me to drive there immediately and leave the other kids with Aunt Janet and Uncle Francis up in Waukon until we knew what was happening. Two hours later, driving on icy roads, we were in Wisconsin at the imposing edifice of the Gunderson Hospital. We weren't used to such a big city; we'd only gone up there for shopping trips. We found the ICU inside the maze of a hospital. Dad was sitting in the waiting room area, leaning forward with his head in his hands. He wasn't crying, but when he looked up, I've never seen him so pale and sad and exhausted. It was like he was being torn apart from the inside out. He was still dressed in his blood-soaked clothing. I kicked myself for not having thought to bring him a clean change of clothes.

He couldn't tell us anything, really, except Mom's head and brain were both very injured and the doctors were doing everything they could to save her life. So, we just sat together, and waited . . . and waited.

The doctors didn't come out at all. Now I know they were saving Mom's life. Pastor Urlaub finally arrived around ten p.m. Dad started really opening up, telling him about the swelling and pressure and fluid on Mom's brain, that they were going to do emergency surgery to relieve it, that they would come give us an update. The Pastor sat with us and we all prayed—not out loud, that's not how Midwesterners do it. But we all knew we were praying. There was no one else in the waiting room. I was glad. It would have felt like they were intruding.

Very late into the night, maybe past midnight—I don't remember—the surgeon came out. I'll never forget what he said to Dad. "If Katherine makes it through the night . . . "

I gasped.

" . . . with the major damage to her skull and brain, she might be able to live a reasonable life," he finished. He went on, "There was so much swelling, and she will likely have severe brain damage. If she does recover, she may never be the same. I want you all to be prepared for this. You can't go and see her now, there's too much of a risk for infection. She needs to rest. We'll come and get you if things change." That's when the pastor stood, had us all join hands, and say the Lord's Prayer. Then he read Psalm 23 from the Bible: The Lord is my shepherd; I shall not want . . .

I started to cry.

The pastor stayed by our side the remainder of the night into the new day. We tried to sleep (and did, fitfully, at last) in the incredibly uncomfortable chairs in the ICU waiting room, not knowing if Mom would make it. It was the longest night of my life. I couldn't even imagine how Dad felt.

The sun came up as always the next morning. It seemed like a joke, like it was laughing at us. It was such a pretty day, when nothing was pretty inside this place. Just the smell of the hospital was nauseating. It's weird how you can smell the blood. We were dirty and tired and hungry, and worst of all, we didn't even know if our mom was alive.

It seemed like hours with no news. Finally, Dad said we needed to eat, but we didn't want to chance going to the cafeteria and miss an update from the doctors. I found a vending machine close by and got something for all of us, I don't remember what. It was dry and horrible, that I do remember; probably crackers, with pop to wash it down.

At last, the surgeon came into the waiting area. We were so afraid. When he shook his head, I thought, Oh, God, you've taken my mother!!

But when he started to speak, my heart filled with thankfulness. "How Katherine survived the night is beyond my comprehension," he said. "In fact, now the swelling is way down. She's awake and asking for you. I'm going to let you go in and speak to her, but only for five minutes each." Dad cried. I cried. Kevin cried. And Pastor Urlaub, he teared up, but said only, "It's the Lord's will."

Separately, we went in to see Mom. First in was Dad, of course. When I walked in, I was shocked again at her appearance. Her face was completely skewed: one part up and one part down. One eye was almost completely closed. It wasn't Mom. But it was Mom. She just looked like she'd had a stroke. At least all the blood had been washed off. But now there was a big place they'd shaved off her beautiful auburn—almost black—hair. And there were huge stitches in her scalp. I think they were green.

The first thing she said to me was, "Oh, Karen! I don't know why everyone is making such a fuss over me, I feel just fine!" Of course, I wasn't going to tell her she didn't LOOK fine. The next thing she said grounded me completely. "Now, dearheart, since I'm in the hospital, you have to make sure Karl does his homework. He has gotten behind in his arithmetic. Make sure he keeps up." I almost cried with relief. This is really MOM. She hasn't lost anything at all! She KNOWS things, and she REMEMBERS. She's ALIVE!

Many years later she shared, "I knew from the very beginning, without a shadow of a doubt, that I would be okay . . . it was just going to take some time. And some things wouldn't be the same. But I would be alive and productive and live a good life. I knew, because God told me."

I won't say the following days were easy for any of us. Since it was the holiday season, Dad decided we were going to put up a Christmas tree in the parlor as we always did. We all wondered, why bother? It wouldn't be the same with Mom in the hospital, and she was going to be there a long time. But he insisted. He went out to the woods with the boys, and they found a fragrant cedar tree and chopped it down. We decorated it in silence. We each added little presents now and then. It just didn't feel right. Dad told us, "We'll have our Christmas when Mom comes home."

I remember that Dad also insisted that us older kids go uptown and do some Christmas shopping. We weren't really in the mood, but I think Dad felt it was something we could do together, even though Mom wasn't there. We were at the end of Main Street, just coming out of a store, when Kevin suddenly started looking very strange. I said anxiously, "Kevin? Are you okay?" His eyes got glassier and became unfocused . . . then his lips started turning blue. I had just called to my dad out on the street that something was wrong, when Kevin fell onto the sidewalk, shaking violently—it was obvious he was having some sort of a seizure. A passing lady saw what was happening, ran over, and said, "I know what to do. Stand back." Later I found out she had a family member who was epileptic. She saved Kevin's life—he was breathing normally and feeling fine within minutes. Still, we took Kevin to the emergency room. This is getting too familiar, I thought. To this day, I think it was the stress of everything that had happened over the past few weeks and how he internalized it all. He was a rock during that period of time, except for that one incident. And I never found out the name of that wonderful lady who helped so much that night. And Kevin never had another seizure.

So, Christmas came and went. We exchanged small presents at home on Christmas Eve. We'd gone up to La Crosse and seen Mom for Christmas Day. New Year's came and went. I spent many evenings in the parlor, listening to music. The tree still was up, lit at night. I prayed a lot and wondered about the future.

We all spent a lot of time at the hospital. Mom was still, according to the surgeons, "not out of the woods." But slowly, oh, so slowly, she was getting better. We found out that her skull had been cracked completely across. Her saliva glands had been severed. Both of her eardrums had been punctured. Her tear ducts no longer worked, so her eyes were always dry, and she had no sense of smell. One eye would never be able to close—the eyelid muscles were so mangled they couldn't be repaired.

She remembers one day that she knew she was getting better: "Your Grandma Sutton was visiting me in my room. All of a sudden, I could smell all these smells. I could smell the oxygen that was being piped into my nose. I could smell the hospital, the food that was being served—everything. I remember how thankful I was. My mother cried with me. And by the way, the hospital served wonderful food."

But there were so many obstacles for her to overcome, the surgeon worried. Dad worried. We all worried.

Eventually, though, after a lot of rehabilitation and under numerous surgeons' care, Mom was deemed well enough to come back to the farm. "You have to be very gentle, and help her a lot," her main doctor said. Well, yeah. She couldn't eat without adding liquid to everything, because she didn't have working saliva glands. She could barely hear and would have to get hearing aids for both ears, which was going to take some time; she eventually got fitted for both.

Dad or one of us kids had to constantly add drops to her eyes, since she had no operating tear ducts. And she was so thin and pale. We were used to a mom who was always working hard, out in the field, tanned and fit and healthy, someone who could always handle herself plus a husband and five active kids.

And maybe that's what brought her through it all: her love of life, her strength, both in body and soul, the support of her family and church, and the absolute love of her husband and children.

So, she came home. And finally, we got to celebrate Christmas together. It was the most meaningful holiday I ever remember, even though it was in late February.

I also remember that day, months later at the supper table. It was summer. Eating was such an ordeal for her. She was slowly working on trying to chew up some food. All of a sudden she cried out, and liquid literally shot from her mouth. Her saliva glands had grown back together! It was like a miracle, because the doctors doubted it would ever happen. Yet it did. But when she cried over this miracle, she still had no tears. She never would. The rest of us cried a river for her.

Mom healed. We healed. Life went on, albeit very differently than in the past. And we all had our way of dealing with it, some of us facing it head on, some of us not so much.

Over the years, people stared. Mom was disfigured, of course. And I could hear them, sometimes, saying things like, "What is wrong with her?" "She looks like a monster!" from kids that didn't know better. These insensitive people enraged me. But Mom never said anything. She just went about her business, as if there was nothing wrong.

One day many years later, I finally asked her, "Mom, how can you stand comments like that? How can you not be angry?" She was quiet for a minute as she thought about how to respond. Finally she said, "At first it *did* bother me. But I know what I'm like on the inside. And God knows what I'm like on the inside. And Dad and you kids and everyone that cares about me and loves me knows what I'm like on the inside. You all love me no matter what. I know that I'm beautiful to all of you. I know that you think I'm worth something, no matter how I look."

It made me think of those teachers who made me think as a girl, that I wasn't "worth it." Now I knew the truth.

The accident happened when my mom was forty-five years old. This year, she'll be ninety-two. The love of her life, my dad, passed away last year. She misses him every day. But she says, "Every day is worth it, dearheart, no matter the troubles. Rejoice in every one."

I know, Mom. You are so beautiful.

UNDERDOGS

ROBERT J. BEGIEBING

I COULD LET MYSELF OFF EASY BY BLAMING MY FATHER FOR THE shit that happened to my friend Tommy and me. It all started back in the late '90s at dinner when my father was telling my mother one of his Jody Harriman stories. Harriman had moved to town a few years earlier and immediately began to make a splash in local politics and land development. Dad's theory was that the guy had "some new money from his family," even though he liked "to swagger about town in the role of self-made entrepreneur."

From my father's tales in those days, I began to see Harriman as a kind of go-getter who writes breathless letters to the town about limiting the school budget, all the while protesting his deep concern for educating the town's youth. In the meantime he sends his own kid to private school. A guy who destroys a large beaver dam and wildlife habitat just because he has dreams of making a killing by developing every square inch of property he bought when he moved into town. But then when he realizes the law and the Conservation Commission won't allow him to develop the few natural wetlands among his holdings, Harriman turns those over to the town so he looks like a hero. "That way," Dad says, "no one will dare challenge his motives when he wants other zoning variances or some favor from the selectmen." Harriman even joins the volunteer fire department. "There is no end," my father tells my mother during one of his tirades, "to Jody Harriman's backdoor meddling, town meeting histrionics, and smarmy ass-kissing."

But that night at dinner, I say, "So, Dad, what are you going to do about this guy?"

"Do?" he says. He's on a roll. He looks at me as if to say, Why aren't you just ignoring me as usual?

"I mean, this guy sounds like a real jerk," I say, "but if he's so bad why doesn't somebody throw a few nails on his road?" An expression I got from Tommy—Tommy "Wise-Ass" Milanaise.

He scowls at me. "You can't get away with that sort of thing, Bill," he says.

"Besides," he continues, "you haven't heard anything yet." Then he starts in on the story that probably got him worked up about Harriman again. The way Dad tells it, Harriman had volunteered to go into a recently abandoned house "to inventory potential assets for the town's coffers." The people who owned the house had fallen on hard times, failed to meet several property tax bills, probably couldn't meet their mortgage payments, and simply bolted.

"So, Harriman goes into the house," my father says, "and finds a small dog the family left behind."

Now my mother gives him a look, like—is this going to be dinner conversation? He glances back at her but continues.

"When Harriman went in, the animal—starved, thirsty beyond measure, frightened, and utterly alone—with his last ounce of strength charged out of some dark corner growling and barking at him. He was a little terrier mix, ever loyal to his absent family, and hardly capable in his weakened condition of inflicting much damage. But our young hero Harriman kicked the dog to death."

My mother says to my father, "Bill! Please!"

"Jesus!" I say, and my mother turns her dinner-table eye on me. My father looks at me, like, put that in your pipe and smoke it. One of his own comebacks. I don't let him off the hook yet though. "But, like I say, Dad, so what are you going to do about this guy?"

"If I hear one more word about that awful man and his ridiculous . . . antics," my mother says, "I'm going to get right up from this table and leave the room."

Well, that shuts us up, Dad and me. My mother then changes the conversation, or their conversation, while I eat in silence.

BUT WHEN WORD starts to leak out about the dog killing, Harriman claims he'd been ambushed by the beast and responded "instinctively in self-defense." Then the story gets hushed up pretty quickly.

Later in the week, Mom out of the house, I ask Dad why Harriman is going to get away with it.

"Harriman's the kind of man who always gets away with it," he says.

What I think really got my father's goat back then was that Jody Harriman, educated just enough to be dangerous, had fooled nearly everybody in town. My father taught English at the state university and had a superb memory. Whenever he was on one of his jags, he loved to quote authors he called "the great skeptics of human wisdom and benevolence." Catullus, Juvenal, Rabelais, Swift, Ruskin, Thoreau, Twain, and Mencken were some of his favorites, and I heard their pithy words from childhood well into my adult life, until my father died in the VA hospital in 2018.

But that night at the dinner table Dad's story about the abandoned dog got to me. I had a dog myself then—a young female golden lab. My best friend Tommy had a dog too—an energetic mongrel he rescued off the street. These dogs went with us when we went fishing, swimming, or messing around in the woods. In those days I was always hanging pictures and posters of dogs, famous or not, on my bedroom walls. My favorite was a huge poster of beautiful sled dogs running right at me through the vortex of a snowstorm.

Anyway, one day Tommy comes over for a bike ride to the beach for a swim, about ten miles from my house, and I tell him the story my father told at the table.

When I see that Tommy never even heard of Jody Harriman, I lay out my father's Harriman rap sheet.

"Bastard!" Tommy says.

"Like Dad says."

Tommy looks at me. "He's going to get away with it, you're sure?"

"I guess so. Least Dad's sure he is."

"Bastard!" Tommy repeats. He frowns the way he does when he gets to thinking hard. We don't say anything for a while. Tommy seems to forget about the bike ride; he paces around with his eyes to the ground. Finally, he says, "Why not make him pay?"

"Us? Like how?"

"Don't know yet. But we can figure something out, can't we?"

We think it over a few days.

My mother says Tommy is "unbridled and unkempt." His family is kind of a mess, except for his Uncle Geno, who seems to be the only one with money (and a fancy house). Mom was always trying to discourage me from associating with Tommy. Still, he was my best friend then, and I would keep telling Mom, "He's a lot smarter than me."

After a few days of thinking, Tommy and I and our dogs hike to our favorite swimming hole on a hot day to talk it over. All four of us jump in immediately. Sally, my dog, is always dominant in the water over her smaller, land-bred friend Rose, Tommy's mutt. When Tommy and I get out to sit on the rocks, the dogs stay in, frisking about with one another and two old tennis balls we throw from time to time. Sally retrieves them, but Rose always tries first to snag the ball out of the water and run around with it, frustrating the hell out of Sally.

"We can't risk doing one thing too big and righteous. We'll end up in juvenile correction," Tommy says, as if thinking aloud. "And we couldn't risk doing the same thing over again, either."

"But we want to give Harriman some payback," I say. "So, what's your plan?"

He thinks a minute more. "Shit yes. We'll have a rip-roar." His face brightens. "Small good paybacks. All different." He gives a few examples.

I turn his ideas over in my head. "Okay," I finally say, "let's get him."

First we make up a half-dozen signs saying DOG KILLER, the big letters cut out from magazines, pasted on paper, and photocopied in my father's study. Then we get the target in our sights. Harriman's pretty wife likes to drive around in her new Lexus. We sneak into the driveway one night when the car is parked outside and unlocked, put a sign under the windshield wiper, and then pour two cups of sand mixed with two cups of cornstarch into the gas tank.

Several days later, we find Harriman's shiny truck in back of the town hall. We're able to leave a sign on the seat and let the air out of two tires before someone comes along and we have to bounce. Another night when the Harrimans are away we break a small window in the house with a rock wrapped in our sign. Then we sit back in triumph.

"I say we lay off this bum for a while," Tommy suggests. "We keep screwing him, we'll get caught. We can always come back. Months, a year from now, when he'll least expect it."

I think about it. "Harriman won't want too much made out of our hits because he doesn't want to stir up memories of his dog murder." I hate to let Harriman off so soon. But I say, "You're probably right. We're pushing it. I bet he's got it all planned by now how he's going to catch us in the act."

"Anyways," Tommy says, "there's other battles to fight."

"Other battles?"

"Other dogs. Why not? It's fun, isn't it?"

"You don't think we'll get caught?"

"Not if we're careful and keep moving. Mostly I'm just talking about getting a few dogs out of jail." He grins.

We sit around for a while coming up with likely candidates: dogs never let off short chains, dogs never out of pens barely larger than their bodies, dogs with tight collars and ropes eating into their flesh, dogs left out without enough food and water.

Next thing we know we're Robin Hoods in the strange country of dog abuse. We take wandering summer bike rides through towns and open country in search of abused and neglected dogs. Tommy likes to show off sometimes by coasting on his bike while standing on the seat and leaning over to grab the handlebars. He does other tricks too, like a cowboy in a circus show. Whenever we pass a river with a place to swim, we jump in. If we happen upon a dog that looks messed up, we note exactly where we are on a road map and then return to the most likely cases to make sure.

Then we plan our strike. Usually we sneak out after midnight. In our backpacks we carry a good lot of Milk-Bones ("Fortified with 12 vitamins!") and bottled water to make friends and help the poor buggers off to a running start. We take Tommy's father's bolt cutters to chains and fences. We undo collars, unhitch ropes. We make and leave more signs: DOG OWNERS ARE

RESPONSIBLE FOR FOOD AND WATER. DOGS NEED EXERCISE. DOGS NEED SPACE AND SHELTER. YOU DON'T DESERVE THIS DOG. Like his father, Tommy's proud of his profanity. His favorite: WHAT KIND OF LAZY, CRUEL, FAT FUCK ARE YOU, ANYWAY? We list the addresses and offenses on notes I print out in Dad's study. Copies of the notes we mail anonymously to our local New Hampshire SPCA shelter. If a dog looks to be sick or the flesh has grown into a too-tight collar, and if on a rare occasion there's a vet or shelter nearby, we tie up the dog with a bowl of water and a half-dozen Milk-Bones outside the office and tape our note on the door. That is if we can move the dog at all either after dark or before the shelter opens. By now we're feeling pretty damned good about our adventures. But we know we're pushing our luck.

And sure enough we get nabbed early one morning about to tie a dog that looked like a famine victim to the locked front door of our local SPCA office. But we're not early enough. The manager yanks his car into the lot and bolts out his car door. He's too fast for us to get away clean. He threatens to turn us in to the police, but ends up calling my father to come and get us. The manager must have been sympathetic to us deep down, because he just talks friendly to Dad. He says he'll get the dog to their vet.

Then the manager turns to us and says, "Don't you two let me even hear of any stunts like this again."

We promise.

"You ever see anything like this, you come in here and tell us about it, the proper way. We all have to follow the laws—even you kids." We don't say we're the ones who sent in those anonymous reports with addresses.

THAT EVENING AFTER dinner, my father sits me down in his study. "You could have ended up in court, you know, if the manager hadn't been a good guy," he says. He looks me in the eye hard. "I bet this wasn't your first 'rescue.'"

"Sorry, Dad," I say. "There were some suffering dogs we helped. It felt like the right thing to do. Wish we could have helped that little guy before the likes of Jody Harriman kicked him to death." He doesn't say anything. I savor the familiar smell of books, leather, and whiskey in the room.

"Of course rescuing something or someone that's suffering is the right thing to do," he says as he's pouring himself a shot of Jack Daniels from the bottle in his desk drawer. "But that doesn't matter. It's how you go about it. And the 'right thing' gets people into trouble all the time. You're fourteen, almost fifteen—too old not to see that by now, Bill. If the manager had gone to the police chief . . . well, imagine then how they'd treat a traffic violation when you start driving. That troublemaker again! You can't just go around wildly like some little kid acting on your impulses."

So, Tommy and I lay off the dog rescue. And we swear we'll never do Harriman again.

But then a couple of months later near the end of that summer Tommy comes over and says he heard his Uncle Geno talking to his father about a guy who breeds and fights dogs. His uncle says he'd placed a few bets himself. He gave it up, though, as a business that made him kind of sick.

"From what he said," Tommy adds, "I think I've got an idea where this guy's place is."

"You got to be nuts, Tommy," I say. "My father is just waiting for me to slip up again to nail me. And you heard what that SPCA guy said about calling the police."

"What, you turning pussy on me?" he says with a sneer. "Look, it's an adventure. We just ride down and check this out. We don't have to do anything, like before, if we don't want to. Just have a look-see and all." He can tell I'm not convinced. "Call the SPCA maybe if we find something."

We take a day that summer to bike down there a few miles from the Massachusetts line. We find what looks like a backyard full of pit bulls on the leafy outskirts of a city about ten miles from our hometown in New Hampshire. We see a man—a stubby, unshaved, mean-looking slob—driving his ATV around. And we see a motorcycle and fancy cars in the drive: a BMW, a Corvette, a Mercedes. So, we ride by and turn home.

Later that week, we go back to check on those pit bulls, and this time as far as we can tell no one is home. We snoop around. In the large, chain-link-fenced-in backyard we see spring polls hanging from trees where we figure the dogs are being taught to lock on and shake and tear. The dogs chained outdoors just sit there watching us calmly. They look well fed, some of them wagging tails, going into play posture. Tommy gives me the finger and his grin and scrambles right over the fence. He takes out a pack of bacon treats. I'll be damned if the dogs don't seem fine with him. One or two he has to stay clear of. He tells me that some of the dogs have scars and legs that look as if they must have been broken and healed bad, then adds that one looks to have her tongue missing.

"Look, they like me," Tommy says, feeding a treat to a couple of dogs he then scratches behind the ears. The dogs wag their tails. "They're tough fighters, all right," he says. "But I bet they're trained just to kill other dogs. Come on!"

Finally I climb over the fence too. We snoop more, the dogs yapping a bit and wagging their tails at us. Then I stand on Tommy's back and look in the window of a converted half barn. I see three treadmills: dog training? A Quonset hut that houses more barking dogs is locked with an enormous padlock—too heavy even for Tommy's bolt cutters—so we don't get to see inside. What we really want to do now is get into the barn so we can check things out, but I'm afraid the owner might come back. We look around some more.

The place is quiet, not a light on in the main house; even the central air conditioner shut off. We start to get our courage up. We throw a lot of Milk-Bones around and then sneak back toward the barn. Tommy stands on my back this time and forces his hunting knife up between the sashes toward the window lock. In another minute I feel his weight lift off my back.

"Holy shit!" he says from inside, and then helps me up.

Inside, we find not only treadmills, but also a refrigerator holding bottles of medications and hypodermics. We find three fighting dog magazines, but they seem to be written in some sort of underground lingo, so we can't really understand much—beyond the photos of champions and action-packed fights. I roll one of these mags up and stuff it in my backpack. We find a big TV and a shelf of what from the titles sound like pornographic DVDs. One of these entitled *Hard High Heels* we pop in the player just for the hell of it. In less than two minutes we turn it off. "Jesus fucking Christ," Tommy says. "Better take this one too for evidence of what we found here."

I know we're both thinking of turning the owner in to the SPCA, like the manager told us.

We walk up a set of stairs where blood stains the carpet and the walls. We meet another padlocked door, but this lock our bolt cutters can handle. Inside, dried blood everywhere, the room is set up like a fight pit, a small arena. We smell stale blood and something else—that sharp, sickening smell of fear wherever animals are confined. The clients must like it that way; it must increase the blood thirst of men betting hundreds of dollars on which dog will live and which one die.

"Tommy," I say, "we better go. And stay gone. Now we've broken in, this guy will be laying for us."

"Yeah," Tommy says, "before we screw up and have every fucking pinkie-ring and lead-pipe wise guy from Boston on our sorry asses." I laugh and figure he's quoting his father.

Just as we're ready to leave we hear a car and look out the window. A huge man with raked-back, well-moussed black hair gets out of his vintage Corvette convertible. He's wearing a slick gray summer suit. We hear him knocking on the door of the house. Before long he comes around and tries to force the gate to the backyard. When he can't get in he just stands there calling heavily: "Vito. Hey, Vito!" We crouch, keeping so quiet we only hear the deep voice starting to get angry, and our own panicky breathing. He shakes the gate furiously—setting the dogs off—and begins walking around the fenced yard.

Then we hear his voice boom again, as if he's calling toward the window we have been stupid enough to leave open. "Vito! You in there?"

Two more calls and then it gets real quiet. We finally hear his car roar away.

"You think all this is mob shit?" I ask.

"Looks like it," Tommy says and grins. "Good Fellas."

We make our escape. But just as we get on our bikes and start peddling for dear life, we hear Big Fella's car screeching around the corner. We're about to head off the road toward the woods when he pulls right in front of us. Tommy's bike bumps the car and he falls off. The guy leaps out and manages to grab Tommy as I dodge off into the woods.

"Lemme go, you big goon!" I hear Tommy scream as I run.

But I can't just keep going and leave my best friend in Goliath's hands. So, I sneak back through the woods. Big Fella has him by the neck and the belt as Tommy thrashes. The goon is barely getting his suit rumpled. A bear holding a furious squirrel at arm's length.

Finally the guy yells, "Knock it off, you little shit!" and shakes him hard. Tommy keeps on, so Big Fella bangs him a terrible one on the back of Tommy's head with the flat of one hand. He lifts his hand to swipe him another good one, but Tommy has stopped flailing and protesting and goes limp.

"Had enough, you little fuck?" Big Fella bellows. He looks around to be sure no cars are coming. Tommy stays limp, sort of sob-breathing. I can't really tell whether Tommy's conscious now. Maybe the big goon broke his neck.

I don't move or try to help yet. I'm not that stupid. Big Fella picks up the bolt-cutters that have fallen out of Tommy's pack and throws them and Tommy into the car. Then he gets in the driver's seat; I see him pick up a cell phone and start making calls. I'm not close enough to hear a thing. I guess he might be leaving a message for Vito and alerting his whole tribe that two kids broke in and blew their cover, broke in and probably took stuff. Only this one kid got away. I still do have the magazine and the DVD in my pack, but he doesn't know that yet.

Tommy is so slumped down in the seat I can't see anything but the tip of one shoulder and the top of his head. Meanwhile Big Fella keeps making calls on the phone. I have movie visions of Tommy being dumped in Boston Harbor wearing concrete shoes, getting his nuts cut off with his own bolt-cutters, being locked in a closet and buggered every day for months. I begin to memorize the car's license plate while I wait to see what he's going to do with Tommy.

Finally he backs the car out onto the road and screeches it over to the driveway of the house. He jumps out, rushes up to a stone wall by the front door, picks up a stone, and pulls something out of the bottom. He opens the front door and goes in.

I dash for the Corvette convertible—about fifty yards away—and thump on Tommy's shoulder. His head turns slowly; his eyes look like somebody waking up, like he really can't move. He's trying to recall what all is going on here. Then I realize he can't use his hands. Finally I open the door. He's handcuffed to the steering wheel. I grab his bolt cutters off the floor and cut him loose. I notice the goon threw his cell phone on the seat in his anger and hurry. I pull Tommy out of the car and grab the phone. With my help Tommy gets up and we try to run. He's clumsy, still woozy. But then he seems to be coming to as we enter the woods across from the house, as if moving fast is clearing his head. Then he bends over, leaning against a tree, and vomits.

"Any way you can climb this tree if I help?" I ask when he's finished. It's a good-sized maple with a few dead lower branches that help us get started. We can only get Tommy up about twelve feet off the ground. He tucks into a leafy notch and I continue to climb toward the top until the branches get too thin to go farther.

I settle in and call 911 on the phone. I tell the dispatcher there's a child who has been beaten and is in trouble and there are some abused dogs here too. I give the address and add the Corvette's Massachusetts plate number for good measure. But I don't stay on the line as asked. "Just hurry!" I say. "Gotta go!"

I can just see the car in the driveway still, door closed as I left it. Within minutes I hear a distant siren and in a few seconds more, Big Fella comes lumbering out of the house with three briefcases in his hands and gets in his car. He peels out, heading away from the sound of the siren.

When the cruiser pulls up, lights flashing, we start down the tree, me helping Tommy, and begin to get our stories together to tell the police. We agree to say that we were just out riding bikes on a back road and happened upon a lot of chained dogs. Our curiosity got the better of us so we looked around. Then, our story goes, we put two and two together and figured out this was some kind of dog fighting setup, but we wanted to be sure before taking a chance on turning in an innocent man to the SPCA—or even a guilty man who might get off and come after us. So, we sneaked around, and yes even looked in, and finally climbed in an "unlocked" window to see what we had really stumbled into. Then Big Fella pulls up and goes after us. Here's our evidence, officer!

THE FIRST THING the cops do is cordon off the house and yard. Then another cruiser comes by to take us back to the station, after first stopping by the local emergency room to have Tommy's head checked out. The doctor says he has the symptoms of a minor concussion. So, a city police detective comes to us in a small room where Tommy is lying on a cot until it's safe to release him.

While we're telling our story, the detective shakes his head. "You kids are nuts," he says. "Do you realize what you're messing with here?"

"Well, we knew he was a bad dude," I say, "but once we figured out what he was up to, we planned to turn him in. Then we got caught and Tommy took his knocks."

"Matter of fact, we've been on to the owner for some time," the cop says. "We almost had enough on him to go in and have a close look."

At that point he pulls out the dog-fighting magazine we turned over. He blows out a whistle and shakes his head some more. "Nobody outside the game gets hold of these things."

Then he pulls out the porno we lifted. "So, what's this?" he says.

Tommy opens his eyes. "Crush porno," he says. "All kinds there, but this one we found out was crush. Just evidence, like the magazine. So you'd believe us."

"Christ almighty," the cop says. He doesn't say it with shock or surprise in his voice. He's probably seen and heard just about everything. But his voice sounds as if he's thinking: just one more crazy thing with this asshole. He turns the DVD over in his hands as if it has dog shit on it. "You shouldn't have taken his property." But he tags the DVD and throws it and the magazine into plastic bags.

When we watched a couple minutes of the DVD we almost got sick to our stomachs. Tommy told me he'd heard the name "crush" somewhere—near-naked women dressed in leather and spike heels stepping on small animals.

The cop shakes his head again and then hands me a pen and paper.

"Here," he says, looking bleary-eyed. "Write up your own account of everything you two saw and would be willing to testify to in a hearing before a grand jury or a judge. Or even in court later, if necessary."

Tommy looks at me, frowns, and slowly shakes his head no. But I want those dogs out of there. So, I sit down and start writing.

"Don't worry," the cop says to Tommy. "They'll never know who talked."

Tommy doesn't budge. "Look," the policeman says, "you know what they do sometimes to a dog that loses a fight but survives?"

"I don't want to know," he mumbles.

"Set 'em on fire, club 'em to death or near death. You want to hear more?"

"Okay, all right," Tommy says in a defeated voice.

Later, the detective drives us to the station and shows us a typed-up version of our statement so we can both read it. Then he calls our folks. Tommy's dad yells into the phone, "Let him rot in jail!" We figure he's drunk, pissed, and inconvenienced. But my old man rushes down to the station, insisting my mother stay home while he handles it.

When he comes in he gives me a look like he wants to kill me.

Dad converses with the cops for ten minutes and then calls his lawyer. His lawyer tells him to hold out till he gets there for our not making a court appearance. If these guys could get to the kids, they would, he tells my father. We sign the statement and Dad countersigns our testimony as witness. He agrees to testify in court, if necessary, to the validity of our written evidence, to our voluntary signatures, on the provision, as the lawyer insists, that we will never be named or appear in person beyond a grand jury.

After the lawyer shows up, the detective finally takes us and all the paperwork to a judge who interviews us in a lazy, pompous way for twenty minutes. He wants to make sure we all agree to everything and that we indeed signed the paper voluntarily. The detective asks the judge if he may say a word. The judge nods.

"These kids had no business, your honor, going in like that, but they did no real damage to property. And for whatever it's worth, we've had a lead on this character for some months now, and it's their report, as friendly eyewitnesses, that could get us inside the place finally, if the court will agree to a warrant. He can afford the best lawyers, so we couldn't go in till we had something solid."

The judge mentions that our evidence probably wouldn't be admissible, but he'll consider it as probable cause for now. He realizes of course the bargain Dad's lawyer requested is to save our skins from Vito's boys.

The judge looks Tommy in the eye. "Sounds as if you have already taken some punishment for this," he says. Then he spends a few minutes exercising his displeasure for our benefit. "This is the first and last indulgence you'll receive from the court," he says. "Don't let me or any other judge see you before him again—for any reason."

On our way out of the judge's chambers, the cop says, "Now go home and lay low, as low as you ever have."

He and Dad shake hands. The lawyer says he'll call Dad later and leaves. The cop says, "I'll be contacting you later too, sir." Dad thanks him; we begin to leave.

But just outside the cop stops us with his voice. "You kids took too big a chance," he says and we turn toward him. "That was too great a risk, you know. But still, we're going to get this evil character, and that's the right thing to do. The wrong, right thing." His face offers the first smile we've seen. "It took guts."

THREE DAYS LATER we read about it in the paper: the police raid, the dogs, the hypodermics and steroids and antibiotics, among other evidence confiscated. The dogs, we read, have been placed in several shelters throughout New Hampshire and Massachusetts; the owner, Vito Manicci, has been arrested with bail set at $300,000. Our names are never mentioned, just a reference to "eyewitnesses" whose report "initiated the police department's full investigation." And Dad has not been called before the courts, not yet. Forty counts of animal cruelty for openers. Also some drug violations. From the way it's written up, it looks as if the prosecutors have all the evidence they need to keep Fast-Money Vito's balls in a nice tight vise for a few years.

And that's the story of our last and best revenge, the final act in our Robin Hood drama. We've slipped through the system about as close as anyone can.

As for the pit bulls, three months later we read that they have been put down finally, even a couple of puppies. The debate over their fate had raged in the newspapers for weeks, but the pit bulls, we're told, had been specially bred and raised to be explosively aggressive toward strange dogs. No family could give them a home. In fact, we read that professional fighting pits (unlike city-gang pit bulls) are trained not to be aggressive toward people. That, Tommy takes pleasure in assuring me, is why we weren't torn to shreds ourselves in the first place. "That and the heavy chains," I say.

But I can't forget those dogs. Some of them wagged their tails and ate our bacon treats and Milk-Bones. A few looked me in the eye, as if wondering whether I might be the instrument of their deliverance. Yet finally neither I nor anyone else could do a thing to save them.

When I first read the newspaper article to Tommy, I can't help myself; I start to cry. He doesn't make fun of me or anything. He just sits there shaking his head and frowning.

"The sonofabitch!" he finally says, heaving a stone at a tree.

I pull myself together. "I'm through taking chances, Tommy," I say. "I'm not doing any of this stuff anymore. There's got to be other ways to help."

He looks up at me, sort of surprised. "Like what?"

"I'm not sure yet. Something."

"You figure it out," he says, "you let me know."

"I will," I say. "Maybe someday I'll be a vet. Anyway, everything's different now." I even see my father in a new light.

*

THAT NIGHT AFTER bringing me home from the station, Dad sits me down in his study again and asks a lot of questions. I do the best I can, and I tell the truth, just as I'm telling it here all these years later.

Then I thank him. "You're putting your own neck on the line, Dad, for Tommy and me," I say. "We know that. We screw up, but then you're the one who could get into the papers for these wise guys to see."

"It's not that big a deal," he says. "Might all be settled out of court. Besides, they promised me anonymity and police protection, as long as necessary."

"You trust them?"

"Enough." He looks to see if I believe him. "Anyway," he says, "I might seem like an old fart to you. I could be your grandfather." He laughs and reaches into his desk drawer for the Jack Daniels. I'm pretty sure he wants to say more.

"Look at it this way, Bill," he continues, as he pours himself a glass. "I survived a tour in Vietnam. I came back, worked a crap job, went on to grind out seven years of grad school on the GI Bill and a teaching fellowship, while trying to raise a family, went through a rough divorce, got married again, started a second family—you and Mom. You know the story."

"Most of it," I say.

"Well, I'm saying I've been through a lot, seen a lot." He takes a first sip. "I'm not going to spook too easily at this point in my life."

I sit there while he takes another sip.

"People can get pretty screwed up," I suggest. "You can't go through your life worrying about whether they might screw you up too."

He looks at me and laughs. "Something like that, Bill," he says. "Something like that."

"But do you think the cop was right, about Tommy and me? We did the right, wrong thing?"

He takes another sip. "You went directly against my admonitions in the first place," he says. He turns the glass around on the desk a few times. "But to blow the whistle on this creep once you were sure what was going on, and at your own risk from the start, yes. You did the right, wrong thing. Should have told me first about what you and Tommy had found. You stayed with it way too long and nearly got hurt."

"But we got the evidence. What they called probable cause."

"True."

"He's a pretty bad guy. That cop called him evil."

"I noticed."

"You believe that?" I ask. "That people can actually be evil?"

He glances at me quick and then looks at the top of his desk. "I don't go in for sweeping theories of good and evil—"

"One person at a time, you mean?" I interrupt him. "Like Jody Harriman," I add, knowing I hit home.

He turns the whiskey glass against the mellow light of his desk lamp. He looks at me, smiles, and finally says, "Go to bed, will you, for Crissake."

OVER THE YEARS I've thought about those dogs a lot. When I recall that my signed statement was my own final step in the death of those pit bulls, only one thought keeps me going: Those dogs, when all is said and done, are at peace. They had been delivered from Mr. Vito Manicci's strange paradise of drugs, pornography, agony, and death.

My father seemed able to live with that. And now maybe I can too.

ARRANGED LOVE

JOSEPH J. RIDGWAY

Bit and harness chaffing,
    always a capricious climb—
Strength sometimes failing,
    seldom steps of sweet rhyme.

He to her left—
    She to his right—
Calmly coaxing
    him and his might.

They knew each other well—
    But it wasn't sonnets
nor lust
    for which they fell.

When he picked up a stone,
    their rhythm fell askew—
She took the extra weight,
    until remaining steps were few.

A life of travail,
    then one night came the shot—
His loss unrealized, until
    morning brought her not.

They paired him with another.
    She was impatient to start.
It was lighter on the load—
    but heavier on the heart.

FROG HUNT
MARIO RENÉ PADILLA

UNTIL COACH MURPHY INVITED HIS BASKETBALL TEAM TO A workout weekend on his 100 acres outside Columbus, Joseph had never been on a farm before. Ironically, his family had recently purchased a newly constructed, split-level home built on Ohio farmland developers had been gobbling up for years east off state route 310. Hundreds of new houses were being constructed elbow to elbow, identical in style and color. The population in the area tripled, and the highway had to be widened and repaved, becoming the asphalt border between the aggressive suburban sprawl to the east of the road and the remaining farms of stubborn farmers to the west—the few struggling holdouts of a dying American way of life.

School mornings, Joseph kissed his mother goodbye at the door, slung his backpack around his shoulders, and walked a half mile down the street to the 310 to wait by himself for the school bus. It was his third week at the new high school the city built to accommodate the area's increase in school-age children. Climbing aboard the bus, he'd head for the back, passing noisy teenagers from all the new developments: Fernwood Village, Country Park Homes, Kendale Greenacres, Cranbrook Estates, Old Woods Farm—names suggesting Edenic countryside living, with forests and wild brooks, as if nothing of natural beauty ever existed in the area before financial investors carved up the land for enormous profit.

Joseph enjoyed looking out the window at all the acres of cornfields, cows and horses of the remaining farms spread out along the west side of the highway. He wondered what it would be like to live in a two-story farmhouse with wraparound porches and weathervanes, nestled within a clump of shade trees with a tire swing hanging from a tree branch. He had an idealized notion of farm life, and loved the pastoral view of barns, lean-to utility buildings, and tractors sitting in abeyance on acres of half-harvested fields. Something about fenced pastures, animals munching grass lazily in the sun attracted Joseph, as did the flocks of chickens clucking about, until scattered by legs of farm kids exploding out of screen doors, always running late for the bus. He smiled watching them shout frantically the length of their dirt access road for the driver to wait, followed by a barking dog or two.

In late September, one such farm boy in corduroys and a blue denim shirt, as tall and thick as a John Deere tractor, made it just in time and climbed aboard. Joseph had noticed him before. He had close-cropped sandy hair on a big square head, and always sat up front with the other farm kids, who kept mostly to themselves. Only, this time, he kept coming down the aisle breathing hard and perspiring, till he plopped himself heavy into the open seat next to Joseph.

"Lord! Gotta catch my breath. Didn't think I'd make it this morning."

"You oversleep?" Joseph tried to sound cool in forced conversation.

"I was up at five." He chuckled, good humoredly. "What time did you get up?"

"Five? Damn, why so early?" He'd only recently acquired the habit of cussing.

"Had to muck out the pig's pen. My dad said if I want to play basketball, I got to work mornings. Practices are after school, when I'm supposed to be working. 'That's the deal,' he said."

Joseph made a mental note. He'd always believed Italian mothers were the strictest disciplinarians—but they had nothing on farm fathers of Franklin County.

"You made the team? So did I," Joseph returned enthusiastically.

"Well, glad to meet ya there, teammate," he said, sticking out his big, fat hand. "I'm Preston."

It felt strange. Most guys his age didn't shake hands. "Joseph," he said with a tougher inflection, shaking Preston's calloused hand that felt like sandpaper.

Then, Preston added with a wink, "Especially since it don't look like we're competing for the same position," elbowing Joseph in the ribs. "Shit, there's Margaret Stoals," he blurted out as the bus pulled over. It was a girl Joseph had noticed and looked for every morning since the first day of school. "Tough girl, that one. Don't piss her off. You in ninth?"

"Yeah"

"Thirteen?"

Joseph nodded his head. "Fourteen in two weeks."

"Don't worry, she'll leave you alone. But I'll bet you anything she sits right across the aisle from us. Watch."

Like Preston, she too was tall, probably the tallest girl on the bus. She had a pretty face, but Joseph thought she looked tough with her short black hair and thick shoulders. Her breasts were bigger than the other girls' her age, and she had perfect, unblemished skin, white as milk, but oddly, a long neck, as if she'd been stretched. And just as Preston predicted, she passed two open seats behind the driver and continued loping down the aisle.

Lowering his voice as Margaret approached, Preston said, "We're both in tenth. She and I were sort of . . . hanging out over the summer." Then, raising his voice, "Hey, Margaret."

"Hey, Preston."

"This is my friend Joey."

Now, Joseph had never had a nickname before—he kind of liked it, the idea of it, the sound of it coming out of Preston's mouth—Joey. He wondered if his mother would approve.

"Hi, Joey. Yeah, I seen you on the bus before. But I haven't seen much of you lately," looking straight at Preston, before sitting down heavily and without grace.

"Well, we're in harvest. The disk ripper's acting up again. You know how it is." Then he turned to Joseph. "I'll see you at practice this afternoon, Joey."

"Sure," Joseph shot back casually, as Preston got up and slid next to Margaret, pushing her to the window. She smiled triumphantly, whispered something in his ear and they both began laughing.

Joseph turned back toward the view of endless rows of corn, heavy with husks, whizzing past. He thought of how Preston had work while he had chores. Strange, other people's lives, so different from his, especially in the South End, working-class Italian community where he used to live: "Better high school for Joseph in the North End," his mother told her hair customers, though it was really a move away from the annoying gossip of family—her husband's a musician, drinks a lot as they all do, and he's Mexican. She should be home more for Joseph—the Italian immigrant code of old-world values and racial conformity. But uppermost in his mother's mind was the South End's constant threat of juvenile delinquency. The poverty, narrow dirty alleys, used brick roads, the old, two-story pillared structures with porches and stoops built by German and Slavic immigrants at the turn of the century, now slowly becoming a black community, the Italians and Europeans moving out. It wasn't the "old neighborhood" his mother played in as a ragged, curly-haired street urchin. But Joseph liked playing basketball with the black kids who befriended him. They taught him how to dribble between his legs and shoot. He also missed his cousins, his church, and parochial school, St. Bartholomew, the heart of the Italian community, the Italian festivals, the old guys in caps playing bocce in the park, old women sitting on their porches with rosaries. Moving from Catholic school with uniforms to the north side of town and a brand new public high school (with lockers) was exciting for Joseph. But learning how to be cousin-less—more or less friendless—during the afternoons was the hard part.

Margaret suddenly exploded with laughter. Joseph watched them giggle as he wondered what exactly Preston meant by hanging out. The way they laughed and talked together disturbed Joseph. Compared to them, he felt like a child. He was short for his age, with dark skin and curly black hair—a gypsy-looking kid who was younger in the ways of things he was just beginning to intuit. But as a pious altar and choir boy, he'd always felt this way, especially around his older, tougher cousins who'd already spent time in reform school. It wasn't Preston so much as Margaret who occupied his thoughts—the sight of her long neck that curved down to her exposed collar bone, her breasts, as big as his mother's, how they jiggled in her tight red and white checkered blouse, how her thighs rubbed together in her jeans coming up the aisle, her too-sweet perfume that arrived before she did, as she and Preston continued to speak of things only they understood.

At practice that afternoon, not knowing any of the other players, Joseph gravitated to Preston. He watched him throw the medicine ball harder than anyone. But then, everyone threw it harder than he did—logged more push-ups and pull-ups too. But Joseph won all the running and dribbling drills: end to mid-court sprints or running ten reps of the school building's three-story stairwells and long hallways. By the end of practice, Preston had everyone, even coach, calling Joseph, Joey—a few adding "little"—though Dean Murphy made it clear that as the new JV coach at Granville High, he was putting together a team that could win: "Joey's on the team because of his hustle and heart, which some of you bigger boys might learn from." Joseph regularly dove for loose balls and took the bumps and elbows without complaint. He had a tough core, always gave back as much as he got. But most importantly, it was his "dead-eye jump shot," as Murphy called it, that earned him a spot, learned in the parks and alleys of the South End, with black kids who, with his dark skin, treated him like one of their own. Throughout scrimmage, Joseph would make baskets, which Murphy would acknowledge, shouting, "Dead-eye, now that wins games."

At the end of practice, Murphy called everyone to center court. "Boys, what this team needs is some physical strengthening. Now I've got a farm." Someone murmured, "E-I-E-I-O," and Murphy smiled. "Okay. That's good. But you boys are soft, with the possible exception of Preston here. Lazy summer days drinking root beer floats at the drive-in I suspect. So, I'm inviting all of you to a 'farm workout weekend.'"

"What's that, Coach?" someone asked.

"Well, come and you'll find out. You'll stack hay bales, dig post holes, repair some fences, feed the animals, but we'll get some games in on my outdoor court, take dips in the pond. I think you could all use a lesson on working together to get a tough job done."

"So, we'll be working with cows and stuff?" another boy asked.

"Yes, I've got some cows and a few pigs . . . and you'll get some of my wife's fabulous cooking. Bonnie's fixing chitlins for your first meal. It's her specialty. Now those of you who want to go have to get permission from your parents. Here's the forms they need to sign."

After showering and dressing in the locker room, Preston said to Joseph, "No way she's servin' a bunch of city boys chitlins. You gonna go?"

"I guess," Joseph answered, tying his shoes. "Don't want to be the only one who doesn't. Hey, what's chitlins?"

"Pig intestines." And with a big smile, he slapped Joseph hard on the back on his way out. "See ya tomorrow, Joey."

Next morning on the bus, Preston said to Joseph, "Heck, I know what workin' a farm is all about," showing him his signed form. "I'm going just to watch you guys bale hay and slop hogs. That's worth the price of admission right there. You ever use a pitchfork before?"

"I rake leaves," Joseph said with a smile. "Isn't that the same thing?"

Preston belly laughed, which made Joseph feel good, knowing he was beginning to find his sense of humor.

"He'll work us all right. But just getting away from my farm will be a vacation."

"Wait, you don't think we'll be working the whole time, do you?" Joseph asked.

"We're not going there just to shoot baskets. My guess is, he's figured out he needs some help with his farm. I'm sure he's in over his head right now. Didn't know what he was getting' into when he bought the place. Heck, my dad's struggling to hold on to ours, developers flappin' around like vultures. Many of his friends have already given up, sold cheap just to get out of debt, and Murphy's buying one? Coach must be crazy."

Friday after school, Joseph, Preston, and five other teammates from a team of twelve stood outside the gymnasium with their duffel bags and permission slips when Murphy drove up in a white school van. Murphy's farm was in the northwest part of the city. It wasn't the typical flatland farm though. Besides acres of corn and furrowed unplanted soil, the area near the house was hilly, and a small clump of trees canopied a large emerald pond loaded with frogs.

Driving up in front of the farmhouse, the van scattered chickens milling in the yard.

"Woah, you almost hit your chickens, Coach," someone shouted.

"They're well trained. Welcome to the farm, boys."

As everyone climbed out of the van, Mrs. Murphy, dressed in jeans and an open-neck white muslin blouse, exited the kitchen door, drying her hands on a waist apron. Joseph's first impression was that she looked like a high school student, more like Murphy's daughter, though he knew Coach didn't have children. She was definitely younger than him. She had golden brown hair and high cheekbones with freckles that framed a narrow delicate nose. Around her neck she wore a little necklace with a gold cross—her face reminded Joseph of holy card depictions of the Virgin Mary. She gave her husband a hug, who announced with obvious pride, "This is my wife Bonnie. Now listen to her, boys. She's the real boss around here."

"Oh, stop it. I'm thinkin' you boys'll be hungry in a couple of hours."

She spoke with more of a southern accent than a Midwest one, and seeing how pretty her face got when she smiled, Joseph's heart dropped without understanding why.

"Yes, Bonnet. Get those chitlins ready. Gonna get them good and hungry first."

"Dinner will be ready when you are. Good to have you boys." Then she turned and disappeared back through the kitchen door.

"Okay, grab your bags and follow me." Inside, they passed through the living room and climbed the stairs. The place reminded Joseph of *Little House on the Prairie*. At the top of the stairs, Murphy pointed and said, "Put your bags in those two rooms."

Each room had a double bed and a couple of cots. White lace curtains covered the windows, softening the afternoon sunlight.

"Now that room," and he pointed to a closed door out in the hall, "that's my room—off-limits at all times. Put your work shoes on I told you to bring, and let's meet out in the yard."

Tying his shoes, Joseph glanced out into the hall toward the forbidden door. Then passing it before heading down the stairs, he touched it.

Outside, they took a small tour of the farm. There were twenty or so cows in a fenced pasture along with two horses, and in a sheet metal lean-to, several pigs, large ones, like those in the *Wizard of Oz.* Joseph remembered how frightened Dorothy got when she fell into the pen—he decided to stay clear. The pond was the highlight. Everyone was fascinated with the croaking, chirping, ribbiting of what sounded like a thousand frogs, though not one could be seen. Kyle, a tall, skinny fourteen-year-old tenth grader with lots of acne scars and big ears that stuck out, a mean-spirited kid who gave Joseph the most trouble of anyone on the team, said conspiratorially to Frank, "Hey, I brought my BB rifle along."

"No shit," Frank returned, an all-American, brawny, square-jawed type whose long blond hair kept falling over his eyes.

A few others who'd overheard asked, "What did you bring?"

"My BB rifle. Thought maybe coach would let us shoot cans or bottles out in the field.

"Hell yes!" and "Alright!" were the general responses.

"Hold on! Now I'm thinking," and he lowered his voice, "maybe we come here tonight and pop a few frogs."

This seemed to go over with enthusiasm. But Joseph fell quiet. He was enjoying the mysterious croaking—the invisible life of the pond—it was something he'd never heard before. He looked over at Preston, who just seemed bored.

Now Joseph, Kyle, Frank, and Carothers, the team captain, and oldest, tallest boy on the team, who, for some reason, everyone addressed by his last name, all chose to work in the hayloft, lifting bales with hooks, carrying them down a ramp to be stacked for tomorrow's use. Kyle and Frank worked as a team and Joseph worked with Carothers. Everyone thought Joseph had volunteered for hayloft duty to prove he was just as strong. No one suspected he volunteered for the hayloft mainly to stay away from the pigs. Preston was put in charge of mucking out the pig pen because he knew what to do. He directed Byron and Jordon, two brothers of German descent who always hung together and did whatever they were told by authority. Preston tried to tell Joseph that carrying hay bales was harder work than cleaning out a pig's pen, but Joseph didn't listen. He wanted to feel self-reliant of Preston—common sense be damned.

But after ten minutes of struggling lifting bales, Joseph began to sneeze uncontrollably.

"What a little wimp," Kyle said loud enough for Joseph to hear.

Murphy, who was supervising the operation, said, "Go on inside and tell Bonnie you're sneezing. She'll know what to do."

As Joseph dropped his hooks and headed for the house, Kyle gave out a fake sneeze, then said loudly, "Hey, Coach, I think I need to go in too."

"Kyle, stop being a pain in the butt," Murphy responded, as he hooked a bale by himself and lifted it with his knee onto the stack.

When Joseph entered the kitchen sneezing, his eyes swelling up, Bonnie turned from the stove. She stood in her element, surrounded by copper pots hanging from a ceiling rack. She set her spoon down and said with a commiserating tone, "Oh boy. Betta come on with me. Looks like ya got it bad. Get it myself on occasions, when I spend too much time in the barns."

Joseph loved hearing her strange accent, the way her lips moved. He caught himself staring at her butt as he followed behind her up the stairs—soft on her feet and in tone, unlike Margaret, who was coarse and loud. Joseph got the impression that Bonnie Murphy had never once raised her voice in anger.

Entering the bathroom and opening the medicine cabinet, she asked, "What's your name?"

"Joseph. But everyone calls me Joey."

"Okay, Joey," pulling two tablets from a box, "take these. See if that doesn't clear it up."

Joseph took the two tablets from her left hand that wasn't spoiled with jewelry, noticing how thin her wrists were, how long and delicate her fingers. She filled a small glass with water and handed it to him. Standing close to her in the small space, Joseph could see beads of sweat appearing on the exposed part of her breasts just below the gold cross, but he quickly looked away. Bonnie smiled. She squirted some lavender hand lotion from a dispenser and began rubbing it into her hands. "Sure is hot and humid out there," she said. "I'll make y'all some lemonade."

Joseph thought how her hair was the same color of the hay he'd been working, only thick and wavy. It framed her face like a halo, making the pools of her green eyes appear deep and mysterious. She was like the farm itself, natural and fresh, yet she seemed a bit fragile too, different from anyone Joseph had ever met. No one in his family looked or acted like her. They were all aggressive, thick-bodied, and emotional, wore their passions out in the open, talked expressively with their hands, and suddenly, he didn't want to leave the house. He sat down on the edge of the tub and began rubbing his eyes.

"So, Joey, other than this bout of hay fever, you having fun so far?"

"Well, it's my first time being on a farm, but I like it." Joseph didn't know what else to say. "You like living on a farm?"

"Me? I love livin' on a farm. Lived on one most a ma life. Except," and she hesitated, "a few years in Loullville, Kentucky. The farm I grew up on was near Fort Knox, the army base there. My father's, and now Murphy's. He's no farmer though. He just knew the life was good for me. That being around animals, especially horses, made me happy."

"I've never been around cows or pigs before. I did ride a pony once at the state fair."

"They're all pets to me. Evenings, I go outside and listen to the sounds the horses make prancin' about in the field, the pigs snortin' at each other, wallowin' in mud for a night's sleep, the cows lowin'. Step outside tonight. You'll see what I mean. You can even hear the frogs croakin' in the pond all the way up here, if you listen closely."

"You sure got a lot of frogs in that pond."

"Wait till you hear them tonight under a full moon. They're magical creatures. If you see a frog sittin' out in the moonlight, make a wish." She smiled like a young girl, then chuckled to herself. "You just might get it. So, feelin' betta?"

"Yes, ma'am, I think so. Guess I should get back with the others."

But he really didn't want to go. He loved seeing her smile. And the way she rubbed her hands together with lavender lotion, the scent, he just wanted to stay in it and hear her talk.

"Those pills'll keep working for ya till ta-morrow. Then we'll give you a couple more."

"Thanks, Mrs. Murphy."

"Now really, I wish you boys would call me Bonnie." She sounded as if she were slightly annoyed being treated like a grownup married woman.

Walking together down the stairs and through the kitchen, Joseph hesitated at the screen door, turned, and stammered, "Mrs.— I mean, Bonnie, are you serving chitlins for dinner?"

Bonnie laughed. Then she stepped close to Joseph and put her hand on his shoulder. It came with the scent of lavender. "Joey, old man Murphy's pulling your leg. Don't pay him any mind. I've meatloaf in the oven, with mash potatoes and gravy. And an apple pie for dessert. How's that suit ya?"

"Sounds great," he returned enthusiastically, with a big smile. "Well, thanks again." Then he turned and went out, heading for the barn.

Yet, with each step Joseph began to burn inside. There was Kyle, ready to start in on him. He always found ways to belittle him about his height, the color of his skin, always making him feel less than. He saw Preston over at the pig pen, thought again about him and Margaret hanging out. Then he thought of the beads of sweat on Bonnie's breasts, just below the gold cross.

At dinner, most of the boys complained about how tired they were, how they'd never worked so hard in their lives, calculated to convince Coach they should just play basketball tomorrow. Looking at Bonnie out of the corner of his eye, Joseph said he loved doing farm work. Preston smiled patiently. Kyle glared. When dinner was finished, Murphy suggested everyone shower and watch TV. "On a farm, we go to bed early, boys. Reveille is at 0500 hours." Rumor had it Murphy had spent several years in the army. "After a hardy breakfast, we've got a pasture fence to repair, the cows need to be brought in from the west field, feed the animals the hay you stacked, then stack more hay—lots of fun stuff." Murphy smiled. Everyone groaned.

Then Kyle spoke up. "Hey, Coach, would it be all right if we went down to the pond tonight? See if we can spot a frog?"

"Do what you want," he said. "But whatever it is, do it as a team. Be in bed by ten, okay. I've got a couple of flashlights."

The boys gathered together in the largest of the two bedrooms. Kyle blurted out, "Man, Mrs. Murphy is hot! What a set of tits. How old do you think she is?"

"Younger than Coach," Frank responded. "Someone told me she was a homeless runaway at sixteen when he met her. She was hooked on some kind of pills or alcohol and stuff and was selling herself for drug money to guys stationed at Fort Knox."

"Well, I overheard my mother say to my dad that she doesn't think they're actually married," Byron said.

"Damn, I wonder what she'd be like in the sack," Frank added.

Then Kyle said to Joseph with a sly smirk, "So, little Joey, what were you and Bonnie doin' inside so long?"

"She gave me some pills."

"Yeah. I wonder what kind." He added, "Hell, you wouldn't know what to do with her if she tore open her blouse and stuck your face in her boobs."

"Keep your voices down," Carothers whispered. Joey turned red.

"Kyle, yer so full of shit," Preston said, as he sat down and lay back on the bed.

"Sorry if you farm boys are a little slow on the trigger," Karl shot back.

Preston just looked back at him with a passive expression. But Joseph felt like jumping on Kyle and tearing his face off. Then, Carothers broke in, "So, we going on a frog hunt or what?"

"I think we should ask Coach about that first," Joseph said firmly.

"Are you kidding?" Kyle said. "They're only frogs. You ask Coach every time you smash a fly? What a wimp. Anyway, he won't hear us. The gun doesn't make that much noise."

"Yeah, he'll be too busy stroking Bonnie's tits behind their closed door. I know I would," Frank said.

Then Preston sat up. "Kyle, let's say you manage to pop a frog with that toy of yers. You gonna eat it?"

"What? Hell no," he shot back. "It's a fucking toad. Would you eat it?"

"Of course I would, if I shot it. Frog legs, buddy. What other reason would I have to kill it? Look, I got no problem shooting animals. I do it all the time. My dad and I shoot pheasant and duck when they're in season. Had to shoot one of my own cows once. But then the meat was on the table. You guys go on ahead. I think I'll stay and watch TV."

"Wait," Carothers cut in. "Nobody has to shoot anything if they don't want. But you heard Coach. We got to go as a team."

"Whatever," Preston said, shrugging his shoulders as he lay back down. "Ain't shootin' no frogs though."

"So, what about you, Joey?" Kyle asked.

Joseph hesitated. It bothered him doing something the coach might disapprove of. Besides, these were Bonnie's magical frogs she loved so much. But he wanted as much to be a part of the group. Accepted. Included.

"Sure, why not," he said. "But you heard Coach. It's late, and he wants us to get to sleep early."

"So, little Joey, is it past your bedtime?" Kyle mocked.

"Shut up, Kyle!" Joseph shot back with such built-up aggression the room froze for a second. Kyle flinched, a bit surprised by Joseph's response, then leaned forward as if to retaliate, but Preston sat up between them.

"Joey's right," he said, staring hard at Kyle. "Coach wants us in bed by ten."

"Okay," Carothers jumped in. "We're agreed then. We won't stay out late. Just long enough to take a couple of shots each."

"Kyle, how you getting that rifle out of the house without Coach seeing it?" Preston asked.

"I'll carry it under my jacket."

"All right then," Carothers said. "Byron, you and Jordon go get the flashlights from coach."

With that, everyone plowed down the wooden stairs, out the door, and into the yard, the excitement of the hunt in the air. Most of the boys had never shot a gun before. It was as if someone were about to release a fox.

On the way to the pond, Preston walked with Joseph and asked, "So . . . you ever shoot a gun before?"

"At a carnival once."

"Well, I've seen the rifle. It's nothing like those guns. It's pretty high-powered. It'll have a kick. You don't pull a trigger, Joey, you press it, steady like so as not to jerk the barrel. Breathe slow and steady, then hold yer breath when you squeeze the trigger. And make sure you take the slack out of the trigger first."

"Okay," Joseph replied, hoping he could remember all that.

"The whole thing seems stupid to me," he added. "You all got one in hundred chance of hittin' a frog with that thing."

Joseph remained quiet as they walked toward the pond. He tried to ignore the loud, mysterious sound of croaking life teeming from the lake, growing louder as they approached the edge of the water. Like most boys, he was curious to know what shooting a real gun at an animal might be like. He felt the night air warm against his neck. Over the pond, the moon appeared through the trees making the water glow, as the bellowing of the frogs, the cacophonous croaking without cessation, seemed to grow louder—as if they were forewarned of the boys' intention.

But Joseph didn't want to think about the life in the water. "It's only a frog for Christ's sake," he kept telling himself. "I dissected one in the eighth grade." Then he looked over at Kyle, who was bragging about the number he was going to kill.

Kyle found a log and lay down like a soldier, positioned himself behind it as if the frogs might shoot back. Byron and Jordon shone the flashlights on the pond, like searchlights for a penitentiary escape. In the light, several frogs could be seen sitting on the bank, their throats bellowing, and Joseph thought to make a wish, but then quickly wiped it away. Resting the rifle on the log, Kyle took his first shot, but the frog didn't move. Checking to see if the rifle was working right, he cussed a bit. How could he miss so badly? He'd been practicing on birds in his backyard. He fired again with the same result.

Carothers grabbed the rifle. "We don't have a lot of time, Kyle. Let others have a shot."

He and Frank took a couple of shots each, and like Kyle, nothing was disturbed, although Frank's frog jumped back into the water from the ricochet. Byron and Jordon declined to shoot because they were enjoying their role as spotters. Then, it was Joseph's turn.

"So, you want a shot, Joey?" Carothers asked.

"We should prop him up on a pillow," Kyle smirked.

Joseph was too anxious and confused to even respond. He stood up and took the rifle into his hands, and using some instinct, handled it with skill. He surprised everyone when, instead of using the log, he remained standing, spread his legs, his feet evenly balanced, as he always made sure they were before rising off the court for his jumper. All the time he was thinking: how horrible it was—what he was wishing for. Byron's flashlight lit upon a large bull frog on a rock in the water. Joseph peered down the barrel, lined up the front blade in the center of the open notched rear sights, right in the center of the frog's bellowing chest. Joseph's hand was steady, his breath even, his chest expanding and contracting quietly, just as Preston advised. He took the slack out of the trigger, held his breath, and squeezed. Shouts rose instantly from his teammates. "Oh shit! Joey, you got one." "Damn, Joey."

"Jesus Christ," Kyle said, "the little fucker got one."

The boys ran to the edge of the pond to see the dead frog floating in the water. Joseph laid down the rifle but didn't move from the spot.

"Dead-eye Joey," Preston said with a smile, leaning against a nearby tree. "Yer a natural. I'm bringing you hunting with me and Dad when we go out for ducks."

And for the first time, Joseph felt himself to be Joey, transformed, his teammates slapping him on the back, speaking to him with admiration—even Kyle. But then, when he finally walked to the other end of the pond and saw the dead frog floating terrible in death, while the croaking of hundreds of living frogs seemed to grow louder, more intense—a chant of mourning for their fallen comrade—something fell inside him. He smiled on the outside, but his heart was revolted by the sight. He wanted to get as far away as he could. To pretend it didn't happen. To breathe again, to feel something beside the darkness of the kill.

"You ought to fish it out and bury it, Joey," Preston said calmly, coming up behind him when the others had already started heading back to the house. "C'mon, I'll help you."

Without hesitation, Preston took his shoes off, rolled up his pants, and stepped into the water. He picked up the dead frog, its limp body hanging ugly from his fingers, and carried it to the bank. They found some sticks and dug a hole, then Joey buried the carcass, covered it with dirt and dead leaves. "That ought to do it," Preston said, putting his shoes back on. And seeing Joey's hanging face, he stood up and added, "It's all right. C'mon."

On the way to the house, Joey didn't say much, kicking stones in the road. Finally, he said, "Thanks, Preston. I didn't think I'd hit one, you know. Just a lucky shot I guess."

"Nah. That wasn't luck. Yer a shooter, Joey." Then he added lightheartedly, "Just make sure you hit your shots during the games."

That night, Joey, being the smallest, was assigned one of the cots. At eleven o'clock, he still lay awake, staring up at the ceiling, listening to the deep-breathing snore of Preston, who was sharing the double bed with Carothers. He couldn't close his eyes. Every time he did, the dead frog would appear before him, his limp legs, his long fingers spread out and tense in death, once able to jump, eat worms, swim about the pond. He imagined he heard the croaking of the frogs through the open window, the white curtains shifting lightly in the breeze, a sad violin. Then, he saw the frog clearly as if someone had dug it out of the ground and was dangling it in front of his face. Its big eyes suddenly opened and his throat began to bellow, making a loud croaking sound, as it stared straight into Joey's eyes, getting bigger and bigger . . .

"Hey, Joey, wake up," Preston said, shaking his shoulder. "Yer dreaming, buddy. Wake up."

"Oh. I . . . I must have fallen asleep?"

"Yeah. That's what we're supposed to do."

"Sorry."

"I hope yer not going to do that all night," he added, as he crawled back into bed, still half asleep.

But Joey couldn't fall back asleep. He kept whispering to himself, "I hit it. I hit the damn thing."

Hearing Preston snoring through his mouth again, he thought of him and lusty Margaret, what they must sound like hanging out, then imagined the soft breast of the dead frog he touched, just before covering it with dirt and leaves, and he felt no interest in any of that anymore. Only Bonnie's holy-card face and delicate hands remained before him, her lavender fragrance deep in his senses— the scent that would remain for him the everlasting fragrance of tenderness and mercy—when the sound of the frogs carried him off to sleep.

ABOUT APPLES
MARGARITE LANDRY

IT SEEMED TO HER ON THE DRIVE TO NEW JERSEY THAT SHE
had done this trip to her father's so many times and so thanklessly,
that she'd be spending the entire day sorting his stubborn laundry
or vacuuming his house. And he'd stand by and insist there was
nothing wrong with his heart or his housekeeping. Yes, today would
be like the others, and send her into a death spiral of self-loathing
and doubt.

The fifteen-year-old Toyota (left over from her marriage)
(spoils of war not entirely worth it) crawled over the George
Washington Bridge in a lane of Saturday drivers on errands like
herself, their GPSs bright on their dashboards.

He'd said on the phone he didn't need housekeeping, but he was
glad of the company. She supposed she needed company herself.

Getting a divorce was not her favorite thing, she reflected, as
she recalled the most recent phone call from her attorney (quarter
of a billable hour) telling her the paperwork still hadn't come back
because her ex hadn't gotten around to signing.

She sighed and turned up the radio, hoping *Wait, Wait, Don't
Tell Me* would provide sufficient distraction to forget both the
money and the disappointment the last few years had brought,
almost like punishment for having Peter, her ex, turn out to be
sleeping with his admin, who'd accused him of sexual harassment
when he'd broken it off.

The world was full of surprises.

Only she, Celia, a marketing slog for a large and only somewhat
morally ambiguous corporation (they made soap with ingredients

that killed coral, but sent their hygiene products to conflict-riven refugee areas), now knew the sting of infidelity, which had come as a surprise.

But she missed his good cheer. Now she dated new men who sat across from her at the restaurant table and prattled about their ex-wives and their children. Or else she'd be waking up with an unfamiliar body in her bed, or their place, wondering what strange universe she'd landed in. Altogether it was wearing her down.

You needed a partner, but the possibilities seemed clownlike and unfamiliar, as if aliens had taken over her love life.

SHE ARRIVED AT the outskirts of Leonia where some of the maples were already turning, a reminder that seasonal affective disorder was on its way. The residential streets were manicured, calendar-photo-like in their landscaping, the houses that spoke of peace within, affluence, expensive cars.

She found her father in his backyard, perched on a huge ancient wooden stepladder that would make his cardiologist faint.

Celia did not even chastise him; they'd been through this before. Since her mother died her father had been on a gleeful mission to defy his own mortality, viz., hence, stepladder, poorly lit cellar stairs, his driving in general, and continuing to chain-smoke despite everyone's giving him handouts from the American Lung Association.

He defied death, he believed, picking his apples seven feet off the ground, and dropping them carefully into a plastic bag from Target.

"You're at it again," she said.

"Don't begin nagging me, Celia, this is one of my few pleasures in life."

She threw up her hands in dismay and wondered how long until he fell off the ladder. "I'm thinking we can go for lunch," she said.

"I can cook something for you."

She demurred, recalling the last time she agreed to that the bread in the sandwich had green mold on it.

Is this the end of life? she wondered, eating moldy bread and not being able to taste the difference? It had, in truth, looked like a normal sandwich.

She set down her tote bag and held the bottom of the stepladder and he glared at her.

Suddenly there was a massive cracking sound and the huge limb on the opposite side of the tree, heavily laden with red apples, swooped down toward the ground on one end, leaving an open crotch of raw wood amid the break on the other side of the tree. She could see the soft, pale fibers newly exposed.

"Don't stand there under that," her father said in dismay. "Goddamn drought." He climbed down the ladder and inspected it beside her. "I was afraid of this. Too many apples. You see that?" He gestured at the ponderous clusters of ripe apples now leaning toward the ground like ornaments on a holiday tree. "You have to help me."

He directed her toward three plastic wastebaskets set on the back porch, marked RECYCLING with circles of arrows showing that nothing is ever lost, if you just tossed your water bottles in the blue bin.

Ten minutes later they were both picking apples and setting them carefully into the recycling bins. Clearly this was going to be a big job.

THE INSIDE OF the house is quieter since her mother passed, and she likes it better. Horrible to say, and impossible to admit to anybody, her mother's constant unhappiness seemed to have come with a will to criticize Celia that never lost its determination. Shoes wrong in childhood. Sit up straight. Your brother's doing so well. Never mind marrying Peter, who had, for all his faults, sided with Celia after most family gatherings here, when Celia would leave the house and get into the car to drive back to Manhattan feeling she'd somehow become a less worthy person.

Even the photo on the piano of her mother's tight smile makes her heart beat a little faster, as if to protect her from her own inadequacies.

Oh, how do we come to be born with these difficult people? Celia looks at herself in the bathroom mirror. She wipes some eyeliner from under her eyes with her fingertips and washes her hands.

They will make lunch now, and it will be dried-out baloney with curled edges, and cheap mayo she can't abide. But no, on the kitchen table he's put a pile of apples and a cutting board and he's paring the skins off and whistling.

"What are you making?"

"Old recipe your grandmother used to make," he says.

"The crisp?" She goes to the fridge and actually finds a new package of supermarket generic butter and sets it on the kitchen table. The refrigerator contains very moldy food indeed. "I thought I'd vacuum," she says.

"Not today, Celia. It's not that dirty this time."

What is he smoking? she wonders. He thrusts a bowl at her.

"I've got sugar in that cabinet over there." He nods his head toward it. When she opens it there are some mouse turds, but the package isn't chewed, so she brings it back to him.

"You need an exterminator for the mice."

"I've taken care of it. I've got Havahart traps in the cellar. Then I drive them to the park behind the high school and I let them out. You have to do it in the dark."

"Because it's illegal?"

"It's not illegal, it's just the neighbors don't like it. Some predator eats them anyway. They have no defenses in the wild."

"Your hands are clean," Celia says, thinking they've gotten their unappetizing discussion for the visit over early. Last time it was the upstairs bathroom shower drain being clogged, and he'd showed her the gizmo he'd bought to fix it.

Okay, he was living alone; the body functions seemed to have become more acceptable after an older person lived alone. A higher threshold for belching, for instance, and not caring about it. A widower, which he was, she was being uncharitable, no question.

"I DIDN'T KNOW this was Ma's recipe," she said.

"She never made it. I often asked her to make it. My mother used to make it. Your mother never made it."

Celia mashed the butter sticks with a fork until they were as soft as he told her was correct. She poured the sugar in and cut it with the two knives. She was almost doing it right, he said, but not exactly. The knives were the wrong kind.

"Did she show you how to do that?" he asked.

"I have been known to bake on my own," Celia said, thinking she should have had children. Maybe she could still have children. A baby. She probably wouldn't be a harsh parent, she thought. Not critical at all, really. Probably spoil the child rotten.

That is my mother's voice, she thought suddenly. Spoil the child rotten. I don't think like that. I will never have that thought about my child.

Her father was lighting the gas oven, and she waited uneasily for the explosion. He said the pilot light had stopped working, because he'd managed to turn it off, six months ago, to save gas.

"It's a scam of the gas company," he said. "I read it in the *Times*. They don't mind if you turn it off."

"They said that in the *New York Times*?"

"I can't remember when. Why are you doubting me?"

"I'm not doubting you. I'm just wondering."

"That's the same as doubting me. I told you people don't mind."

"I'm not going to argue."

"Good," he said.

The peeled apple slices were turning rust colored in their stack in the middle of the table. She bumped elbows companionably with her father while they finished the dish (Pyrex bowl with remnants of previous dish still in corners). (How could he live like this?)

He brushed his hands together in satisfaction.

"I've got to build a brace for that tree," he said.

"What if you use the stepladder?"

They sat on the back steps, watching the broken tree in the sunshine.

"I brought you some food," she said.

"What are you, Meals on Wheels? I don't need food. I go grocery shopping."

She made a face. You're welcome, goddammit, she thought. He'd never be grateful, it was too much to expect. The patriarch never says thank you. The patriarch will explain to you you've spent too fucking much on it, and you're stupid. She sighed.

Her father lit a cigarette and put the match in a tin can, a system he'd maintained since her childhood.

"You shouldn't smoke with high blood pressure."

"We were having such a good time, and now you bring this up."

"I do," she said. "Because you know I'm right."

The timer buzzed for the apple crisp, which was only slightly burnt, but hadn't she warned herself mentally that 400 was too high? And hadn't she decided not to say anything?

"CELIA," HE SAID after they ate, "I have family pictures for you. I'm cleaning up my file cabinets because I'm old."

"I live in an apartment, Dad. It's better if you keep them."

"Salvation Army," he said. "That's where they'll go. Someone will wonder who we are, and then throw them in a dumpster. This is what is going to happen."

"I told you to go to the doctor. What is it?"

"Maybe a bit of angina. I ran out of the pills."

"God, Dad, I'll just go to the pharmacy and get more. It's no trouble."

"Mortality," he said. "I don't like it."

She was overeating, third serving of apple crisp, but somehow it calmed her down to think she was ruining her diet.

"What about the photos?" he asked.

She shook her head.

"Your mother is in most of them. I suppose that's making you stubborn."

"I'm not stubborn."

He shrugged. "Dumpster. Too bad."

"All right, I'll take them. But I'll stick them in a closet."

"There are some of me."

"I'll keep those."

"I need to explain them to you," he said, rising and pushing back his chair.

"Not today, Dad. Maybe next time I come." Her voice sounded shrill even to herself.

He sat back down. A silence. Then he said, "Do you need money?"

"I have a job." The sunlight filled his kitchen, bleaching out the failures of housekeeping. The stack of washed Styrofoam containers earmarked for recycling. The dish sponge that should be sent to the Centers for Disease Control.

"You're not answering me, Ceel. Do you need a loan? A life scholarship."

I am waiting to get the exhaust on the car fixed, she thought, but I'm not going to tell him it's two grand.

"No, thanks," she said.

He was boiling water for coffee, which he made out of instant. "You don't want your mother's pictures," he said, still turned away from her.

"It doesn't really have a good vibe," she said.

The water boiled; the teaspoon clinked in the mugs when he stirred.

"I was the one who loved you," he said.

The instant coffee granules whirled around on the surface of the water in the mug, a whirlpool of bits that should have been real coffee, instead of this thing she would not ordinarily drink, and drank only to please him.

"I know it," she said, sipping, scalding her tongue.

"I'm putting the crisp in the refrigerator," he said.

It reminded her of Peter announcing what he was going to do. I'm going to brush my teeth now. I'm going to move this lamp so I can read.

Was that being married, where you had to announce everything except, I'm going to meet my admin now, and we're going to a conference room where we'll lock the door. Was that what it was like to live with somebody?

You couldn't really tell what was normal in a marriage, there were so many ways to do it.

"My shrink says I have low self-esteem," she said suddenly.

"I don't believe in it."

"Low self-esteem?"

"No. Shrinks. Too much whining. Look at you, why would you have low self-esteem? You have a job, and you look good. Men stare at you. I saw that when we went to the restaurant last time. Men look at you with interest."

"Marriage is different," she said.

"Tell me about it. You think your mother was easy to be married to? She was not a happy woman. A woman who is not happy makes a terrible wife."

"And mother."

"Of course. On the other hand, she was very intelligent. We thank God for small favors. I like that. Talking about Tchaikovsky so your head would spin around for the joy of it. She was smart. On the plus side, you've inherited her brains, Celia, that's a benefit."

"I'm ecstatic to know this."

"All right, be sarcastic. I thought it was a good thing. You were bright as a button."

"I never satisfied her."

He drained his coffee and set down the mug. "Correct. You never did."

"I don't suppose it was my job. My therapist says that. He said it wasn't my job."

"Why does he make it into a labor negotiation? Your job. Not your job. It just is."

"I hate my divorce."

HER FATHER, DISMAYED by the brink of the abyss to which she has brought the conversation, gets up, gathers her mug, and pours more hot water and instant coffee in it.

"This will cheer you up," he says.

"I don't think so, Daddy." It's only caffeine, the depressive's go-to drug, she wants to tell him. Totally suitable for a visit to Leonia, where people don't weep about divorces, if they're unfortunate enough to screw up and get one.

Maybe, to judge by the perfect lawns, they never get divorces. Too chaotic. Too inefficient, to divide the marital property. At least she can keep the car, which is in need of an exhaust system. That could be symbolic of some deeper failure between herself and Peter. Flunking inspection because of a failed carbon emissions test. My life.

* * *

FIFTEEN MINUTES LATER her father is dragging the wooden stepladder across the grass toward the apple tree, and she's afraid of him lifting the bough so it can rest on top of the ladder. It seems the tree has broken from being too fruitful, she thinks. Under the shady tree, her father smiles at her doubtfully.

"Come on now," he says. "I love you. One out of two ain't bad." He gives her a hug and thumps her back gently. She rests her head against his chest, home of his aging heart, and she thinks of all the complexities of love, its peaks and valleys and surprises. He keeps her there until she has had enough and is ready to break away and move on.

LATER SHE IS driving back to Manhattan with three plastic bags of apples in the backseat, rustling around in the wind from the open window. These gifts from her father, who had put them in her hands with the assurance he'd selected them carefully, both new-picked apples and drops, and couldn't she use them both, he'd asked her, both the bruised and the ones perfect from the tree. "Some are good for cooking," he'd said, "others you eat, of course, if you have any sense."

The George Washington Bridge looms distantly, and the on-ramp is fit to raise her blood pressure. The sun is beautiful on the river, and for a split second she sees it.

CURTAINWALL

B.N. WILLIAMS

The city loomed indescribably high,
Far higher than it ought to,
The dusty,
Sepia tones a contrast
To the clouds that clung, too heavy to support their weight.

They were wrong colored clouds, painted
Sickly tones of green and orange
That rained wrong colored rain onto the vacant streets below
Collecting
In wrong colored pools that gurgled unhappily
Rejecting the viscous silence.

The silence was shattered by the sound of the sky
Breaking
Coming down in russet shards of glass
That had nothing to crush
And no one to harm
In the overwhelming emptiness.

The shards fell end first
Planting themselves in the ground to emerge
From the wrong colored water
Ringing
With the voices of constellations.

They stood, gazing skyward
At the darkened space where centuries had passed
And they had watched,
Unheeded,
As the world below them was slowly strangled.

And they would mourn for millennia.

VESTIGES

MORELL E. MULLINS

THE BELL OVER THE STREET-SIDE DOOR JANGLED, INTERRUPTING daydreams about my sons and South Dakota. I leaned around the desk to peek into the waiting room.

The figure standing in the doorway reminded me of a mushroom's shadow. April sun glared behind him, and a cowboy hat perched on his head. He paused like a man uncertain about his goal. Then a shrug of his shoulders pulled him inside.

I stood up gradually, knees aching.

"In here," I called and edged to where he could see me.

He surveyed the waiting room, as if dimness, wooden chairs, and a vacant receptionist's desk might contaminate him. Coal-black sunglasses hid the upper part of his face. A dark suit bagged down from narrow shoulders.

He tilted his head toward the noise from outside. Behind the strip mall, the zik-sik of hand saws mixed with the pounding of hammers. A faint odor of lumber and sawdust seeped into the office. The old strip mall was a poor investment, but the corpse of the stock market was worse.

"My tenants make furniture," I explained. "The power's off, and they're using hand tools."

I expected him to turn around and leave. Instead, he waddled toward me. It wasn't a fat man's waddle. He was tall and narrow, shuffling from side to side like someone with a hidden deformity.

The window air conditioner behind my desk gargled back on, and the overhead light glowed. With the return of electricity, the power tools outside resumed their whine.

The man stopped at the doorway. He clutched a large manila envelope in his left hand.

"Mr. Lon Turpin?"

"That's me."

I stepped forward. His posture stiffened, and he leaned away. I figured he wanted me to keep my distance, so I didn't offer to shake hands. Pointing him to the padded chair across from my desk, I returned to my own spot, with the air conditioner cooling my back.

Moses, lying out of sight behind my desk, rumbled a low warning. The man stopped beside the chair, rigid. He should not have been able to hear the bloodhound over noise of the air conditioner, but I was sure he did. His thin lips tightened.

"Mr. Turpin, I am told you have expertise in a particular kind of missing persons case."

Another damned granny dumper. I waited for him to continue. Or walk out.

I'd drifted into investigations to buy dog food and pay the utilities. Maybe one day I'd get another stretch of genuine legal work, but I doubted it. For the past twenty years, nobody'd much used lawyers or courts. Meanwhile I kept paying bar dues and hoping.

"Several local nursing homes recommended you," the man finally said. "Our grandmother has dementia. She has been missing for four days."

"From what facility?"

"Some distance away. But we believe her destination to be in this geographical area."

"From what facility, and why would she be heading in the direction of Two Rivers?"

"She's missing from a facility in Pennock. A person matching her description was seen yesterday, in a rural area fifteen miles or so from Queen's Bayou, where she grew up. You know the place?"

I nodded.

"She frequently expressed a wish to go home."

Something familiar yet unfamiliar about his accent distracted me—like an extra *s* or two hidden among the syllables. He also hesitated between words, as if talking required a conscious effort. The voice itself reminded me of a retired cop I knew. He had taken a .22 hollow point in the throat.

"Pennock is sixty miles southeast of here," I said. "Mostly abandoned rice farms between here and there. It's a tough hike on foot, especially for an old woman."

"The onset of dementia occurred somewhat early. Physically, she is a strong and healthy individual. Quite able to traverse . . . rural terrain on foot."

Between the oversized sunglasses and ragged voice, I had trouble getting a feel for how much he was lying.

"Tell me the circumstances of her disappearance, and have you filed a missing person report?"

"She was gone between one a.m. and six a.m. Circumstances unknown."

"Four days ago," he repeated when I stared at him. "No one observed her leave. We wish to avoid filing a missing person report. The potential for family embarrassment is substantial, and we prefer to avoid complications."

"Do you have a picture of her? Information, age, so forth?"

The man approached my desk. Moses growled, audible this time. Usually the dog would have limped around the desk by now, wagging his tail and friendly.

The man dropped the manila folder on the desk and retreated, walking backwards. He snaked around the guest chair like a man with eyes in the back of his head.

"If you've talked to local nursing homes, you know what I need."

"Items of wearing apparel, preferably night gowns, underwear, something with a strong scent on it for your dog."

He reached into a coat pocket and pulled out a clear plastic bag containing soiled underwear. Only then did I notice he wore leather dress gloves. He stepped toward my desk again—slowly. I nodded at the chair, and he dropped the bag on it with a hiss of relief. He surprised me with a question.

"Do you carry a firearm?"

"Is your grandmother dangerous?"

I did not like the sound of this granny.

"No."

The denial popped out too quickly. I stared at him.

"I prefer that you not carry one," he added.

"Maybe you should find another investigator."

He quoted a fee. The amount was more than my total net for last year.

"She suffers from a form of dementia which makes her unpredictable. We would be more comfortable knowing that she would not be accidentally shot if she became upset."

"I would be more comfortable not getting killed by your granny if she got violent. She's not feeble if she can walk maybe fifty miles over deserted countryside in ninety-degree heat. I couldn't do it. She's tougher than I am. Anything else you should tell me? Like, a butcher knife is missing after she wandered off?"

"Nothing like that. It is very important to . . . the family that she be returned discreetly."

"Half the fee upfront. Preferably in gold, but cash will do. I don't take credit bits."

He reached inside his suit and pulled out a thick wallet. Gloved fingers tugged out a stack of hundreds. Moses growled when the man placed the money on the far edge of my desk. The bills had grit of some kind on them. They were dry, but wavy from having been wet in the past.

His sunglasses confronted me. A tiny patch of skin, the size of a fingernail, curled away from one cheek, like failing makeup. The skin underneath appeared to be rough. Pockmarked?

"I need your name and telephone number," I said.

"I will phone you to check on your progress."

"And if I find her before you call me? I need a name and phone number. I can't babysit a dementia patient while I'm waiting for you to call."

I picked up a cheap pen with a funeral home's advertising on it. He stiffened but gave me the information. Piers Jeffress. When I handed him one of my last cards, he shoved it into a suit pocket and shambled out of my office. I followed and watched him in the shimmering April heat. He bent to open the rear door of a large black sedan. The tinted windshield matched the black paint—and his sunglasses. A bulge in the hood showed that it had been modified to run on syn-gas.

He'd barely pulled away from the curb when Tammy, the contract mail carrier, arrived. I walked out to the modified golf cart. Her wide hips overflowed from the driver's seat. Packets of mail stuck out of a paper grocery bag leaning on the passenger side.

She nodded, jaws working as she chewed tobacco. Her hand reached toward me, and I pulled out a twenty.

"Long way out here," she said. "Looks like your gov'mint check come. Worth extra for trip way out here, seems to me."

She leaned over and spat brown slobber close to my sandals. Contractors could lose your mail easily. She knew it, and she knew I knew it. I could probably get her delivery contract terminated for taking extra money, but I might wind up with somebody worse. At least she came out here twice a week. Dependability nowadays was worth paying for.

I added a twenty, and she pulled a bundle of white and brown envelopes from the bag. I sorted through them quickly. The check from the Disability Administration was in the usual tan envelope— a subsidy for housing and being trustee for my developmentally impaired tenants.

Nobody in the remnants of the national government needed to know that Serafina, James, and some of the others were mis-classified. The feds diagnosed them as autistic, and I wasn't going to kick a gift horse in the ass. Besides, Serafina and the others were better off if I didn't call attention to them. As I told my law clients, back when I had law clients, "don't try to explain. It just confuses everybody. Leave bad enough alone."

IN THE OFFICE, I paged through the granny file, enjoying the air conditioning while it lasted. Granny's records were on expensive paper, with the facility's name at the top. The paper rattled when I turned the pages. Better quality than nursing homes generally used.

I looked for photographs of her and found one hopelessly blurred specimen. The medicals and legals for involuntary commitment were in order, which meant nothing. I personally knew more than one corrupt MD and enough hungry lawyers to fill a large courthouse. I couldn't rule out control of granny's money as a motive for her commitment, and for the family's failure to report her missing.

On the other hand, her biographical data confirmed why she was headed in this direction. She'd grown up in Queen's Bayou. Advanced dementia patients often returned to vestiges of childhood memories. Okay. The commitment might be legitimate.

Why didn't Jeffress—and others in the family—go look for her around Queen's Bayou themselves? Score another point for bona fide dementia. If they simply wanted to control her money, and knew where she was headed, they would keep the search strictly in the family. Besides, if they'd done their research, they also knew about Queen's Bayou. Decades ago, it was a low-density gated community. Now the population was squatters, meta-kristal cookers, and serious criminal fugitives. Many of them had outstanding warrants that no sensible deputy would serve.

Mr. Jeffress struck me as the subspecies of inbred gentry who avoided sweat or threat. Why do it yourself when you can hire inferiors to do it?

I'd need my shotgun, and Wade Sexton for backup. I hoped the telephones were working. A call to the sheriff's office too. I counted out some money. Three hundred for Wade, and one hundred apiece for a pair of deputies who would simply make themselves visible out there. Two hundred for Sheriff Greenwald to authorize the deputies. I wanted to give the impression that the family was well-off but not rich. No sense whetting anybody's greed or curiosity.

I put the rest of the client's cash in my office safe and went next door. Moses limped along, in perfect heel position.

As usual, Serafina sat at the rear of the showroom, behind a table covered by old computers and flickering lights. Also as usual, she stared toward the storefront with a faraway expression, watching things I'd never see.

Two children sprawled on the floor a few feet from her. They played silent games with lots of hand motions and mumbling. Serafina, by ways known only to herself, had created an AI system housed in the three-foot-wide array of computers on her table. It was one of the few AIs functioning in the county. After the most recent electro-mag pulse, it might be the only one. I addressed the AI.

"Nestor?"

"Yes, Mr. Turpin. I am operational," the AI responded.

I handed the government check to Serafina.

"Please scan this check for deposit. Then phone Wade Sexton. Then Sheriff Greenwald."

I plunked down two tens for the calls.

After scanning the check, Serafina noticed Moses and cooed. She asked him the usual questions and looked behind me with the usual faraway expression. Moses wagged all over and laid his slobbery chin on her knees.

"Moses. U come see Serafina? Poor Moses. U has three legs. What happened to u other leg?"

The lights faded out, leaving us in brown-shaded dimness. Serafina pressed her finger to a depression in one of the computers on her desk.

The computers resumed their glow. My own office, and the rest of the strip mall, remained dark. Hammering and hand-sawing resumed from out back.

"Nestor, while you are making the telephone connection to Wade Sexton, please display Queen's Bayou, and predict behavior from oral input. Subject sixty-year-old white female, suffering second degree neo-altheimic dementia, physically fit . . ."

Nestor hummed. Serafina drifted to the back door and opened it with a shove.

"Moses's here!" She looked up toward the sky when she spoke.

The hammering stopped. James ambled into the office, sawdust caked on sweaty coveralls.

"Give treats?" he asked me.

"One from each of you." I held up one finger.

"Phone connections not yet established," Nestor interrupted. "Task of display and prediction completed," the AI added.

The printer clicked. Sheet after sheet of discount store paper whispered out onto the floor.

"James," I said, as I started picking up paper.

"Sir."

I spoke slowly for him.

"Please fix . . . paper tray . . . on printer."

"I can. Fix anything."

"Yes, you can fix anything. Remember: fix the printer tray."

James turned toward the printer. A familiar expression hovered on his face, part questioning and part grimace, then solidified like marble. I'd seen him do this before. Staring at the machine, he figured out how to repair it.

WE TOOK WADE'S four-wheeler to Queen's Bayou. Moses and I, and a shotgun, squeezed into the rear storage space where Wade carried small cargoes, like marijuana.

He hopped off and helped me extract myself. My knees throbbed, and my calves twisted from a mild charley horse. I put Moses's harness on him and introduced him to granny's underwear.

"Used to be some really good fishing out here," Wade mused. "Now look at it. Not even swamp. Scrub land with a muddy trickle through it. They say the water table's about gone. Like somebody pulled the plug."

Shrubbery and ragged patches of grass occupied the depression once filled by water. An invisible past, and visible skeletons, surrounded us. Fragments of boats resembled gray bones dropped from the sky—a stern here, a bow there. The hardwoods still standing along the former shoreline bore few leaves. The pines grew stunted, crooked, and a yellow shade of green.

The remains of a dozen houses formed a rough circle around the old inlet. Some had burned down. Others had collapsed. As far as I could tell, somebody lived in the one directly across the way. Two dogs on chains slept near a shed to the right of the house. Rottweiler mixes, looked like.

The patrol car pulled up, gravel popping. Doors opened, and the deputies got out. Both of them carried shotguns.

"Morning, Robert," I called. "Morning, Elvis."

The deputies strolled up, and I gave each of them a plain white envelope. They were gaunt, underfed men. Fat police were mostly a thing of the past. Robert Carter was pale, with an Adam's apple that wouldn't stay still. Elvis Moreno's complexion was brown sugar.

"Find." I gave Moses one more sniff of granny's underwear and handed my shotgun to Wade. He locked it to the driver's seat on a chain and picked up his assault rifle. I started down the slight incline, toward the house of the sleeping dogs.

"I wouldn't go there, was I you," Elvis joked.

"Safe enough, with deputies in sight and Wade at my back."

"Wouldn't bet on it if they think you're the law."

"Do we look like the law?"

"Yes, sir. You do look like law, even without me and Robert standing here. You look like the law."

I gave Moses the command to track silent. He headed toward the house, which seemed to be collapsing in slow motion. Nose to the ground, he tugged me toward the sagging porch. Granny had been here. This shouldn't take long. From the way Moses pulled toward the front door, she might be inside.

"Hello in the house!" I called, and glanced toward the two dogs. They were dead. Blood-soaked mud surrounded their bodies.

Without taking my eyes off the front door, I yelled for the deputies. "Better get over here, gentlemen. We got a possible crime scene."

I'd paid them to meet me out here and just stand by, but this was different. They were still cops.

Deputy Robert called into the house and tried the door. It swung open, and he darted in. Elvis ordered us to stay on the porch and followed Robert.

The house muffled the deputies' cursing.

"What is it?" I eased through the front door.

"Better stay outta here."

"You guys know me and Wade. Besides, Greenwald appointed us special deputies after he was elected."

"Don't touch anything," Elvis ordered.

I drifted into the living room.

To my left it looked like somebody had sprayed gore, bone, and brains halfway up the wall. On the floor, a roughly circular patch of blood was soaking into the faded carpet. Somebody had gotten in the way of a shotgun blast, or been doing oral surgery with explosives.

More blood had spattered in streaks on the floor and couch, starting two feet from the patch on the carpet. Moses tugged toward the visible kitchen and back door. I held him while the deputies checked the house for occupants.

"Maybe you better leave, Mr. Turpin," Elvis said. "Whoever did this probably still around. We're calling for backup."

"Moses can help. He's on the old lady's scent. I figure somebody has taken her body out of here."

"This is an active crime scene."

"He'll make your job easier. I've been shot at before. So has Wade. And we're special deputies."

"So you told us."

We waited. When another pair of deputies arrived, Moses surged out the back door, still in silent mode. He lunged up a low hill as fast as a three-legged hound could go, which kept us at a rapid trot. His nose stayed near splotches of maroon on the rocky dirt. Near the crest of the hill, Moses stopped, and we froze at the sounds from the other side of the rise.

Shovels chipped rocky dirt. Men mumbled indistinct words. The other two deputies circled around. After a few stretched-out minutes, Elvis and Robert went over the hill in a rush. Cursing, orders to stop, and the sounds of running followed.

Wade and I topped the hill and walked down to the bodies, a pair of them. They lay beside a half-dug shallow grave, wide enough for both. The old woman's dirty, blood-soaked nightgown once upon a time had reached her ankles. With her head swathed in bloody bath towels I couldn't see whatever remained of her face. One bony hand reached out, as if beckoning. Her deformed fingernails reminded me of claws. The other corpse was a man with his neck bones visible through a ragged set of lacerations and sun-drying blood.

The deputies returned from their half-hearted pursuit. Out here, disengagement was a good idea. Too many residents were kristal cookers addicted to their own product, or violent people who would kill, rather than go back to prison.

"Was only two of them, so not likely to come back anytime soon," Elvis said.

We walked back up the dwarfish hill. It was better to be on what little high ground there was.

THE MEDICAL EXAMINER arrived a sweat-soaked hour later with a couple of techs. He and I knew each other from kinder times. He had been a junior assistant ME, and I had been on the local prosecutor's staff.

I explained what I was doing out here. He knelt by the woman's body, touching her hand before he lifted part of a towel. He looked up at me.

"Going to call your client?"

"Sure."

"Can you wait until I get her to the lab and do a prelim?"

His voice wavered, maybe from overwork. Last I heard, the county cut his funding and eliminated his assistant MEs.

"The family expects me to call," I said.

"I need to check some things. Give me the family's phone number. I'll handle it."

"Okay."

I'd never get the other half of my fee anyway. I followed Wade back to his four-wheeler.

AFTER NIGHTFALL, I walked Moses outside around the strip mall. The bushes rustled from three different locations. Moses growled, and I hurried him back in. I sat in my office, everything on hold, like when a friend has died and you're waiting for word on the funeral arrangements.

Serafina or James banged on the wall from next door, summoning me. When I arrived, Serafina touched the computer and went back to bed.

"You have a call from the medical examiner," said the AI.

"Lon?"

"Yes."

"I need to ask you some questions."

"Sure, but I never saw the old lady when she was alive."

"Not important. I've seen her. Describe your client."

The ME's voice shook. The telephone land line hissed. In the background, some lab device or other clicked.

"He was tall, maybe six foot. Thin, wearing a black suit a couple sizes too large for him. Sunglasses, a big cowboy hat."

"What else?"

My mouth turned dry.

"He wore leather dress gloves. He also seemed to be wearing makeup. A bit of it peeled off a cheek. What's going on?"

The ME didn't answer.

"Have you called Mr. Jeffress yet?" I asked.

"No, and I do not want you to call him either."

"Why not?"

"How secure is your line?"

"About as good as any nowadays."

"I'm going to call some people in National Security."

"Why?" I asked.

"You don't want to know."

"'Want' doesn't count. I saw her hands out there, and a guy with his throat ripped out. And two dead guard dogs, with their throats in the same condition. I need to know what's going on."

"She's the strangest corpse I've opened in thirty years."

"Tell me more."

"The organs are different, especially the reproductive organs. Looks like they were for laying eggs, like a bird. And the skin. The skin is vestigial scales. Do you understand? Not really skin. I'll let you know when I hear from the—"

The line went dead, not unusual during the day, but this was night.

"Nestor, please call him back."

A few minutes later, the AI spoke. "The line is unconnected. My scanner informs me of reports on police radios regarding an explosion. County office building."

"Keep me informed, Nestor. And please call Wade Sexton when you can get a line."

I didn't want to overreact, but I remembered earlier, when I was walking Moses outside. Hopefully, Wade wasn't stoned to the point of giggling.

Nestor turned on the main radio station for me. A reporter already was interviewing the mayor.

"We would have seen a lot of fatalities if the explosion happened during the day."

The medical examiner's body had been recovered.

I consulted Nestor, feeding him all the information I had, and requesting recommendations. His response began within three minutes. It pulled together everything in his database, including stuff I didn't know was there, or anywhere. His opening words confused me.

"Hypothesis: The tipping theories of dynamic ecological change and species fluidity propounded by Richard Helmich, Xuan Xian, and Sombat Singh suggest the possibility of rapidly emergent species derived from stocks of small populations."

"Explain the relevance of those theories," I requested, "and in plain English, please."

I suspected that I would not like the answer.

"Summary, with caveat: This is an oversimplified explanation. The Helmich-Xuan-Singh theories predict periods of extreme and rapid evolutionary change in periods of ecological stress. New species will diverge from current stocks within a short period. Some may possess higher-order intelligence."

Nestor continued his explanation. I clutched the edge of Serafina's desk. She and James were sound sleepers, but Nestor automatically spoke in low volume after bedtime. The more Nestor talked, the more the skin on my arms and neck tightened.

My client and his kind likely descended—71.9 percent probability, said Nestor—from bipedal reptiles in swamps, starting a million years ago. Fast-forward 970,000 years. Avoiding humans required more and more intelligence. Living in small, mobile groups, they provided the stuff of legends—like Scape Ore, Honey Island, and the Loveland Frog.

"Shall I provide annotations?"

"Please continue the summary, Nestor."

With human populations expanding into their tropical and subtropical swamps, the bipedal reptiles had faced extinction. Only the most intelligent survived. Their genetic pool became dangerously small.

Then pandemics decimated human populations. Environmental shifts wrecked human infrastructures. Electro-mag pulses crippled human technology.

Ecological vacuums resulted. The reptiles reproduced by laying eggs, so their numbers could have increased exponentially in five decades.

"Tonight's explosion, and the vehicle in which your client was a passenger, indicate a user level of technological sophistication on a parity with those of the United States circa 1950, roughly the level to which humans have regressed. The reptiles can survive temporarily, with some discomfort, in the arid conditions prevailing in this geographical area.

"The explosion also indicates a willingness to kill any human who is perceived as a threat. Your knowledge of their existence constitutes a threat."

I continued to listen. Under current climate conditions, their habitat could not spread above the 35th parallel, where winters could be fatal to most of them.

Nestor hypothesized the existence of other rapidly emergent species. Like the yeti and bigfoot. Legends and myths. In the oceans, cephalopods and cetaceans. At first I paid little attention. Then he mentioned certain humans currently misdiagnosed as high-functioning autistics. Of particular interest to Nestor: Individuals such as Serafina were capable of interfacing directly with advanced AIs.

"Something entirely new," I said.

"Not quite. The potential always has existed. The technology to create me is relatively recent. Based on available data, a few other bonded AI-human pairs share common developmental experiences and a future evolutionary path. Likewise, James and his line have interesting potential. The offspring of Serafina and James—"

"Please implement your recommendations for tonight," I said. "I need to talk to Wade Sexton."

"By the way, I appreciate your courtesy," Nestor replied. "You always intuited that I am sentient and treated me accordingly."

* * *

WADE ARRIVED AROUND two a.m., driving a twenty-foot truck, with the name of a local company fading on its sides. Deputy Elvis, in civilian clothes, rumbled behind on a motorcycle. He rode with assault rifles in scabbards rigged in front of each leg, and a guitar strapped to the top of the luggage carrier. He grinned at me.

"Wade called and told me," Elvis said. "Asked me to be outrider to South Dakota. I didn't need any convincing. I saw what was out at Queen's Bayou, Mr. Turpin. If there's more of them things, I don't want to stick around here."

"It's just a theory."

"Theories don't tear out people's throats and blow up county buildings. Wade said your computer figured the lizards don't like places that have real winter. I've been thinking about South Dakota anyway. Lotta boom towns up north hiring experienced law enforcement and security. Your sons up there could help me find a job. Down here we already had kristal cookers, addicts, and criminals with no respect for human life. Barely human to begin with. Now I find out we got some kind of monsters with lizard grannies that can kill folks bare handed. This ain't home no more."

"'This ain't home no more,'" I twisted out a smile. "Sounds like a country-western song."

"I might make up one on the way north," Elvis said.

Wade went into his old military instructor mode. James, Serafina, and the other strip mall tenants packed. Woodworking tools, computers, supplies, and personal belongings fit comfortably into the truck, leaving plenty of floor space for sleeping bags.

Moses cuddled between Serafina and James. The hound always liked going for rides, and this was going to be a long one. I pretended to address James and Serafina.

"Take care of him, you two."

Wade grunted his understanding. He wrapped the money belt, full of my cash and gold coins, around his waist before putting his shirt back on.

"Come with us, Lon," he said.

"I'll be on the road tomorrow."

"Driving what?"

"Whatever I can steal or buy. I kept some money out."

"Service stations few and far between. I think we got enough syn-gas in the extra tanks to get most of the way without stopping. Most likely you won't."

"I'll manage. Besides, maybe I can negotiate with them."

"Come with us. We'll be a hundred miles north of here before dawn. They ain't gonna follow us."

"I can't risk that. I told you what Nestor said about Serafina and the others. They have to be kept safe."

"I don't figure our future's that bad, Lon. Humans been around a long time."

"That's probably what the dinosaurs said. Look at the mess we've made, and without being hit by an asteroid. Get Serafina and the others to South Dakota. Look after them. Like you'd look after Adam and Eve when they were children. Compared to them, Nestor says, you and I are just apes who like to hear stories."

"That's not very flattering."

"No time for flattery. Besides, they're going to need us for a while. If nothing else—to pull the triggers. Nestor says they have an aversion to violence. Get them away from here."

"We'll need firepower to take care of those damned lizards," Wade persisted. "I'll be picking up Shawn Brown to ride shotgun with me in the truck. Come with us. I'm not comfortable around auties."

He still didn't understand. I tried to explain it again.

"Not all of them are autistic. Serafina, John, and a few of the others are something else. Besides, they all grow on you. They're better people than most."

Wade persisted. "What's to keep the lizards from attacking us on the road, with or without you staying behind? Not to mention human highway gangs. We may need that shotgun of yours."

"Nestor says I'm their priority. If I go with you, they'll follow. Nestor and I are betting they don't understand what he is, or how he interacts with Serafina and her children. Eighty percent probability. Also ninety percent probability that the reptiles have only a half-dozen individuals here locally. They figured to recover Granny, kill me, and go back to their home. Not enough of them to go after me and your bunch both. I may kill all of them, or enough to make the rest give up. Who knows, they may be willing to negotiate."

"Talking don't fit with anything we seen of them."

"The one this morning talked with me."

"Yeah, but negotiate?"

"Wade, they've had interaction with humans in the past. Somebody must have taught them how to speak our language. To survive this long, they have to be rational."

"If they've survived, it's not by trusting us. What's Nestor told you about the odds of them talking it over with you?"

"Fifteen percent or so."

"How much 'so'!"

"Plus or minus five percent."

Wade snorted.

"You better come with us."

"Worth trying to talk to them. You never know. Now finish loading up Nestor and his housing."

"If they're watching from the bushes, they'll figure something's up. If they're smart, they'll come after us too, so as to not take any chances. You should come with us."

"Like I told you—probably no more than half dozen of them here. I'm their priority because they're sure I know about them. They won't divide their forces. But keep alert."

"I'll stay with you."

"Take Serafina and the others to Eden."

"First time anybody ever called South Dakota Eden."

I SAT BEHIND my desk in near darkness. My right hand stroked the shotgun on the desk. A 9 mm with an eighteen-round clip was in my shoulder rig, extra clips on my belt. Shotgun shells with double-O sagged my shirt pockets. Flashlights and military surplus night goggles lay on the desk in front of me.

I watched the infrared monitors Nestor helped rig before we'd packed him away. Two forms edged toward the front door. The cameras picked up one out back. Scraping noises came from two sets of clawed feet on the roof. At least five of them total. Was there a number six out there? I wondered how good their night vision was.

ANGELS IN THE DARK

JANE SHOENFELD

I'll get in trouble if she finds me looking through her things.
I know what I want from her drawer.
All the way in the back, she has a pin cushion.

> I am outside hanging laundry and I see her through
> the bedroom window.
> She puts her small hand and forearm inside the armoire.
> It's a narrow drawer that I rarely open.
> She removes the antique cushion that I kept
> when Mother died.

The drawer makes a squeak when I pull it out to get
in the back where the red, shiny cushion is.
It has sections that are pulled together with a button in the center.
Each part looks like a slice of jelly candy.

> I see my daughter pull a needle or a pin out of the cushion, then
> push the whole thing back inside
> and shut the drawer. The pin cushion has plump sections
> like the segments of a blood orange.

I take the needle with the big hole in the top because
I want to hang it
in the closet in my bedroom. I heard about angels
dancing on the head of a pin.
I think there are angels in my closet. Everything in the closet is mine.
There's not a lot of dresses, but there's enough to wear to school.
There's a blue plastic raincoat and the heads of some dolls
that broke.
I put one of the doll's heads in the pocket of the raincoat.
It's hard to get the yellow string from my mother's
sewing box through the needle. I hang it from
a little gold hook in the dark part
of my closet. I wait for the dancing angels, but all I see is the needle
with the hole in it that looks like a tear.
(Even though my father said there was no such thing
as magic, I know there is.)
On Sunday when I wake up, I remember that it is angels on the
head of a pin,
not a needle,
so I have to go back into my mother's drawer
in the bedroom
she shares with my father.

> I see my daughter go back into the armoire again
> a few days later.
> This time she removes the entire pincushion and takes it
> in her room.

I take the whole pincushion. I push all the pins, except for one,
in as far as they go and hide it in my closet. I am inside my closet,
when my mother comes into the room looking for me.

My daughter is in her closet.
My ruby-rose pincushion is on the top shelf behind
a stuffed star that she stole from the Christmas tree.
I ask what she is doing and when she tells me that she wants
the angels in her closet to dance on the head of a pin, I tear up.
I can see she expects I will be angry with her as I often am
when she gets into my things. Instead I look at the pin knotted to
a thread
and say I can see that the angels are getting ready.

My mother sits down on my bed and
pats the spot next to her.
She puts her arm around my shoulder and
pulls me close.
I like the jewelry on her ears. The lamp with a neck like a goose
is on and it is shining on the jewelry
and I touch her earrings.

I remove one of my earrings and hand it to my daughter.
I tell her that she can get her ears pierced and have a pair of her
own earrings,
whatever color she wants.

She is holding me. I feel sleepy and I put my head in her lap.
I never put my head in her lap. She is skinny, too much like a pin.
I see the soft, grey flannel of her slacks and her
yellow fuzzy socks and
I feel her hand on my hair. I hear her breathing and in the back of
my eyes,
when I scrunch them shut, I see the angels dancing.

FIRE

FAITH SHEARIN

One week after you died all the fire alarms
in our apartment went off though there was

no fire; this was the middle of the night
and my siblings had come to stay; my brother ran

from room to room, his robe open, pulling noise
from the ceiling. Sometimes I dream

of the batteries falling, the exposed wires
like your veins. Just that morning

my sister had folded all your clothes into an armoire
in the living room and locked the door. Afterwards,

I went into the stairwell, ran my hands over the cold walls.
Remember that last spring we spent together

in our mountain cabin when your campfire
blossomed in the wind, its embers alive in our meadow?

By the time we called for help those flames
had nearly reached our door, the grass outside

like a pride of lions; we were spared that April but now
a new blaze has begun in the rafters of the afterlife:

smoke blowing over the bed where we once slept together.

SHOCK TREATMENT
MALCOLM R. CAMPBELL

THEY DROVE HIM WESTWARD AWAY FROM TALLAHASSEE'S safe hills, westward through the panhandle counties where King Cotton once reigned, westward through pine flatwoods where wiregrass and fire sustained the world, through Quincy where Coca-Cola money brought prosperity one hundred years ago, through Chattahoochee where a psychiatric hospital of some controversy and the Apalachicola River provided conflicting approaches of respite to the world's cares, through Marianna where both Florida's Caverns and the now-shuttered reform school were out of sight and out of mind, and thence straight on to the uninspiring Georgian plantation house where Mistress Harkness died of melancholia waiting for her husband to return from the Civil War.

During Reconstruction, the beautiful mahogany wainscot, delicate wallpaper, and priceless furniture were stripped away, allowing the spacious rooms to be broken up into small, confined spaces suitable for the insane. Locals called it the Cottondale Crazy House because it took in creatures judged too far gone for the then-called Florida State Hospital for the Insane at Chattahoochee and later, for youths judged too incorrigible to be reformed with leg irons and flogging at Marianna's Florida School for Boys.

When management saw more profit in the elderly, Harkness Asylum became Harkness Rest Home without the expense of changing the facility or the staff. The manager, Miss Sullivan, who grew up in Quincy, added a Coke machine, a new sign, and an elevator to carry nonambulatory residents to the second and third floors. In an early pamphlet, now out of print, the board of directors

216

said the facility was "The modern ice floe, a practical and reasonably humane solution to the disposition of the elderly."

When his children dropped him off, Miss Juliette Sullivan, MSW (according to her name tag), stepped outside through the entrance portico's delicately fluted columns and said, "Welcome, Mr. Warm." Her gray hair matched the gray of the stone walls but was less elegant.

They shook hands and she led him inside. As he struggled with an ancient Samsonite two-suiter, his son and daughter shouted, "We love you, Daddy," and drove away in his new Phyronic Blue Metallic X5 xDrive50i BMW. The car was all they needed to convince a judge Luke was mentally incompetent, spending the fortune they planned to inherit.

Miss Sullivan pointed out the warren of offices to the left of the front door. "You need an appointment to go in there. Fort Knox is easier to penetrate." She pointed to the dining room to the right of the front door. "You eat when we tell you to eat." She smiled and added, "Or you starve. God forgive me for saying it, but starvation is a disgusting sight."

"May I see my room?"

"Follow me."

The elevator raised them up to a second-floor hallway that belonged in a black and white crime film where people were killed in the middle of the night accompanied by voice-over narration that explained, "If you died here, you weren't anybody and nobody cared." There was no red blood on the faded carpet from those black and white days. Thieves or movers had crammed his worst bed, a dresser from the attic, and the lumpy easy chair from the garage into the whitewashed space. The Venetian blinds were dusty and askew, providing a slanted view of the scrub oak and saw palmettos that hid the highway and the rest home from each other.

"Decorate this room to suit your tastes if you have any," said Miss Sullivan.

"There's no place for my books," he said.

"Pity," she said.

She left the room without closing the door. No doubt, resistance was futile. He blew the dust off the blinds and wished he hadn't. The mass-produced, folk art "Home Sweet Home" painting on the wall was crooked. He left it that way.

"Howdy, neighbor."

A petite black lady clad in a pale pink dressing gown stood in the doorway with two glasses of iced tea and a smile that welcomed the world with an exuberance beyond Miss Sullivan's understanding.

"Hi, I'm Luke Warm."

"Is that a name or a condition?"

"Yes."

"I'm Lily White, your next-door neighbor. I make the best sweet tea in our prison."

"Sit, we'll celebrate our new friendship."

"Thank you. What are you in for?"

"Buying a new car with money my kids want."

"Old story," she said, handing him a glass so cold he feared frostbite. "My family got me committed because I forget stuff."

"What stuff?"

"I don't have a clue. I do remember nurse Ratched—that's what we call the Sullivan honky—telling me you got put in this room because your people don't like my people."

"My kids, who say they love me, don't know that my will stipulates that ninety percent of my estate is going to the Southern Poverty Law Center."

"Glory!"

"I used to be a lawyer in Tallahassee. When my wife died, I lost my heart. My colleagues actually called me heartless. I won a lot of cases being heartless. Where are you from?"

"I've been told my people once worked this property as slaves and got beaten," she said. "I've been told my daddy worked here when the Harkness people took in the insane and everybody got beaten or got shock treatments in that room at the end of the hall and forgot who they were. Got married and got beaten in between kids. He liked making kids but he had no finesse." She gave him a hard look that ruptured her smile. "You look more like a coach than a lawyer: stocky, those muscles, glory, and your hair cut so close I can hardly tell if its gray or blond. Did your wife, may she rest in peace, ever tell you if you had finesse?"

He smiled, thought back to the days when a Home Sweet Home sign on the wall meant something. Finesse wasn't a word Mary ever used so he didn't know if he had it. She did say, "You have tenderness inside you, Luke, on rare occasions."

"No, Mrs. White, she never spoke of finesse. She worked late at the high school. I guess that was a clue."

"A woman comes home early when her man's got finesse," said Lily. She tilted her head slightly, more east to west than south to north. "Did you hear that bell?"

"No."

"Dinner bell. If we're late, we get beaten or get a shot that makes old ladies like me feel dead."

"You better go on down to dinner, then," said Luke. "I'm going to sit here and settle in."

She stood and fetched away his empty iced tea glass and walked out into the hall. Then she turned around and leaned against the door jamb and said, rather like a first-grade teacher to a child, "Don't get too comfortable. You're in a gloomy wood, astray."

"Gone from the path direct," he replied.

"So, you know."

After darkness fell, he went to bed. He did not sleep. Life left him with too much unfinished business to sort out in a room with no place for books. The doctor who told the court he was incompetent, didn't tell him how long he had, said eccentricity had no proven time line for a prognosis. His children brought him to Harkness Rest Home because it was inexpensive and distance offered them, Samantha and Edgar, a viable excuse for not visiting. They had busy lives, places to go, people to see. A new Beamer in the driveway. The wine cellar was full. The yard service was paid in advance. His assets were sufficient to pay for his care. If his life were a noir film, somebody wearing old lace would give him arsenic and release him from this gloomy wood.

When the moon rose onto the partly cloudy sky, he saw her standing next to his bed in a ragged nightgown, Lily White, with her hair down like a shining waterfall.

"I'm tired of being alone," she said. "Let me slip in there with you."

When he pulled back the rough sheet and thin blanket, her nightgown dropped to the floor and she came into the bed and lay next to him, trembling in the crisp chill of the autumn night. Her breath was sweet in his face and her hands pulled him close into herself.

"You have finesse, Luke."

LILY WASN'T THERE in the morning. Moonlight had altered the room, leaving it more spacious. Luke showered, shaved, and dressed with fresh attention to detail and went downstairs in time for breakfast. He didn't see her in the hall or the dining room and ended up at a table with three men he hadn't met. They were talking about the shock treatment room at the end of the hall.

They introduced themselves when he sat down with a full plate of cold eggs, limp bacon, burnt biscuits, and lumpy grits. "Fred Bannerman, Clyde Wilcox, Jimmy Kouba, Lucas Warm," they said in turn, shook hands, and dipped their heads to each other as though they had once been part of the same army unit or chain gang.

"Lucas, you look more fit than most," said Fred. His hair was as white as the driven snow.

"Thank you."

"You're welcome to join us for a round of golf after breakfast," said Clyde. "It's great exercise and it'll give us a chance to fill you in on the house rules."

"I read the orientation booklet."

"Yeah, the official stuff. Don't cook in your room, don't crank up the volume on your TV in the middle of the night—the usual. I'm not talking about those." Clyde leaned over like he was going to share national secrets. "Traditional rules."

"I grew up with them," said Lucas.

"I'm sure you did," replied Clyde. "Keep them in mind. If you don't, Marty Baxter will pay you a visit. That's the last thing you want."

"Anyways," said Jimmy, "we were talking about the old electroshock therapy room at the end of the hall. It's still dangerous: don't go in there."

"What's inside?"

"Nobody knows—rusty lobotomy knives, broken-down brain burner machines, ghosts maybe." Clyde said. "Guys curious enough to look never come out."

"I quizzed that Sullivan dame about the room, and she told me it was a storage closet," said Jimmy while he dribbled coffee down the front of his old shirt. "'Storage for what?' I asked her. Right before my eyes she turned into Elsa Lanchester from *The Bride of Frankenstein* and brushed her tongue against my ear when she whispered, 'The dead.' I stuck my head in the shower for twenty minutes after that."

"I would have requested a spray bottle of Lysol," mumbled Fred.

"If I were running this place, I'd lock the door," said Luke.

"Think about it, Luke," said Fred, "losing residents cuts expenses."

That notion killed the hope he felt after the night with Lily. As though his thoughts could summon her, she appeared at the far side of the room and sat at a table for two with a soft-boiled egg and a glass of orange juice. When the men finished their breakfast and went off to play golf, Luke walked over to say hello.

"You must be the new guy," she said as he approached.

He laughed. "Like you don't know."

"Have we met already? I'm bad with names."

"Are you serious?"

"No, I'm White Lily, like the flower," she said, and reached out to shake hands.

Her hand was warm, but her expression was cold.

"Lucas Warm," he said.

"Welcome to the penultimate stop on life's journey," she said. "Enjoy your stay."

Dismissed, he turned away. She said she was committed because she forgot stuff, but dumb oaf that he was, Luke thought her short-term memory would include him. He should have played nine holes of golf. He should have done lots of things going way back to his childhood when his mother's maid, Francine Whitehill, brought her daughter Lillian to work and they became best of friends in the garden and on the playground until they kissed each other at such a young age they had no idea what it meant, it was something they saw on TV, and when Francine caught them doing it, she flat quit and went to work for somebody else. How had he forgotten until this moment that day on the seesaw when he and Lillian smiled deeply at each other and vowed to be friends until they died—before fate drew them into separate lives? He didn't recognize her yesterday when she welcomed him with sweet tea. She didn't remember last night or yesterday and that truth was a fit subject for fiction, a story called "Shock Treatment" that would end badly. The hurt of "we love you, Daddy" was insignificant compared to "Have we met already? I'm bad with names."

He took the stairs to the second floor because exercise was good and he wasn't in a hurry to get there. Empty room, no books, no attraction there. The faded sign above the purported storage room said "Electroshock Therapy" nailed into the wall during the era when the procedure was often used as punishment. The two words didn't belong together and would have provided little hope to the sheep-to-the-slaughter. Somebody had carved the words "No Exit" into the heavy wood door with a knife. The words were quite legible in a style of penmanship the schools no longer taught.

He paused beside a utilitarian wood bench next to the door where patients once must have queued up to be shocked. At this point in his life, there was little left in the world that could shock him, so he reached for the doorknob.

"Don't fly away!"

Startled, he whirled around. "Oh, Lily, I thought I was alone."

"We're each alone here," she said weakly. She looked older and smaller than she did in her forgotten yesterday. "You'll be more alone if you go in this closet."

"What's in there?"

"Eternity."

"Death, you mean."

"Since nobody ever comes out, there must be a monster inside wearing a white attendant's uniform with a blue sticker that says 'Hi, my name is Miss Sullivan.' Most think it's a euthanasia program that takes our money and cremates the evidence."

"You're remembering a lot for a person who forgets things."

"I can't forget the closet because everyone talks about this room day and night."

"At the moment, eternity has more promise than Harkness Rest Home."

So small she was, still wearing her pink robe—malnourished in spite of the bad food. Her well-lined face and her gray hair held few hints of the child she once was. And how she pouted when her mother pulled her off the low end of the seesaw, sending Luke on the high end crashing down.

"Suicide is a sin," she whispered, "if that's what you're speaking of."

An old man with a walker came out of a room nearby, paid no attention to them, and shuffled toward the elevator.

"Baxter," she said. "Can't forget him because he takes things from people."

When he disappeared, Luke said, "Everything has been taken from me."

"Doesn't surprise me. I can't be sure, but I don't think I ever had anything except a bed and a toilet in my people's house."

"I'm sorry," he said. "Dignity is not for the old."

"Everyone at Harkness is white except me. Baxter reminds me daily that I'm Miss Sullivan's token African American, installed to facilitate government funding. So, I make my own dignity because I'm ignored. I keep myself clean. I make my bed. I walk in the yard. I'm a model prisoner."

"I'm not. I don't play well with authority figures. I prefer the quiet of my rose garden and the company of my books."

"I played in a rose garden when I was little," she said. Then she laughed. "But what do I know? I dream every night that I played in a rose garden. Perhaps I am dreaming now because I have forgotten your name. That's the way of dreams."

"Luke," he said.

"I don't know what we're talking about, Luke. I like it though. Nobody talks to the black lady in the old folks' home. If you walk through that door, I'll be alone again."

When she put her arms around him, he thought of last night. She wept. Baxter saw him drying her eyes with a white handkerchief.

He scowled, stood up straight like he used to be somebody, and pushed the walker toward them like a battering ram.

"What's going on here?" he asked.

"We're hugging," said Lily.

"Do you think I'm blind? I can see that."

"Okay," said Luke, "now that we've cleared that up, return to your room."

"You're new here?"

"Sure."

"I don't like your tone. My name is Baxter. Ask around. People will say I'm one you don't want to mess with."

He pushed the walker against Luke's knees. He pushed his eyes against Lily's body, like weapons.

"You came to us. You're the one doing the messing."

"We're getting off to a bad start," Baxter said.

"I wasn't looking for a start," said Luke.

Baxter pulled a steak knife from his back pocket. When Luke reached for his wrist, Baxter stepped back. "Lucky you, new guy, it's time for my meds. I'll give you a free pass this time because you don't know the house rules. Stay away from each other, and you'll live in peace. Elsewise, you'll wake up dead."

"Why now," snapped Lily. "I've been here for years and you haven't threatened me."

Baxter put the knife back in his pocket, sighed, crossed his arms, kept his eyes on her like she wasn't worth spit.

"Life's good when folks know where they belong, know their places, and don't question the wisdom that created those places." He glanced down the hallway and when he saw it was still empty, he whispered, "Up to now, none of the white boys here has shown any interest in you no matter how lonely they may be. They respected God's rules. Luke is an ill-mannered heathen, probably has a glossy photo of Satan in his wallet, and cares nothing for his heritage. He lost his mind last night when you went to his room."

"You don't know shit from Shinola," said Luke.

"You underestimate us," said Baxter. "We see everything that happens here."

"Just what are you accusing me of doing?" asked Lily.

Baxter laughed. "Unleashing your feminine wiles. Since white men cannot resist them, save those wiles for darkies."

"Is that still the way of the world outside, Luke?" asked Lily.

"Not in most places," he said.

"It's the way here," said Baxter. "Stay on the right side of God, and you won't be harmed. Transgress, and vengeance will be swift. I'll give you five minutes to say your goodbyes. Then one or both of you two will march his or her ass away from this bench."

"Thank you for letting us know," said Lily.

"My pleasure," said Baxter, even though his eyes, the animal's true male gaze, said otherwise.

He took his time walking back down the hall to his room.

"We'll never be safe now," said Luke when Baxter was gone.

"My fault," she said. "I am drawn to you because I think I knew you in the past."

"My mother owned that rose garden, Lillian Whitehead. It came to me earlier today like a dream that finally clears itself to the waking mind."

"That name, I don't remember," she said. She leaned against him. "I'm so cold. But happy."

"Happy?"

"The rose garden is real. Most things I think are real, aren't real."

"I want to hug you and keep you warm."

"You can't. Baxter's door's open. He's probably standing just inside following the second hand around the dial of his watch."

"I'll leave this place," said Luke. "You'll be safe then."

"They'll catch you." She laughed. "That's a guess. If I ever saw them catch anyone, I've forgotten it."

"Each day is fresh and new for you. I'm envious."

"Don't be. It's a curse not to know yourself, don't you realize that?"

"I know. Seriously, I know. When I was a kid with a friend named Lillian, I didn't know who I was. All I knew was sandlot baseball games, catching tadpoles in the creek, helping Mother in her garden, and taking that yellow bus to school bright and early every morning. Those were sweet days, but they didn't prepare me for the world."

"I'm an old lady, Luke. Praise the Lord, I remembered your name this time. I expect my momma taught me the world was all black and white with no tolerable gray. The old days weren't really as sweet as catching tadpoles in the creek. I expect Momma told me about men, too." She put her hands around his hands almost like they were praying. "Miss Sullivan told me my momma was a conjure woman. Warned me not to hex anyone. I reckon I don't know how. Did I hex you last night with my wiles?"

"Absolutely not. We were two lonely people abandoned on an ice floe. The good Lord blessed us with a moment of grace. I'm sure of that, Lily."

"If the good Lord had grace to spare, He'd allow us to grow older together. You'd remember for me. You'd tell me what happened yesterday. Oh, Luke, I think Baxter and his friends have chased the good Lord out of this place and now our time is up."

He pulled away from her clasped hands lest he hug her. "I'll leave tonight."

"No need," she said.

Lily opened the electroshock door and leapt across threshold like a frightened deer. The room swallowed most of the light from the hall. Luke wasn't prepared for such a palpable void, but if he had been prepared, he would have also expected banshee cries, the smell of death, and dust and old songs.

Before she vanished, she smiled shyly like the child he knew on the teeter-totter. He was too young and ignorant to follow her then. But today he was the eccentric king of the ice floe, a minor god outside the ken of Baxters, Sullivans, and kids saying "we love you, Daddy." Yes, he was in a state of grace. Before the electroshock door slammed shut, he followed Lily into the great freedom.

THE DETECTIVE

OLIVIA NALDER

I WAS SURE I HAD NEVER SEEN SUCH A LARGE MAN, A BARGE with a mustache. Or was he the iceberg? He certainly was cold. He was talking to me, asking me endless questions, but I didn't hear him. Was it truly all flesh that filled out his hulking form, or was it the layers of his uniform? And did detectives actually wear trench coats, as he did now? At least, I assumed, by association, that this must be a trench coat. Did he always don it, even on sweaty days like today, or did he somehow know of and humor my childish fascination with all things mysterious? Did he know my cat's name was Miss Marple and that I wanted to put a happy end to Sherlock Holmes's bachelorhood as soon as I was of age, just as he seemed to know everything else? My mind was surging with just as many questions as his.

He sat across from me in our very ordinary kitchen, something like wisdom beaming out from beneath his heavy lids and forested brows. I let my long hair fall in front of my own eyes, hoping maybe he would not observe just how scared I was. Though I am sure he heard my thrumming heartbeat and noticed my feet wrapped at impossible angles around the legs of our little green secretary chair.

Do detectives see the world as endless processions of evidence that continually need gathered and herded into patterns? Do they look for motives and lies lurking in every glance, where everyone else is content to see smiles and friends?

My mother may have been even more nervous than I was. I don't think I realized quite what it meant to wring one's hands until I spied her in the corner, clasping and unclasping her palms and rolling one over the other like she was making invisible little loaves of bread.

"Are you sure the nose was thin and small?" he asked evenly in a voice that matched his bulk.

No, I wasn't sure! I wasn't sure of anything. And the more questions he asked, the more unsure I became. I remembered a golden afternoon, a dusty country road, and the sweet smell of horses. My friend and I zigzagged slowly home and somehow found ourselves in the barrow pit alongside a pasture, basking in the shadows of two chestnut mares. Their fuzzy noses tickled the flats of our hands, and we couldn't contain our giggles. We each wanted a horse of our own more than beauty, or a suntan, or appliqued jeans, or anything else in the world. Her father had bought her a llama in lieu of an equine. But llamas spit and try to scrape their riders off on fences and leave horse-shaped holes in the hearts of little girls.

So, we stopped and stroked the necks of the beautiful beasts and tried to feed them milkweed, perhaps their least favorite food. But as the divine creatures they were, they obliged by wrapping their lips around each purple bloom before discreetly letting it fall to the ground. They nodded their regal heads at us periodically and we lowered our eyes in return. It was like having tea with the queen. We were in some kind of heaven, oblivious to the world. Then our reverie stopped short. My friend whipped her head around and dropped her milkweed. An older sedan had silently pulled up alongside us and cast a new shadow. A face stared out, smiling awkwardly. It was the face that a large, lumpy detective was now trying to replicate in his notebook.

Are all detectives such good artists? He had done a rapid but incredibly lifelike sketch of a perturbed-looking middle-aged man. Nothing particularly salient leapt out from the face on the page though, and as the questions continued, the man's visage blurred into that ubiquitously bland "Caucasian male of medium build and medium height and medium hair color," who seemed to commit crimes simultaneously all over America. I could make out a cloudy vision of the man's face when I closed my eyes, but how difficult it was to separate that vague whole into all its concrete and unique and requisite parts. High cheekbones, a bulbous nose, a low-set brow? What exactly even was a low-set brow? The features the detective rattled off in question form were all like pieces of numerous jigsaw puzzles mixed together, and I had no idea how to assemble the correct picture from the jumbled mess. The only distinguishing feature my mind clung to was a thick and ugly burgundy scar that shot down the center of the man's throat. But even that . . . a scar? How clichéd. How unlikely. Was my nine-year-old mind taking creative license with something as serious as an attempted kidnapping? I often feel that self-awareness is such a curse.

The detective switched from questions to transparent slides of countless facial features that he quickly slid on and off the basic sketch. "Did he have a mustache? A beard?" he queried, as three or four different shapes of facial hair whipped on and off the suspect's face with the flick of a wrist. "I— he did have a hairy face," I said, tentatively. "But short and scratchy. Not like any of those." He intuitively knew what I meant and confidently placed a slide of rough stubble over the man's chin and cheeks. The drawing instantly looked more like the face I remembered from a few afternoons prior. Or did it look more like the face my suggestive imagination had fabricated?

I squinted my eyes and tried to stretch my mind back to that dusty road. My friend got a closer look at the man than I did. She was pretty and confident, with that kind of heedless confidence that often goes with prettiness. When the driver of the car waved us over, she stepped up to the opposite window, still about ten feet back, while I stood expressionless and rigid, farther behind her. I let her do all the talking, as usual. Their conversation was muffled but I saw her back stiffen, and then she jumped a bit and grabbed my arm to hurry me along. "We need to go," she whispered urgently. And I felt in the pit of my stomach that she was right. We became skittish rabbits, the tremors and twitches in our muscles and eyes moving ten times faster than our leaden legs. The car followed slowly alongside us, the window still rolled down.

"Come on!" he shouted solicitously. "It's a long walk and you know you need a ride." We kept our faces averted as much as one can and still walk a straight line. We quickened our steps, taking longer strides but still did not run, as if invisibly bound to that code of politeness and decency that said not to leave while someone was talking to you. That is rude. Besides, where would we go? It would take too long to try to squeeze through the tightly strung barbed wire to our right, so we walked, trapped between the car and the fence. From that day on, if ever I walk alone, I always eye the wire on fences for barbs and try to decide if I could easily slip through, or if I need another route of escape.

A pencil dropped and brought me back to the kitchen. "Are you sure?" he asked.

Why did he keep saying that! Didn't he know how much of my life was ruled by uncertainty? Didn't he know that I was nine and insecure? Didn't he know that all someone had to do was suggest I wanted waffles too, or that I didn't actually want to wear that dress, and instantly, suggestion became my reality? I was sure of so little.

And as the precocious, bookish type of child I was—dubbed by all my friends "the philosopher"—I already knew the concepts of relativity and subjectivity and perspective and sifted all my thoughts and feelings through those holey metrics. Can one ever trust their own mind?

I read an article the other day about the fluid and shifting nature of memory, and how each time we recall a past event from the files of our brain, we shape it into the memory that best serves us at that current moment in time, and then refile it in its new form, the original and "true" memory lost forever. Memory is like history, then, continually rewritten by the victors.

"Concentrate," I scolded myself and rattled my brain back into focus. My stare homed in on a piece of fuzz stuck in the detective's massive mustache, which rivaled his bushy eyebrows. It wiggled and bounced as he opened a hidden mouth to speak again. "Are you sure?" he repeated. I simply nodded my head absentmindedly. I was tired. I think he knew that, this all-seeing eye of a man. He let out a sigh and slowly closed his notebook. "That's all for today then. Thank you," he stated in a voice that tried to sound cheerful and self-assured and like he had actually pulled useful "evidence" from my feeble recollections. The boulder stood up and shook my hand, a huge paw wrapped around thin, piano-player fingers. He glanced at my mother. "You will be notified of any developments."

We were never notified of any developments.

The days that followed the detective's visit were fraught with untethered emotion and faceless fears. My thoughts flitted around like nervous birds, not sure where to land. Part of me ached to hear our old rotary phone ring. I wanted the detective to say, "We have our man." I wanted to see my mother's shoulders relax in relief. I wanted her to let me outside again. I wanted to want to go outside again. I wanted my shapeless specter to materialize into something real and tangible, like a man. I wanted proof of the soundness of my sensitive mind. I wanted to be that reliable witness that Sherlock would have smiled at. But then, I also inexplicably didn't want them to find this person. I was tortured with some nameless unease or guilt or something. Is this the witness's curse? It was like there was now an invisible affiliation or allegiance to this man, knit simply through having had an interaction with him; some sort of due diligence I owed him, to tell his story correctly. I felt like I had to be fair. But how could I be, when he had not actually done anything other than offer, persistently, two young girls a ride, and all I had to base my accusations on was a feeling? That wasn't "fair." A crime almost-committed is so much harder to name and define than one with bruises and bodies and broken bones.

Afterward, when I couldn't sleep, I pondered how strange it is that the innocent mind unswervingly seeks to fit the actions of all mankind into the same box as our own motives or outlooks. It is stranger still how tirelessly a child tries to assign all humans humanity. This man's actions chilled me to my core on that hot afternoon and frightened me for years to come. But it all seemed so at odds with what I expected from a grown-up and fellow-man. I still can't decide if I should have dug deeper into my memory in search of the precise shape of his nose, or if I should have let him slip, ghostlike, into anonymity, as I did.

Months later, there was a call, but not from my detective. It was a news agency. In response to an uptick in local kidnappings, a journalist wanted to interview my friend and me for her piece on "awareness." I still couldn't bring myself to trust my words or my memories, so yet again, I let my friend do all the talking during the interview, while I stood a pace behind. As I stared at her back, my thoughts darted again to the past, to the roadside fence and then to my friend and me atop the sedge hill we finally fled to, fear pulsing through every vein and our chests heaving painfully. Our small ribcages bent over, in part to remain hidden, in part because we had no strength to stand erect, we frantically tried to make sense of what had just happened.

A few eternal moments earlier, as the sedan crept alongside us, we had glimpsed a break in the fence and spoke to each other in silence, as best friends do. At precisely the same instant, we both broke into a run for our lives, moving as one, our legs tearing out from under us. We were thinkers and dancers and readers, not runners. But terror is fuel. Every inch of my skinny body burned, but the fire seemed far away and inconsequential. So, we kept running without looking back. I veered to the left, up the root beer–colored hills that somehow seemed like an upper hand. Finally, our energy gave out and we slowed to a lope. But as soon as we turned our eyes downward, there was the sedan, parked by a barn, and the medium-everything man was out of his car, rabidly searching for movement.

My burning muscles turned into a tepid sickness that pooled in my joints and made everything feel heavy and slow. Neither of us could move. The man raised his hand to his temple, like a salute, and scanned the hills. Then his gaze stopped, in direct line with our hidden spot in the sage. I saw every feature in clear and terrifying relief. Everything snapped violently into sharp focus.

For days and years, before and after, I had contemplated this man and the accusations my gut had leveled against him. I held court with myself and debated all angles of my perspective. I struggled to put him to rest in the proper place within my mind. But he kept rearing his head, and each time, it looked at me as it did below the sage.

Gradually, it is no longer politeness, or fear, or philosophical speculation that guides my memory. Truth no longer seems theoretical, but visceral, and I feel the warm sickness in my stomach when I remember him. In that moment on the hill and every single moment it has revisited me over time, I know I was looking evil in the face. And when my hard-to-shake conscience doesn't muddy my perception, I see his high cheekbones, and low-brow, and purple scar, and I know he had a small, thin nose. I wish the detective would ask again.

SEVEN

LISA M. NOVAK

MAMI HUGGED ME WHEN THE G.I. JOE TOOK ME AWAY. WE spent five days walking to the river and when we crossed the G.I. Joes took us to the building and then we sat in a chair and they wrote stuff on papers. Mami told me don't be scared, she'll get me when she has the papers for America and then we'll go to Tia Yoli and Papi will be there and I'll get my Ninja Turtle bike. It's the one with Donatello on the handlebars and it looks real cool and I can't wait to ride it. Mami said it's for my birthday when I turn seven next month.

The G.I. Joes took me down a long hallway and they put me in a hot smelly cage with a bunch of other kids. I was pretty smelly too and I thought they were gonna make me wash but they didn't. It was a cage like I saw at the zoo when Mami took me, only it was a cage on the inside instead of on the outside. I wondered if this was a zoo with kids and the animals come and look at us. Some of the kids are just babies like Ramon. He must be real scared without his mami. He keeps crying and we all feel sorry for him.

THE G.I. JOES don't say nothing to us. They give us food and take us to the bathroom every day, but they don't say nothing to us or look at us. Even though I say Hi G.I. Joe they don't say nothing. Mami said I have to listen and do what they say and practice my English so I try but they don't say nothing to me.

RAMON GOT HIS first tooth today. He cried a lot and Hector said it was his tooth coming in that's why it hurts. Ramon keeps us all

234

awake crying and he's got so many more teeth to come in. Maybe they'll let us out of the zoo before more teeth come in. I remember how Mami was so happy when my sister got her first tooth. She chewed on everything, and Mami gave her a squishy toy to chew on and held her and rocked her. I didn't have no squishy toy but I picked up Ramon and held him for a little while, but he kept crying and crying and crying and nobody else wanted to hold him. So I put him down because I didn't want to hold him no more.

PEDRO SAID HIS mom is coming for him and taking him to New York. We think he's a liar because his shirt is all ripped up and he got no bag or nothing. He always rubs his eyes and his hair is in his eyes because it's too long.

JUAN TOOK HIS first step today. We all laughed as he wobbled and wobbled. Then he fell back and grabbed the cage with his fat little fingers, and laughed and laughed and laughed so much, that spit came out of his mouth. Then he got up and took some more steps and fell. He did this all morning and then we didn't think it was funny no more 'cause he was smelly 'cause he did a caca in his diaper and some of it got on his leg, and the G.I. Joes didn't give us no more diapers until dinner.

EFRAIN SAID TODAY is his birthday and he's five years old. I think it may be my birthday today but I'm not sure so I don't say nothing. When the G.I. Joes bring us food I save my cereal bar and give it to Efrain for his birthday. I hope it's not my birthday because I don't want to be in a cage for my birthday. There's no cake and no presents and no piñata and nobody sings "Feliz Cumpleanos" and my mami and my sister and my friends aren't here either.

JESUS LOST HIS first tooth today and I felt sorry because we don't get pillows for him to put the tooth under and get his gift. Also, the G.I. Joes don't let nobody come to the building, not even El Raton de los Dientes, so Jesus didn't get a gift for losing his tooth. When I lost my first tooth Mami said she was proud of me and no one said they were proud of Jesus.

* * *

I WAS MAD today. Carlos stepped on my hand when I was sleeping, even though I wasn't really sleeping, I was just tired. They leave the lights on so it's hard to sleep but Carlos could see my hand and didn't have to step on it. I yelled at him and called him a maricone even though I know I'm not supposed to use that word but my mami isn't here so I can curse. The G.I. Joes don't care if anyone curses. I'm mad because Mami said in America she'd get me my own bed that looks like a race car and I wouldn't have to sleep on the floor.

I HIT EFRAIN this morning because he did a caca and it stinks. He didn't ask us to help him sit on the toilet and if he asked we would have helped but he didn't and now it really smells. He started to cry and later on after they brought lunch, a G.I. Joe came and took him out of the cage.

TODAY WHEN THE G. I. Joes came they gave us all pudding cups. We were real happy because we didn't never have pudding here and they let us have two. Then they gave us towels and told us to clean our face. Then some men and ladies with glasses came and said Hi to us and wrote stuff on yellow papers. I'm not sure where Ramon is because I don't hear him crying. I think the G.I. Joes took him out of the cage before the ladies with the glasses came. I hope they didn't give him any pudding because he always makes caca and he always smells.

After the ladies with glasses left, Jose threw up and it looked like caca because it was brown. A G.I. Joe came and put some powder on it and we all tried to stay away from the pile but there was no room so we made Juan sit on the wet spot since he was the smallest. And he only cried a little, then went to sleep.

I got a stomachache so I went to where Juan was sleeping on the wet spot and threw up. It was brown like Jose's throw up. Some of it got on Juan's hair. He looked at me but didn't cry or anything. He doesn't try to walk no more. Nobody does nothing no more.

MY HEAD IS itchy and I don't want to scratch it no more because it hurts and I think I made it bleed.

* * *

THIS MORNING I tore my blanket up because it makes too much noise. It's like tinfoil they used to wrap food in. I tore Hector's blanket and he smacked me in the head. So I went to some of the smaller kids and tore their blankets and they didn't do nothing because I'm bigger than them.

I DON'T THINK my mom is proud of me no more because she left me and she said she loves me and she'd come back and she was proud of me because I was brave even though I cried when the G.I. Joes took me to the cage. I don't cry no more but I don't think she's proud because she didn't come back for me. And I curse now.

ONE DAY THE ladies came back with more paper and they asked us to draw pictures. We thought it was stupid but we did it anyway. I drew the cage and G.I. Joes and a big pile of caca. They asked what it was and I said it was a big pile of caca only I didn't say caca I said shit because Hector says shit all the time. And I like saying shit.

HECTOR SPIT AT the G.I. Joes today. They took him out of the cage and didn't bring him back. Maybe if I spit at them they'll take me out of the cage but I don't know where they'll take me. I'm scared it will be a really bad place and then my mom won't know where I am if she ever wants to come get me.

THEY BROUGHT RICARDO into the cage yesterday. He had on a Mutant Ninja T-shirt and it made me mad. I slapped him in the face because I was supposed to have my Donatello bike and I didn't like seeing him wearing the Mutant Ninja T-shirt. He cried and cried but I don't care because the G.I. Joes don't do nothing so I can hit anyone I want. Then I took his cereal bar.

THEY TOOK ME and Jose out of the cage today and drove us to another building. They took us into the bathroom and let us wash in the sink and gave us different clothes. We got white T-shirts and gray sweatpants. The G.I. Joes threw our old clothes in a big black garbage bag because they were ripped and smelly and had throw-up and shit on them. They put us on a bus with a bunch of other kids and drove us for hours to another place for kids. The kid behind me said they were taking him to his mom and Jose said shut up dumbass, they're not taking anyone to their mom. And I said yeah, shut up dumbass.

When we got to the building they put us all in a big room that had some baby toys and chairs and desks. Me and Jose sat in the corner with a few other kids. Some of the kids played with the toys. Then they brought us some food on a cardboard tray. It was a ham and cheese sandwich and some carrot sticks and grapes and a chocolate chip cookie. I said I wanted a cereal bar and so they brought us some cereal bars and I took three.

We don't know where we are, but we don't see any G.I. Joes here. And it don't smell. These people look like the ladies with the glasses that made us draw pictures and some of them look like doctors. They asked us a bunch of questions like what was our name and where we were from, and how old we were and if we knew where our parents were. I told them my name and that I was seven and that I don't know the answers for the other questions.

This building has lots of rooms and windows and beds with pillows, and they told us that we would each get our own bed. They asked what we wanted to do, if we wanted to do arts and crafts or play or watch cartoons. I asked if the bed had real blankets or the tinfoil blankets and they said real blankets and I asked do they turn the lights off at night and they said yes. They asked if I wanted to color or have some more food, but I told them I didn't want to play or to color or watch TV or have more food. I wanted to go to bed with a real blanket and a pillow and to turn the light off. I didn't want nothing else.

SUNDOWNING

AUDREY DIPLACIDO

The lion knows not what *is*.
he's grown resistant to the
smooth and familiar;
moves cautiously among those
in his colorless zone of comfort.

Sleep bullies him awake at night.
triggers risky behavior that links him
to danger; blurs the natural
need for social sustenance.

Withdrawal is a new best friend.
he lacks recognition of significant others
yet, still, she shows daily
to remind the lion of what *is*.

She shaves his beautiful face.
pulls an old T-shirt over thinning shoulders,
slides clumsy feet into worn running shoes to
cue up images of lionized athleticism.

She chats home, children, acquaintances.
keeps silent on wounding words
from clueless friends claiming
he's too young for what clinically *is*.

Music, she observed by chance,
adds recognition to vacant, green eyes.
an aide offers a bruised boom box
to stream fave songs forward.

She plays well-loved rhythms
almost manically most days.
she places a hand over his; closes her eyes
to inhale the melodies from their back story.

Lusty vocals dance her back to
a place when joy ruled.
she lets out a deep breath of love;
prays that in this moment
her lion feels what *is*.

THE SPIDER GOD

C. M. BROWN

ELEANOR KNOWS SHE SHOULD SELL THE HOUSE. HER conviction is strongest in the mornings, when her shaking hand lifts a mug of black coffee to her lips. The comforting bitterness just highlights how comforting and how bitter each room of her small slice of city has become. Every inch of her life bears Edmond's gentle fingerprints, from the empty placemat across from hers, to the worn bible still dutifully holding her husband's old reading glasses.

Though she isn't a young woman by any standard, Eleanor only became intimate with time when she started to lose Edmond. She has since learned that the terrible thing about time isn't its inevitable march forward, but how it lingers like cologne in the air. Some days the ghosts dancing in her hallways are the only things that keep her going. But it's a purgatory, too: a coffin smelling of dried roses.

She knows she should sell the house because now all she smells are those dried roses, all she sees are ghosts. She wakes each morning wrapped in a burial shroud of her own memories. But today, like every day, she doesn't hobble to the nearest realtor. She instead finishes her coffee, letting the warmth seep into her bones, and follows her own footsteps.

Her routine leads her out into the world with nothing but a light woolen jacket to protect her thin arms. The world that greets Eleanor is dull and winding; it is clay walls under a flat blue sky. Her knees ache as she shuffles through the sand scattered across cobblestone paths.

There is little in the way of passerby, but she is kept company by the modest statues that line the walkway. They age in stasis, their stone faces tilted to the sky. She sees herself in the erosion of their bodies caused by sunshine and warm rain. She sees Edmond in their empty eyes, staring ever skyward.

Her mind drifts with each rough step. Perhaps it is pointless to sell the house and banish her dancing ghosts, because they dwell in all the silences between her more productive thoughts. Like always, her mind is filled with him.

More than fifty years ago, she had rejected dear Edmond. Eleanor wasn't about to be silenced like her mother was silenced— by that slow suffocation that is marriage. Or at least not before she had finished college, before she had smelled the sweet Paris air and felt the vastness of the desert beneath the sun.

And Edmond, her patient husband, had waited for her. He had offered to take Eleanor to her orchards of crisp apples and terrible towers of dead men's labors. His hands had grown calluses with trenches gouged between them, but his eyes had grown wrinkles from the vivaciousness emanating from his smile. She was entranced.

When they were married, she felt like a foal walking on unsteady legs. He had laughed at her anxiety, her desperation to remember everything her mother had told her about how to run a proper household. About how to make a good wife to this man who had become her world.

"Silly wife," he had said, smiling indulgently down at her, "I would have married someone different if I did not love you as you are."

Now Eleanor takes the stairs with difficulty, each more painful than the last. She should sell the house because it is too far from her destination. She is old now, somehow, and this pilgrimage is likely to end badly one day. They have no children to help steady her when she sways.

Edmond had wanted children, and Eleanor, too, once she had realized her husband would include their children in their dreams instead of choosing one over the other. But it was not to be their blessing in this life. Over many years they had made peace with this, though she'd never managed to dispel the image of a young round face with Edmond's blinding smile.

But that face will only ever exist in her mind. She should not sell the house, because she has never been good at making friends. And when her purgatory ends, the ghosts in her hallway will be her only company.

Eleanor triumphantly makes it down the stairs to blessedly flat ground. Her destination slowly rises from the horizon like a mirage. The pockmarked building is starting to feel like home now, too, and it welcomes her like a fellow convict. It is a network of terracotta caverns nestled at the bottom of an hourglass, that hourglass that is too big for anyone to turn. Sand drips from holes in the terracotta, helpful care providers brushing it into piles along the walls.

Edmond's cavern is filled with paintings and photographs of the places they've been. Scrapbooks are piled on novels of philosophy and science, tomes that rarely failed to make Edmond's face light up though he couldn't remember why. She smuggles him in old-fashioned candy that tastes like root beer, and sometimes challenges him to find it amongst the books and neatly pressed shirts. He doesn't move much anymore, so she indulges his sweet tooth without the games.

The sand completely dominates his cavern now. There is nowhere to hide it anymore. It swirls around her husband like a wake of vultures. He does not respond as she traces his face that does not really look like his face. His polycarbonate glasses are balanced on his nose.

A spider crawls from the unseen depths of the cavern while she claims her usual seat. The spider's legs—light and swift—cast small ripples across the sea of sand until it stands towering before her. They have become very acquainted in these meetings, the spider and she, so she does not bother to start their conversation until her knees have stopped throbbing.

It is always the same questions, and always the same answers.

"Are you righteous?" she asks the spider. Its eight eyes gaze back at her, but it does not respond. "Are you righteous, dear spider? Can I take comfort in you, when there is no comfort for me left here? Are you righteous, and can righteousness be cruel?"

Her eyes travel to Edmond again. She is ashamed of her thoughts. She begs, begs for him to come back to her. She has offered everything to the spider, everything she has to give. Each day she offers it again: her life, her devotion, the pennies she has to spare and the ones she does not.

"You are not worthy," it hisses quietly, so quietly she is unsure if the words come from its mouth at all.

So, she threatens the spider, screams at it for its cruelty. Spits at its many glittering eyes. She wants to fight, to punish it, to quench this aching helplessness that wakes her in the middle of the night. This urgent feeling that she must do something, that it is her turn to save him and she is failing.

She loses Edmond a little more each day. But like the memories floating in the air of her house like dust motes, he will not leave her. And that is the most horrible part of this purgatory; when the threats fail, she begs the spider to take her husband whom she loves more than air. She begs it for release from this grief that started many years ago but will not end. This grief that leads her here each day to trace her husband's face, this grief that causes her to take joy when he has enough sense to bat away the hand of a stranger. He does not bat her away any longer.

She wonders if this is punishment for her selfishness. She wonders if she could save her husband if she loved him enough.

"You are not worthy." And she cannot tell if it is the spider's words or her own. If it has ever spoken to her at all.

The clock chimes its daily alarm, jolting Eleanor out of her thoughts. Each day it becomes easier to lose herself in her mind. She should not sell the house, because then her only home will be here, in the dregs of an hourglass. The ghosts here do not dance.

The spider scuttles back over the sand, going wherever spiders go when one's not thinking of them. Eleanor traces her husband's face.

"Until tomorrow, Edmond. Until tomorrow, spider."

Eleanor stands on shaking legs, smoothing out her jacket and taking a deep breath. It is a battle to wade through the sand, but she makes it to the door as she always does. Perhaps tomorrow she will get a better answer.

www.ingramcontent.com/pod-product-compliance
Lightning Source LLC
Chambersburg PA
CBHW030252200626
46816CB00002BA/614